Barcham
The Tree Specialists

D1688089

Time for Trees | Edition 4

Time for trees

A guide to species selection for the UK

With all the current threats to our trees in the UK, never has there been a more important time to plant more trees to build a more diverse and resilient landscape to combat the effects of climate change and an increasing number of pests and diseases. Planting a tree is a significant investment of time and resources, but the benefits for everyone's health, wellbeing and enjoyment is huge. Before we begin planting, selecting the right species of tree for the right place and choosing a species or cultivar with suitable attributes for the site and space is one of the most important factors to consider.

If we get it wrong and fail, the investment will be wasted, and time lost, but today with all the technical information available online and in reference books, there is no excuse for getting this process wrong, especially with books like 'Time for Trees' which will help and assist the planter through the selection process. This wonderful new edition is packed full of very useful information including the dimensions of trees at maturity, soil preferences and their ornamental attributes in terms of bark effect, leaf, flower and fruit. The technical information is supported by high quality colour images making it an extremely useful guide for selection within the UK. There is also additional guidance on planting and aftercare so now there is no excuse for planting the wrong tree in the wrong place and it failing to establish.

Tony Kirkham MBE, VMH
Head of the Arboretum,
Royal Botanic Gardens, Kew

Time for Trees | Edition 4

Contents

About Barcham 4

About the author 5

Environmental credit rating 6

Size matters 8

Plant Healthy certification scheme 10

ISO 14001 certification 12

Establishment and watering 13

The importance of mulch 15

Tree listings 17

Trees for a purpose 329

Top Trunks guide 332

Honey bees need trees 340

Planting guide 341

How to find us 342

Terms and conditions 343

English to Latin translator 345

Tree index 347

Photography and text copyright Barcham Trees Plc 2021

About Barcham

Barcham Trees is located between Ely and Soham in the Cambridgeshire Fens and in sight of Ely Cathedral. We have specialized in the production of containerized trees and over the last 35 years have supplied over 1.5 million instant impact trees into the UK landscape.

We grow our trees in our field unit before harvesting them into our patented Light Pots for sale the following planting season, by which time they have a root system geared for success and rapid establishment. We have 225,000 trees in production each year and our nursery covers 300 acres. We don't buy trees in from other nurseries to supplement our orders, our stock availability is subject to what we have grown ourselves.

Barcham proudly hold two Royal Warrants, one for Her Majesty the Queen and one for His Royal Highness the Prince of Wales.

We are accredited with the environmental standard ISO 14001 as well as having 'Plant Healthy' status for our strict biosecurity procedures that we have in place.

Our staff are highly trained, many of them to degree level in arboriculture, and we employ over 100 people in the planting season.

We have two purpose-built reservoirs, filled by harvesting the annual rainfall that falls on our site. These hold a combined 80,000 cubic metres of water.

Visits to Barcham are most welcome, by appointment, as we love to show off our full range of trees. We grow over 500 different varieties of tree at saleable sizes between 10-12cm girth to 25-30cm girth, in pot sizes ranging from 35 litre to 1000 litre.

Over the next few years we have plans to plant our own 18 acre arboretum here at Barcham to showpiece the varieties we grow.

'The best time to plant a tree was twenty years ago. The second best time is now'

We look forward to seeing you at Barcham!

Acknowledgements

Many thanks to our magnificent staff here at Barcham who grow, sell and distribute our trees throughout the length and breadth of the UK.

Look out for further information online...
www.barcham.co.uk   www.barchampro.co.uk

About the author
Mike Glover

Mike Glover graduated from Writtle Agricultural College in 1990 with a Higher National Diploma in Commercial Horticulture.

The following year he was awarded the Wilfred Cave Scholarship by the Royal Bath & West Society to study 'Instant Garden Techniques' in California.

Returning to the UK, Mike took up a position with Barcham Trees, where he is now Managing Director. In 2003 he patented the Light Pot in both Europe and the UK with the aim of producing trees with sustainable root systems geared for long term transplanting success. Barcham Trees is now the largest nursery of its type in Europe.

Our thanks go to Howard Gregory Dip.Hort. (Kew) for volunteering to proof read and keeping me on track with nomenclature.

UK providence seed collection

Germinated in our seed beds

Potted into 5 Litre pots to grow on in our triple span polytunnel

Grown on to harvest size in our fenland fields

Nurtured to sell in our patented Light Pots

Supplied with roots that are geared for rapid establishment

Barcham Environmental Credit Rating

Every tree planted is a credit to the environment. During the process of photosynthesis, trees absorb carbon dioxide and release oxygen and in the process store carbon to form the basis of their structures. When I first started growing trees over thirty years ago this always fascinated me as we are the opposite by consuming oxygen and expelling carbon dioxide as a by-product. It has a near perfect completeness about it, a symbiotic relationship in fact. Animal and Plant Kingdoms working together in balance.

However, our species has shifted this balance, consuming too greatly by producing technologies that are destabilising our environment and shifting us into unchartered waters in terms of climate change. At the beginning of the COVID 19 pandemic the BBC attributed extreme weather as 'possibly' linked to climate change but there has been a very interesting shift in the media in 2020 with it now being talked of as a certainty. We are getting summer storms with winds exceeding 50mph, periods of extreme drought, flash floods, and the new term 'Tropical Days', where the temperature exceeds 30 degrees Celsius. It used to be unheard of to get 40 millimetres of rain in one go, now it is the norm; we get so many storms that we are putting names to them; and the temperature continues to rise.

Living in a relatively benign country in terms of climate, the UK has been experiencing inconvenient weather up to now but nothing that we cannot live with. Parts of the world that were already operating under more extremes will be tipped over the edge in terms of disruption. Every tree planted is making a contribution to redress the balance and if everyone in the UK planted about one a year, and looked after them to secure their establishment and well-being, we would have at least 750 million more of them in ten years' time. We need them and they need us.

With all this in mind Barcham Trees have commissioned specific research by Treeconomics in Exeter to look at the hard data gathered by internationally recognized measuring systems such as 'I Tree'. Numbers can now be modelled on how much pollution filtration, water capture, carbon sequestration and carbon storage a genus will achieve over its lifespan. We have modelled this mostly to 300 years but there are many big hitting genera such as Sequoiadendron (Redwood), Quercus (Oak) and Taxus (Yew) that can carry on doing their job of both capturing carbon and storing carbon for centuries after this time period if we protect them.

On average we have grown our trees for about 7 years before we release them onto the market. We have taken into account their environmental cost of production in terms of carbon used for transport and even tractor fuel and water abstraction. Depending on the genus, our trees break even in terms of carbon storage by the time they reach about two years of age so when you get them they are already positively contributing.

Our environmental rating system.

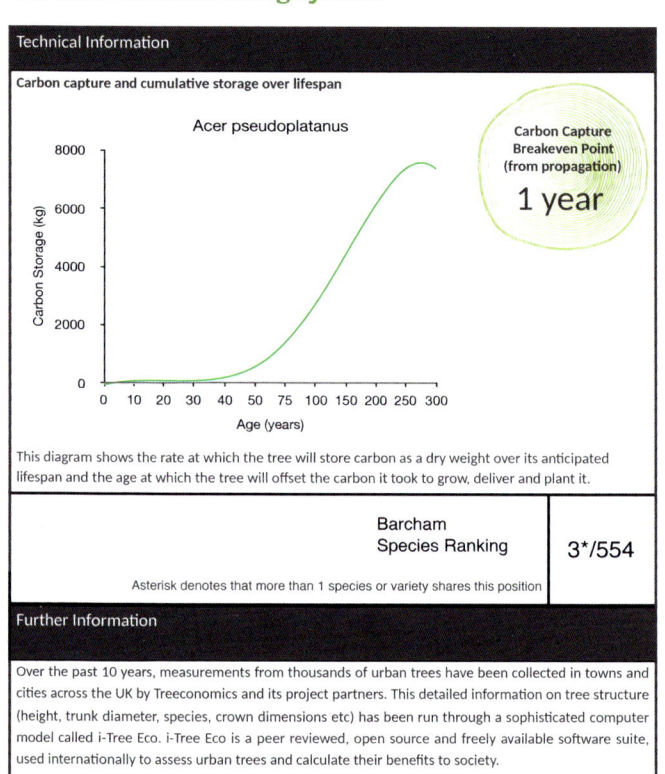

Technical Information

Carbon capture and cumulative storage over lifespan

Acer pseudoplatanus

Carbon Capture Breakeven Point (from propagation): **1 year**

This diagram shows the rate at which the tree will store carbon as a dry weight over its anticipated lifespan and the age at which the tree will offset the carbon it took to grow, deliver and plant it.

Barcham Species Ranking: 3*/554

Asterisk denotes that more than 1 species or variety shares this position

Further Information

Over the past 10 years, measurements from thousands of urban trees have been collected in towns and cities across the UK by Treeconomics and its project partners. This detailed information on tree structure (height, trunk diameter, species, crown dimensions etc) has been run through a sophisticated computer model called i-Tree Eco. i-Tree Eco is a peer reviewed, open source and freely available software suite, used internationally to assess urban trees and calculate their benefits to society.

For further information and detailed methodology go to: www.treeconomics.co.uk/treecarboncertificate/

All trees contribute but some live longer than others and attain greater sizes. The bigger the tree the more carbon is locked up. A Malus (Apple) tree may live for 70 years where as a Sequoiadendron giganteum (Giant Redwood) can live for over 3,000 years. Also, rates of carbon sequestration can differ per genus over their lifetime. We have fed this into the model and come up with a scored rating to environmentally value a tree so the best environmental option can be chosen to suit what space allows.

It has never been easier to choose your trees with greater clarity.

Our environment ratings

All plants contribute towards carbon sequestration, but trees amass the most wood to lock this carbon up and store it. So, trees of great age that grow to huge sizes are the ones that count the most in this regard. Our ratings range from the top environmental 'A' grade to the less contributing 'E' grade. The woody trees are all within the A-C grades with smaller trees and shrubs making up the lower grades. Sycamore is an 'A' grade environmental asset whilst a Crab Apple is a 'C' grade. However, both are contributors to the environment, and it depends on the size and aspect of your planting position as to what genus you can opt for. A poor scenario is to plant an 'A' grader in too small a space so it can never fulfil its contribution. Data to assess the quality of contribution has been collected and analysed over thousands of mature samples within the UK landscape.

The data used to model this has mostly come from trees in urban settings or trees in well populated rural locations. It should be noted that trees in the open countryside that can access greater soil volumes and that have greater space around them will grow to larger proportions and therefore store more carbon. It is estimated that the UK's largest trees will store about three times the volumes shown in our modelling.

Underneath each of our tree descriptions in this publication we have put a corresponding Environmental Credit Rating so if this is your main driver for planting, you can choose your trees with greater clarity.

Modelling is developing all the time and is never perfect, but at the time of going to print we are confident that the methods used are the most reliable available. What we do know for certain is that all trees contribute positively by locking up carbon from our atmosphere, carbon that we all are putting there in the first place; carbon that is changing our climate beyond the thresholds we have evolved with; and this is the single most important challenge of our time.

Trees are planted for multiple reasons, whether it be screening, legacy, aesthetic beauty, commemoration or environmental. Whatever the reason they are all contributing to carbon storage.

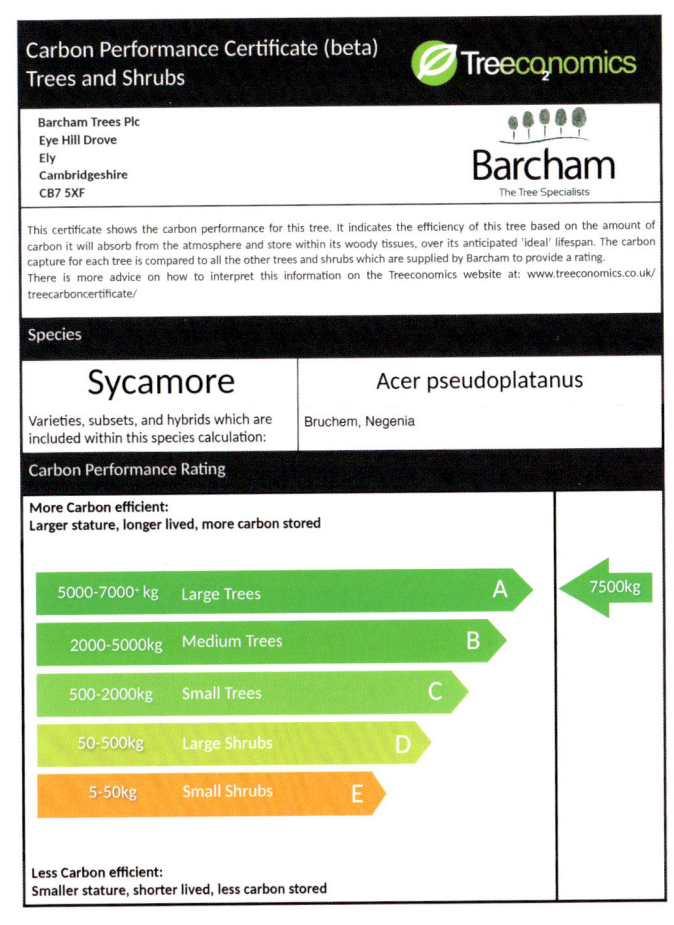

→ **For carbon scores per variety please refer to pages 332 to 339 in the back section.**

Size matters

Over recent decades, there has been a great emphasis on a 'day one' instant impact look with the size of tree grown and dispatched going off the charts. Some trees are so big that only one or two fit on a 40-foot articulated lorry that travels thousands of miles from continental Europe to reach their new homes. There is little or no environmental gain in these. The trouble is that this obsession for size has been transposed across all genera. It's fair enough to buy a tree at semi mature sizes if they go on to live for at least two centuries but what's the point of buying semi mature Malus (Apple) or Prunus (Cherry) as these only live for about 70 years in the first place. In environmental terms it is like starting to invest in a new Olympic athlete when they turn 40. What is more, a short lived tree planted at huge sizes has lost its juvenile vigour and reacts very poorly to this process giving the end user a miserable result rather than the utopian day one orchard they had been promised and imagined.

A tree supplied at an age too old and too large to make an environmental contribution does not make sense. We do not see the point in planting a tree that has a life expectancy of under 100 years at much over 16-18cm girth, our 'large' size. By then it is about 10 years old, so it still has 90 years' worth of environmental contribution to go. Better still, buy these from a nursery who has grown them from scratch rather than an imported tree with a hefty carbon footprint already attached.

For longer lived trees, there is a good case for planting at semi mature girth, our 'instant' size, but surely in this day and age when our environment is at such a knife edge, not at the super-sized girths of 30cm and 40cm+ girth that need large carbon guzzling machinery to transport and plant them, negating their environmental worth from the start.

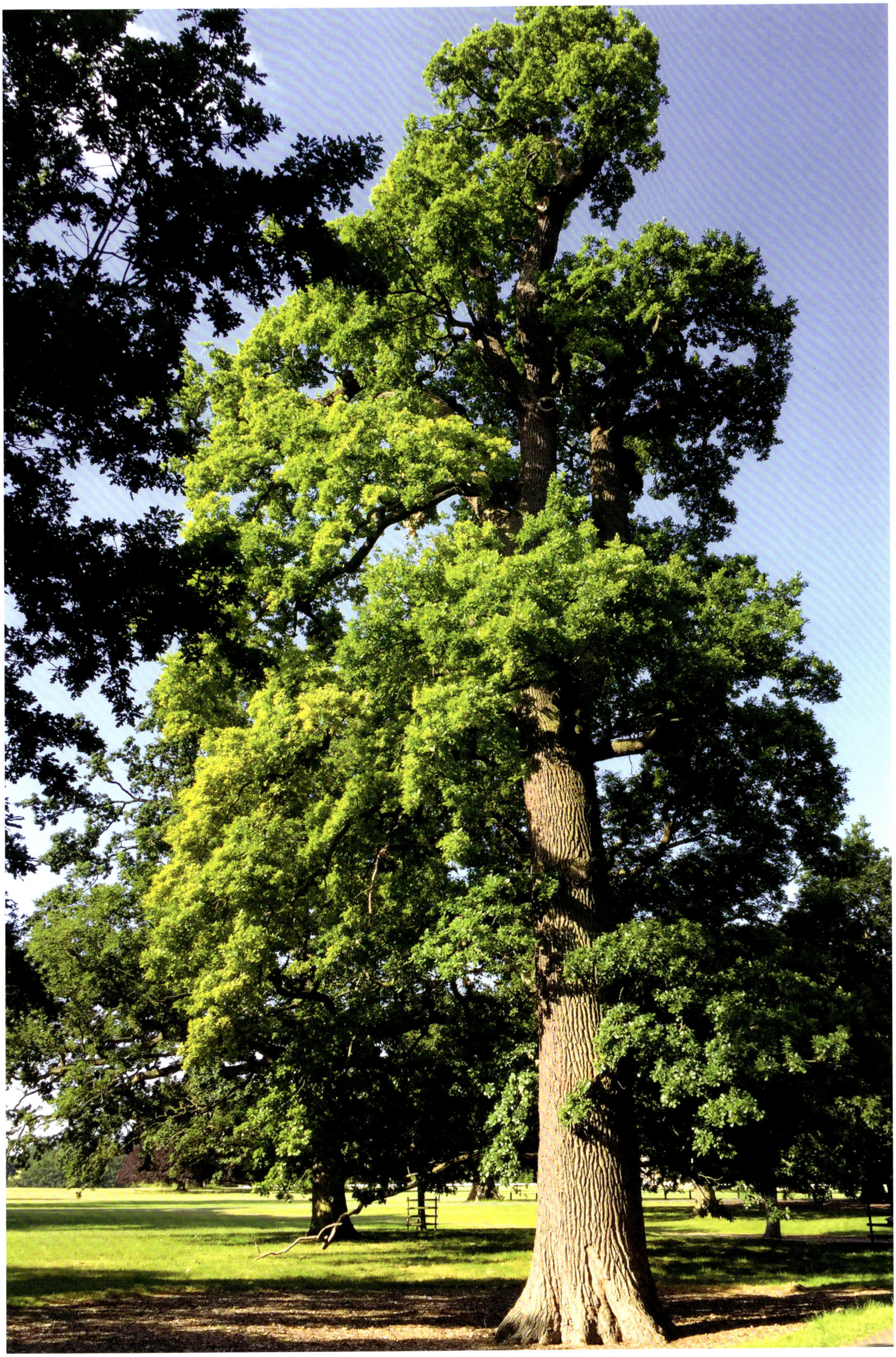

Above left: Field production (Carpinus) Above right: Same Carpinus in pots on the unit a year later.

BIOSECURITY
ISO 14001 and the 'Plant Healthy' Certification Scheme

Plant Healthy

At last biosecurity is beginning to gain traction and industry practices are gradually changing. Take Olive for example, such a glorious tree, unrivalled in what it does aesthetically and so beautiful in structure. However, with the arrival of the plant disease Xylella Fastidiosa into Southern Italy in 2013, the Olive population in that part of Europe was decimated and the production of Olive Oil supporting thousands of families was lost. A lot of tree diseases are genus specific like Ash Die back, but the thing about Xylella is that it also wipes out numerous other genera and particularly favours Laurus nobilis (Bay), Prunus dulcis (Almond), Quercus suber (Cork Oak), as well as mainstream shrubs like Lavender and Rosemary.
We took the decision to stop growing and selling these varieties in 2015 not wanting to risk the UK treescape and our own production for short term commercial gain.

Xylella Fastidiosa has now spread to Germany, France, Portugal and Spain but thankfully there has been no recorded case in the UK… *yet*.

There are still many plant brokers importing Olives into the UK, at great risk to our environment, driven on by demand from specifiers and individuals who have no idea of the catastrophe that could so easily result. I am pleased to say that DEFRA is getting a grip on this and making it a lot harder for Olives to come into the country but we will rest easier when they are prohibited for good, along with the other host plants that Xylella Fastidiosa favours.

The need for strict biosecurity is so important for the health of our nation's trees. This is why the new kite mark scheme 'Plant Healthy' has been launched in the UK, auditing nurseries to make sure they have strict biosecurity procedures in place. We were certified onto this scheme in September 2020. Unfortunately this doesn't stop poorly judged imports via 'white van man' into town markets every week up and down the UK but DEFRA has these traders on its radar and will hopefully put in legislation to get everyone to comply with stricter biosecurity standards.

At Barcham, we do not trade any plants for immediate resale. All of our saleable stock is vitality checked and passed as healthy by DEFRA before they are released onto the market each September, having been grown here at Barcham. Many of our trees are started from UK provenance seedlings and raised in our triple span polytunnel before being planted out in our field unit to grow on to harvest size. They are then lifted and containerized into our patented Light Pots to ready them for sale.

Our white Light Pots allow a small amount of light penetration through to the root system. This triggers a phototropic and geotropic response where the roots grow away from the light and obey the pull of gravity. When they are planted out their roots are not impeded by each other's growth and are able to explore the soil effectively, allowing rapid and sustained establishment. The same cannot be said for trees grown in traditional black containers where the roots spiral into a knotted mass of compromised tangled roots that twist into knots with secondary thickening, destabilizing the trees' anchorage when its top becomes too large a structure for its compromised roots to support.

With the threat of multiple pest and diseases being imported into the UK by traded trees, it becomes more important to devise planting plans that offer a defense against host specific problems. Oak Processionary Moth, Ash Die Back and Dutch Elm Disease are good examples of how a single tree variety can all get wiped out by one event. Genus diversity is the key to future proofing your planting. If one genus accounts for only 10% of your arrangement you are limiting your exposure to total losses further on down the line.

Ironically, the need for greater genus diversity puts pressure on demand and triggers more imports but if you go with a nursery with certified 'Plant Healthy' status you will be on the right side of things. The incidence of importing a problem goes away if you buy from UK nurseries who have grown their plants rather than brokered them. Always good to ask!

Barcham
Has been certified with ISO 14001

In 2018 the management team at Barcham set itself the aim of ISO 14001 accreditation. We looked at all levels within our business in terms of environmental aspects and impacts and set ourselves rigorous objectives and targets such as increasing our recycling levels and reducing the use of peat.

We looked at the business in its entirety, rather than just scope the parts of our operations that we can take an easy win from. Even our coffee machine came under scrutiny and is a good example of the environmental con that we are all living through. Every day we were feeling very cozy about disposing our coffee cups into the recycling thinking we were doing the right thing but it turns out that these 'may be recycled' items could not be recycled at all, certainly not in the UK anyway. So, we ditched the machine for a traditional china cup option that can be washed up in perpetuity. The irony is that the machine that supplies these delivers a far superior coffee and even the pods that feed it are recycled.

But this is the way of it.
The more we investigated, the more savings we made in both economic and environmental terms. This standard has also brought the business closer together. Everyone has been involved communication within the business has become so much more inclusive and worthwhile.

Suggestions for improvement are no longer forgotten with time but are logged instead and fully discussed each month to assess. We collectively decided that we can do the right thing environmentally for our 300 acre business and if we choose to take this home to our private lives so much the better.

Our eyes have been well and truly opened.
Businesses displaying recycling logos on their packaging are invariably misleading. It is trendy to appear environmental but the greening up of businesses still has a heavy pinch of corporate greed rather than doing the right thing for the environment.

As far as we are aware Barcham is the only wholesale tree grower that has achieved ISO 14001. We have incorporated our biosecurity policy and procedures into the standard and hope others will follow our lead on this.

ISO 14001 is exacting and daunting in the first instance. It can give management teams palpitations in terms of perceived financial outlay to achieve. However, it represents a cultural shift within a business and delivers very good value for money if embraced wholeheartedly.

Certificate Number 17587
ISO 14001

Barcham
Establishment and **watering**

With climate change upon us we are experiencing more weather extremes that are tough for newly establishing trees to cope with. In May 2020, most of the UK had high temperatures and only 3mm of rainfall. This came at a pivotal time for recently planted trees as their limited root systems were geared for rapid growth over this period. A Spring drought abruptly stops new root growth which can't access the water needed to sustain them.

During this time, a tree is like a pump, primed for action. Water is wicked out of the trees' vascular system as they photosynthesize and produce new water rich foliage and flowers. If they run out of available water its like a candle running out of wax. With these climate extremes now in play, we need to step in to give our newly planted trees a helping hand.

There are many different methods and ideas for watering trees but often these are over thought. For all the right reasons we want the best for establishing our trees in the first couple of years after planting to give them a great start. However, we can over complicate things and end up veering away from how trees have evolved in nature to access the water that comes their way.

Taking it back to basics, trees have evolved to take rainfall as their source of water. Generally, this is very slow in terms of output, it can rain on and off all day but only provide 10mm. But we all agree that the trees look better for it. Rain is slow release water. The rate at which it is delivered gives vital time for the soil to grip the water as gravity takes it down through its profile. Canopies of trees have time to channel the flow downwards and, in the process, slows it down still further to where its roots system can access it later on. The woodland floor mulch slows it down yet again and keeps it from evaporating as soon as the sun comes out. Mulch also prevents the soil from capping after a relentless pounding of rain to make the soil more receptive to its flow.

So, what do we do?!

We pour on buckets of the stuff all at once and walk away thinking good job done! Think of a hanging basket. You water it with a litre of water from a jug and two thirds falls from the basket onto the ground below. That water is now useless to the plants it was intended for. If that litre of water was applied as a block of ice and left to melt over the next few hours, not one

The Barcham hydration bag

Example of how mulch should be pulled away from the collar of the tree.

drop would fall through the basket as the compost has had the time to grip it. The plants can now access the entire litre of water as it is within their root zone. Now, I'm not suggesting you put ice all over the place but it's a good way to make the point that slow release water is what's needed. (Having said this, I have used ice now and again to water trees and it works very well!!)

So, how should we slow water down so that the soil can grip it for the roots to access it? People think water pipes are a great idea, single use plastic protruding out of the soil line after the tree is planted so water can be applied 'down to the roots'. But the roots are most active and effective on the surface. Using a hosepipe to feed a tube is just going to get the water to sprint through the soil profile with very little being delivered to the right place. Fast release of water can also make a horrible mess of the soil structure below ground. Roots need oxygen and water blended in measure and too much water too fast squeezes out the oxygen from the soil, rendering it useless for tree roots to colonize it.

What about using water retaining gels that the roots can access later? The first thing I think of when I hear about these sorts of products is how many water absorbing gels occur in the soil in nature and have trees evolved happily with this type of stuff in place? When push comes to shove and it gets dry, what's going to want to hold the water, a root system or a water absorbing gel? I don't think I'm a technology luddite, but you can see the point that veering away from how trees have evolved will probably give rise to negative consequences.

You can't get away from it, the best way to slow water down is to mimic rainfall. In my garden I water using a watering can, with a rose attachment, to sprinkle water to the mulch and down through the surface of the soil. A six litre watering can of water, applied every three days, is much more effective than lashing huge volumes on at a quicker pace.

I can do this at my leisure in the confines of my small garden but when time is more pressing, I can mechanise the job by using a garden sprinkler that I can walk away from and this slows the water rate up even further, more akin to a heavy rain shower so I'm now really getting to where I want to be. About 20 minutes per tree via a sprinkler is a great way to water garden trees.

But you can't set off a garden sprinkler in a town or city street or where you haven't got a hose point to feed it. This is where Tree Hydration Bags work well. These sit on top of the root system, hugging the stem like a waistcoat. Once filled they expand with 70 litres of water that is then dripped out the base over the next three to five hours. Incidentally, they also act as a rabbit protector, weed suppresser and mulch mat. Practically they have to be filled by a bowser or hosepipe to make them preferable to hand watering, but they are another great way of slowing up the flow of water for the soil to have time to grip it.

This is all assuming your soil is free draining. If watering puddles on the surface and can't escape, tree roots will drown, and the canopy will fail. Drainage solutions are needed to sort this scenario out, something more radical than a layer of gravel at the base of the planting hole which will make no difference at all if water can't escape.

The importance of **mulch**

A good width of organic mulch around a newly planted tree is a great way of keeping competitive weed growth at bay and creating a buffer zone of retained moisture at soil level.

Ground based organisms travel up through the soil and into the mulch to feed before returning, keeping the top of the soil moist. A mulch also gives a wealth of fungal activity, re-creating an abundance of balanced activity associated with woodland floors.

Trees have evolved to thrive with this balance in place. But we have a tendency to spoil this party. So often I see trees surrounded with decorative rocks, coloured stone chips, an array of plastic liners, decking or even concrete, paving slabs, or tarmac. These non-organic coverings can entomb a tree to a life of slow failure. They can deprive the soil of water, killing off the balancing life in the soil that a tree needs to thrive. They are sterile, not organic, the opposite to a woodland floor. They can reflect both heat and light back into the canopy of the tree with scorching effects. Trees haven't evolved with these inorganic decorations so it's not surprising they do poorly under such circumstances. Trees don't want hygiene, they want a balanced blend of organisms to support them.

Mulch is definitely the way to go but there can be too much of a good thing. Somewhere around four to six centimetres of mulch spread over a metre diameter and pulled out from around the trunk of the tree is enough to do the job. This will need topping up every season as it degrades. It is tempting put a greater depth of mulch on but again, beware of deviating away from what nature intended.

The closer we can mimic nature the more your trees will thrive.

Our favourites to include within a tree planting scheme are hardy Cyclamen, (Cyclamen hederifolium), in both pink and white floral forms, Snowdrops and Bluebells. The cyclamen emerges with flower in September through to November and keeps its attractive foliage until April / May. Snowdrops push through for February / March and Bluebells flower in May. Between the three of them you can achieve a great show of colour for up to 9 months of the year and they retreat back to nothing so they are the most maintenance free plants you could ever hope for.

ABIES fraseri
Fraser Fir

Introduced by John Fraser in 1811 from the USA, this stately evergreen can reach up to 15 metres in the UK with a spread of about 8 metres. The biggest recorded in its native environment has reached 30 metres tall by 17 metres wide. Its pyramidal habit and dark shiny leaves, which have two silver bands on their underside, make it the Christmas Tree of choice in many south eastern states of America but it has always been third to the Norway Spruce and the Nordmann Fir over here.

It grows well on most free draining soils and produces small purple tinged cones that mature to dark brown. The leaves are only about 1.5cm long and in our experience of growing them in East Anglia they can extend growth of up to 40cm per year.

Mature height: 12-17m | Shape of mature tree | Evergreen trees | Eco impact rating: B

ABIES nordmanniana
Nordmann / Caucasian Fir

Introduced from Northern Turkey in 1840, this striking conifer has risen steeply in popularity over recent years for being a tree that doesn't drop its needles. Arguably the most attractive of the firs it can grow immensely tall with some specimens in Europe attaining 85m in height.

Its tiered branches support dark green leaves 2-3cm in length with cones that can grow up to 20cm. It is very robust and disease resistant, but our advice is to plant after the 25th December for municipal plantings! Like most firs it tends to scorch up in very hot climates but is well suited for growing in the UK.

Mature height: 17-22m | Shape of mature tree | Evergreen trees | Eco impact rating: B

ACER buergerianum
Trident Maple

Native to Eastern China and Korea, this very pretty maple was introduced in 1890. It forms an oval to rounded crown at maturity and is well suited to streets or gardens.

New spring foliage emerges a rich bronze colour before hardening to a glossy dark green by summer. Greenish yellow flowers are borne in March and maturing trunks flake to brown / orange colours to provide a patchwork of winter interest. Autumn colours can be variable but seldom disappointing with leaves turning yellow through to red before falling. It is considered a slow to medium grower and is fully hardy down to -25 Celsius.

Recent arborist opinion coming out of the USA place this as a highly prized urban tree. Its increased popularity is not only due to its seasonal interest but also its durability. For the UK it represents an alternative to Acer campestre types

7|12			C
Mature height: 7-12m	Shape of mature tree	Urban trees	Eco impact rating

ACER campestre
Field Maple

Native to England, but not in Scotland or Ireland, this small to medium tree of rounded form was widely used in the Middle Ages for making musical instruments. In autumn, its leaves turn not just clear yellow, but also red and golden brown.

It does best in rich, well drained soils, but is equally at home in virtually any soil type, and will readily tolerate drought, soil compaction and air pollution. A versatile, resilient and attractive species with a wide range of uses. Available both as multi-stem and single stem.

Field Maple also makes an excellent hedgerow plant. Being native, it is very 'wildlife friendly' and it can cope well to rough pruning during the dormant season to keep the hedge to shape. Many of its clones listed next are far more suitable for urban and street planting as they form crowns of more regular shape than that of their parent.

- Mature height: 10-15m
- Shape of mature tree
- Multi-stem
- Eco impact rating: B

ACER campestre
Arends

This cultivar of Field Maple has a much more regular and oval habit than the species. We were first introduced to it in the mid 1990s and placed it into our range soon after as its habit ticked all the boxes for urban planting.

It does best in rich, well drained soils, but does well in virtually any soil type, and will readily tolerate drought, soil compaction and air pollution. Compared to Norway Maple types, Acer campestre clones have much smaller leaves so are a better prospect in the urban environment at leaf fall.

- Mature height: 10-15m
- Shape of mature tree
- Urban trees
- Eco impact rating: B

ACER campestre Elegant

This cultivar of Field Maple is, in our opinion, the pick of the Acer campestre clones for street planting. It retains a compact ascending habit, is vigorous in growth, and gives uniformity if planted in an avenue. Many clones are tricky to tell apart at maturity but Elegant's stubby thick growth makes it easier to distinguish. I have seen Elegant over 25 years old and they were about a third as wide as they were tall.

It does best in rich, well drained soils, but does well in virtually any soil type, and will readily tolerate drought, soil compaction and air pollution. Typical of its type, it can go a glorious yellow in autumn and is a great host to a range of native wildlife. There are some great specimens performing admirably in UK cities which is comforting for urban planners when selecting this clone for planting.

| Mature height: 10-15m | Shape of mature tree | Urban trees | Eco impact rating: B |

ACER campestre Elsrijk

This cultivar of the Field Maple is named after the park in Amstelveen, Holland, where it was discovered in the 1950s. It differs from the species in that it has a more regular, oval habit. At maturity one could mistake it for straight forward Acer campestre but one with a lovely compact shape.

It does best in rich, well drained soils, but does well in virtually any soil type, and will readily tolerate drought, soil compaction and air pollution. A medium sized tree which we particularly recommend for urban and street plantings, its foliage turns a magnificent clear yellow in autumn.

| Mature height: 10-15m | Shape of mature tree | Urban trees | Eco impact rating: B |

ACER campestre Lienco

New to Barcham in 2011, this superb tight headed clone is ideal for a tidy street tree in an urban environment. Many clonal selections are produced by growers, but most are too like existing varieties to be worthy of special interest. This selection stands out as one to watch as it ticks many boxes for city planting.

Selections of our native Acer campestre are a marvellous compromise to planting indigenous trees within our urban settings as they are tough and relatively low maintenance. Good for wildlife, the leaves turn a glorious yellow in the autumn and it thrives on most soils.

- Mature height: 10-15m
- Shape of mature tree
- Urban trees
- Eco impact rating: B

ACER campestre Louisa Red Shine

A most attractive small to medium tree with a rounded habit. The new leaves are flushed with crimson before turning mauve / green as the season progresses. There are very few trees with native origin that have this degree of leaf colour and as it has smaller leaves than the red clones of Norway Maple it provides softer contrast on the landscape.

It does best in rich, well drained soils, but does well in virtually any soil type, and will readily tolerate drought, soil compaction and air pollution. An ideal subject for streets, parks and verges, it has been used with great effect in London in recent years. Each growth flush is rewarded with red to crimson leaves so there is plenty of interest throughout the summer.

The foliage display turns to yellow with hints of orange by the autumn to round off eight months of succession leaf interest. Being of native origin it is also a good host to insects and birds. We planted one of these outside our offices at Barcham in 2006 and it has developed beautifully.

| Mature height: 10-15m | Shape of mature tree | Urban trees | Eco impact rating: B |

ACER campestre Nanum

A top worked variety with a very dwarfing, rounded habit. Its leaves are smaller than those of the species and they form a very dense crown.

It does best in rich, well drained soils, but does well in virtually any soil type, and will readily tolerate drought, soil compaction and air pollution. Very good for streets and residential plantings, or any site where space is at a premium. This clone has long been in cultivation and was introduced in the 1830s.

- Mature height: 5-8m
- Shape of mature tree
- Urban trees
- Eco impact rating: C

ACER campestre Queen Elizabeth

This American cultivar is also known as Evelyn and was introduced in the mid 1980s. It is fast growing, has a relatively narrow habit and is larger and darker leaved than the species. The ascending branches are produced at angle of 45° to the dominant central leader. Pretty much identical to the branded clone 'Streetwise' in our opinion.

It does best in rich, well drained soils, but does well in virtually any soil type, and will readily tolerate drought, soil compaction and air pollution. An excellent choice as a street tree, it has a tighter habit than Elsrijk and was first brought into general cultivation by the well-known Frank Schmidt nursery in Oregon.

- Mature height: 10-15m
- Shape of mature tree
- Urban trees
- Eco impact rating: B

Acer campestre William Caldwell

Cloned from a seedling raised on the William Caldwell nursery in Knutsford, Cheshire in the super hot summer of 1976. This nursery is sadly no longer in business but its name lives on with this upright form that is proving popular as a self maintaining urban tree where space is restricted.

Thriving in most free draining aspects, it can colour up nicely in the autumn on acid soils with leaves turning orange and sometimes red. On alkaline soils the leaves are more likely to turn buttercup yellow in line with its Field Maple parents.

- Mature height: 7-12m
- Shape of mature tree
- Autumn colour
- Eco impact rating: B

ACER cappadocicum

This broad spreading maple has five to seven-lobed green glossy leaves that turn a glorious yellow in autumn. The bark is veined with a hint of yellow when young and it is a native of Western Asia to Himalaya.

Tip die back is commonly seen on these genera during establishment, sometimes causing a complete collapse of the plant, and this is generally caused by verticillium. This fungus accounts for many in the maple family and is carried on water so is difficult to avoid. Like Acer rubrum, the susceptibility is probably caused by inadequate availability of trace elements such as manganese.

- Mature height: 12-17m
- Shape of mature tree
- Autumn colour
- Eco impact rating: B

ACER cappadocicum Aureum

A smaller tree than its parent, Acer cappadocicum, this attractive tree flushes a bright yellow in the spring and retains this splendour through to the autumn. It prefers sheltered conditions and is not tolerant to urban pollution.

It is particularly effective when planted against an evergreen backdrop as the foliage provides a vivid contrast. Best planted on sites offering good light levels but not in areas with reflected light bouncing off hard surfaces.

This tree is difficult to grow and establish but the rewards are great if you succeed. It is rarely seen at maturity in the UK and if you are in doubt about its suitability to your planting scheme but still want a yellow foliaged maple, consider using Acer platanoides Princeton Gold or Acer pseudoplatanus Worleii as tougher, but just as pretty, alternatives.

- Mature height: 7-12m
- Shape of mature tree
- Yellow foliage
- Eco impact rating: B

ACER cappadocicum Rubrum

Also known as the Caucasian Maple, this cultivar dates to at least 1838 but remains rather uncommon. It is a medium to large tree with a rounded habit. The young, dark red leaves turn green and then back to red, gold and yellow in autumn. This superb autumn colour lasts for many weeks.

Although best on moist, well drained soil, it is adaptable and flourishes in either full sun or light shade. It is best grown with a little shelter from strong winds. A good tree for avenues and verges, but not good where soil becomes compacted.

- Mature height: 12-17m
- Shape of mature tree
- Autumn colour
- Eco impact rating: B

ACER x freemanii Armstrong

Selected by Newton Armstrong in the States in 1947, this small to medium tree has a tightly columnar habit, making it very useful as a street and car park tree. It is half Acer rubrum and half Acer saccharinum, but the latter dominates with autumn colour of orange and yellows rather than glorious scarlet.

The toughness of its Silver Maple parentage makes it a better bet than Acer rubrum and its cultivars when manganese is not present in the soil. It tolerates urban conditions but as a warning note is very susceptible to glyphosate (Roundup) so beware.

- Mature height: 7-12m
- Shape of mature tree
- Autumn colour
- Eco impact rating: C

ACER x freemanii
Autumn Blaze

This is a cultivar of a naturally occurring hybrid of Acer rubrum and Acer saccharinum, named after Oliver Freeman, who made the crossing at the US National Arboretum in the 1930s.

This vigorous, oval headed, large tree has dark green, deeply indented leaves, which turn rich flame red in autumn. Acer rubrum is often specified for this effect but very rarely does well on UK soils as it is dependent on the trace element manganese which it can only access at low ph. Autumn Blaze possesses the prettiness of rubrum but the toughness of saccharinum so it is the much safer bet.

This variety is very highly thought of in the United States where there are nurseries, principally in Oregon, that grow little else to satisfy their domestic market. It is a highly dramatic tree, rivalling even Liquidambar for autumn colour. As a word of caution, it is slightly brittle, so planting sites exposed to strong and persistent winds should be avoided.

Mature height: 12-17m | Shape of mature tree | Autumn colour | Eco impact rating: C

ACER x freemanii
Autumn Fantasy

This charming clone resembles Acer saccharinum more than Acer rubrum with its silvery summer leaves and upright oval habit giving a pleasing effect. Introduced from the USA by Bill Wandell of Illinois and new to our range in 2010.

Its real delight comes in the autumn when the leaves turn a gorgeous red to crimson making this a highly prized ornamental tree. Suitable for both parks and large gardens, it thrives on most soils though it finds it tougher on arid ground.

- Mature height: 12-17m
- Shape of mature tree
- Autumn colour
- Eco impact rating: C

ACER ginnala
Amur Maple

Its common name derives from the Amur River, which divides China and Russia. One of the very best trees for autumn colour, when its foliage turns a stunning red, it is also very early into leaf in spring and produces yellow-white fragrant flowers in May. This is a small to medium tree with a rounded habit and is good for parks and public gardens.

It flourishes in full sun or light shade and in most soil types and has the added advantages of being wind and drought resistant. I have had experience of planting this in the north of Scotland and they performed poorly so if planned for north of Glasgow beware!

- Mature height: 7-12m
- Shape of mature tree
- Autumn colour
- Eco impact rating: C

ACER griseum
Paperbark Maple

A small tree, but a magnificent one! Originally from China, from an early age the bark peels to reveal cinnamon coloured under-bark and the trifoliate leaves have attractive reddish tints in autumn. Introduced by Ernest Wilson in 1901.

This maple does well in sun or partial shade and appreciates a sheltered position. Growing tips generally frost out over winter giving the tree a very rounded habit. It does best in moist, well drained soil, and is not drought tolerant. Nutrient rich, wet soil can inhibit autumn colour.

It is always tempting to plant a tree as pleasing as this in a hard area subjected to reflected heat and light but in view for all to see. It is so important to match the tree's physiology with complementing planting locations for the plant to thrive. This tree will fare poorly when surrounded by hard surfaces. I have one in my garden, planted in 2002, and it is performing admirably under the dappled shade of larger trees.

| Mature height: 5-8m | Shape of mature tree | Bark interest | Eco impact rating: C |

ACER negundo
Box Elder

A medium to large tree, which is particularly fast growing in its first few years. A row of these makes a good screen or windbreak, and it is well worth considering where there is an incidence of honey fungus as it shows good resistance. Its compound leaves, more like those of an ash, make this species unique among maples.

A good choice for heavy clay soils and for waterside plantings, it performs just as well in lighter, drier ones. It also tolerates air pollution and soil compaction as well as withstanding periodic flooding. Native of the USA, this tree is a real tough performer.

- Mature height: 12-17m
- Shape of mature tree
- Clay soils
- Eco impact rating: B

ACER negundo
Flamingo

This male clone, raised in Holland in the 1970s, has young leaves that have a wide, soft pink margin which turns to white. Best displays of foliage appear when plants are hard pruned in winter. We supply bottom worked standard trees as it tends to break out when top worked onto a negundo stem.

A good choice for heavy clay soils and for waterside plantings, it performs just as well in lighter, drier ones. It also tolerates air pollution and soil compaction. Very adaptable and recommended as a garden or verge tree.

- Mature height: 7-12m
- Shape of mature tree
- Variegated trees
- Eco impact rating: B

ACER negundo Variegata
Variegated Box Elder

Introduced from a branch sport off a nursery in southern France in 1845, this striking garden tree must be well maintained to continually reward with its stunning display of silver lined variegated leaves. As with 'Flamingo' we grow this tree as a bottom grafted specimen as it gets too congested and heavy if grafted at the top of an Acer negundo stem and is then prone to collapse. The trick to keeping this tree in order is to heavily prune each winter to encourage vigorous and vibrant regrowth. If left alone, the tree tends to slowly revert to green.

Suitable for most soils, this tough tree is best for gardens where they can be kept an eye on. Don't let me put you off; the foliage display is stunning if you butcher it once a year!

- Mature height: 7-12m
- Shape of mature tree
- Variegated trees
- Eco impact rating: B

ACER palmatum
Japanese Maple

The Japanese maple was introduced from its native land to Britain in the 1820s. Also, a native of both China and Korea, this magnificent tree can outstrip size expectation if left alone in an area large enough to accommodate.

A delightful, small tree for a sheltered position such as a courtyard or an urban garden. It has a rounded habit and its deeply lobed leaves turn shades of yellow, red and orange in autumn. They do best in rich, moist, but free draining, loamy soils. It is remarkably self-reliant post establishment for seemingly such a dainty tree.

- Mature height: 3-8m
- Multi-stem
- Garden trees
- Eco impact rating: C

ACER palmatum
Bloodgood

A superb Japanese maple with long lasting and unfading reddish-purple leaves that turn a glorious red before they drop in autumn. This clone won the Award of Garden Merit in 2002.

Recognised as one of the best clones of its type, it also produces beautiful red fruits and is particularly hardy even in the coldest of winters. We grow this as a full standard tree with a rounded crown, so it is best suited for gardens and parks. It thrives on most soils.

- Mature height: 3-8m
- Shape of mature tree
- Multi-stem
- Red/purple foliage
- Eco impact rating: C

ACER palmatum
Dissectum Garnet

A lovely cut leaf deep purple Japanese maple that was raised in Holland around 1950 and won the Award of Garden Merit in 2002.

It is a strong growing form with good autumn colour. We grow this as a full standard tree with a rounded crown, so it is best suited for gardens and parks. It thrives on most soils. When grown under the shade of other trees the leaves are darker green than purple so make sure it has plenty of light to trigger the true colour of the summer foliage display.

- Mature height: 3-8m
- Shape of mature tree
- Red/purple foliage
- Eco impact rating: C

ACER palmatum Fireglow

Developed around 1977, this is thought to be an improved clone of the superb 'Bloodgood'. In truth there is little to choose between them so try not to agonise over the choice!

We grow this as a multi stemmed bush with a rounded habit, so it is best suited for gardens and parks. It thrives on most soils. The glorious display of summer leaves provides great contrast in any garden so time should be taken to carefully select its planting position to achieve greatest effect. As a rule, the eye picks up on deep reds and purples first, if you place it further back in your landscape it draws the focus through your garden rather than blocking off the view behind it.

- Mature height: 3-8m
- Multi-stem
- Red/purple foliage
- Eco impact rating: C

ACER palmatum Osakazuki

The best of all Japanese Maples for red autumn colour, this clone won the Award of Garden Merit in 2002 and was introduced in the 1880s.

An attractive, small tree for a sheltered position such as a courtyard or an urban garden. It has a rounded habit and its deeply lobed leaves turn shades of yellow, red and orange in autumn. They do best in rich, moist, but free draining, loamy soils. A stunning tree that never fails to impress.

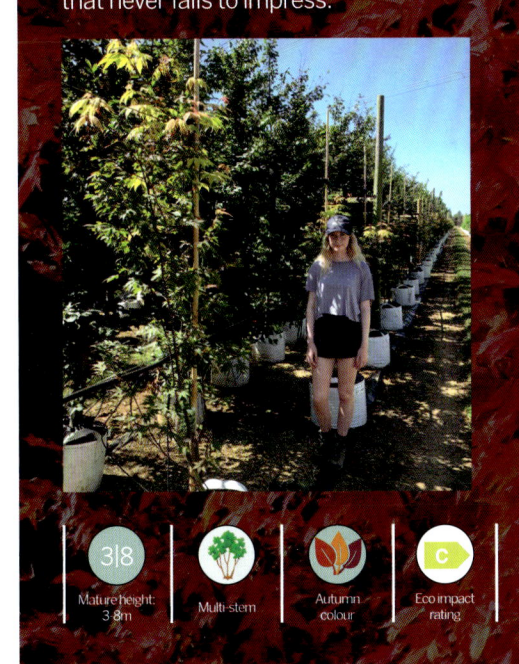

- Mature height: 3-8m
- Multi-stem
- Autumn colour
- Eco impact rating: C

ACER palmatum purpurea

A superb tree for those who like purple foliage, this clone was introduced in the 1850s but has since been unfairly superseded by improved selections such as Bloodgood.

It makes a small tree for a sheltered position such as a courtyard or an urban garden and has a rounded habit with its deeply lobed purple leaves turning shades of luminescent red in autumn.
They do best in rich, moist, but free draining, loamy soils.

- Mature height: 3-8m
- Multi-stem
- Red/purple foliage
- Eco impact rating: C

ACER palmatum Red Emperor

There are so many Acer palmatum types available on the market it is tricky to settle on the best one. However, 'Red Emperor' is hard to beat! Like Acer palmatum Bloodgood, it is slightly more wine red than dark red in the summer months and is slightly later to emerge in the spring. Preferring a neutral to acid soil, this clone is both vigorous and hardy, eventually making a sturdy bush up to seven metres in height by five metres broad.

Best on free draining soils, 'Red Emperor' should be given a sheltered sunny position for best results. We are often asked about growing these in permanent decorative containers and, like all trees, they eventually run out of soil volume and gently decline when pot bound. By autumn, the deep red foliage can turn a luminescent crimson before falling.

- Mature height: 3-8m
- Multi-stem
- Red/purple foliage
- Eco impact rating: C

ACER platanoides
Norway Maple

An imposing and fast-growing tree of great size and the parent of the many cultivars listed on the following pages. The yellow flowers appear in spring, ahead of the leaves which turn yellow and sometimes red in autumn. A native tree of Norway and Europe, but not of Britain, and used widely in parks and streets.

Many of its clones are more suitable for urban and street planting as they form crowns of more regular shape than that of their parent. If planting north of the M62, we would recommend using the selection 'Farlakes Green' as it is the toughest on the market and looks just the same. It does well on most soil types, tolerates air pollution and resists drought. Its clonal selections are generally preferred as seedling plants can grow to large proportions and create maintenance issues in streets and urban corridors.

- Mature height: 17-22m
- Shape of mature tree
- Urban trees
- Eco impact rating: A

ACER platanoides
Cleveland

In cultivation since 1948, this selection has an upright habit and an oval head of branches with big, dark green foliage. It has never really caught on in the UK, with varieties like Emerald Queen and Columnare preferred, but in our opinion this clone should not be overlooked!

Considered as one of the best clones for street planting by arborists in America, it does well on most soil types, tolerates air pollution and resists drought. It has an excellent autumn colour of golden yellow and retains its oval to rounded habit through to maturity.

- Mature height: 12-17m
- Shape of mature tree
- Urban trees
- Eco impact rating: B

ACER platanoides
Columnare

Raised in France by Simon – Louis nursery in the 1850s, this slow growing cultivar has an oval / compact habit and is superb as a street tree because its columnar form needs virtually no maintenance. The crown stays closed even when the tree is mature.

It does well on most soil types, tolerates air pollution and resists drought. The Dutch have confused matters by calling several similar types 'Columnare', but we reckon they are all distinctly different so beware!! From Barcham you will get the original and what we think is the best clone.

- Mature height: 12-17m
- Shape of mature tree
- Urban trees
- Eco impact rating: B

ACER platanoides
Crimson King

A large and most impressive tree with a well-rounded form, it looks good from spring through to autumn as its red foliage turns gradually to maroon. A seedling of Schwedleri, it was raised in Belgium in the 1930s.

It does well on most soil types, tolerates air pollution and resists drought. The yellow flowers contrast impressively against the dark emerging spring foliage. We so often see this tree planted in avenues too close together but there is no need as it is quick to grow. Ten metres should be the minimum planting distance but planting in bulk can give too much of a good thing in that the dark leaves tends to gobble up all the light and create a sombre environment below.

A tougher and quicker prospect than Purple Beech, this can be planted on the boundary of a site to draw the eye through the landscape. Dark leaved trees can be superb for defining the overall effect of the landscape but only if used sparingly. Too often I see this tree planted in areas where it will have to be felled before maturity as the planting position is too small to accommodate it.

Mature height: 12-17m	Shape of mature tree	Red/purple foliage	Eco impact rating: B

ACER platanoides Crimson Sentry

Derived from 'Crimson King' in Oregon in the mid 1970s, this far smaller tree is far more appropriate as a garden tree with its stubby ascending branches supporting purple / red leaves that can give great contrast without taking over valued space in restricted areas. It is a tough tree, thriving on most free draining soils light or heavy.

Visually very striking, emerging leaves are redder than crimson and autumn turns them to a mix of orange and reds before leaf fall. We quite often grow this tree as a low crowned half standard as its columnar shape is best shown off with the lower branches retained.

- Mature height: 5-8m
- Shape of mature tree
- Urban tree
- Red/purple foliage
- Eco impact rating: C

ACER platanoides Deborah

Another seedling from Schwedleri, fast growing Deborah comes from Canada and makes a large tree with a rounded form. Introduced in the 1970s, the spring leaves are bright red, gradually turning to dark green. When the second flush appears, there is a superb contrast between the red and the green foliage together.

It does well on most soil types, tolerates air pollution and resists drought. The leaves have a distinctive wavy margin and colour to a rich orange / yellow in the autumn. Most suited for parks, verges and large gardens.

Its newly emerging flush of spring red leaves are particularly effective against the profuse yellow flowers that are borne in April. For those of you who feel 'Royal Red' or 'Crimson King' are too much, 'Deborah' offers a superb compromise.

- Mature height: 12-17m
- Shape of mature tree
- Urban trees
- Eco impact rating: A

Telephone 01353 720 748 | www.barcham.co.uk | www.barchampro.co.uk

ACER platanoides Drummondii

In cultivation since 1903, this form produces magnificently variegated foliage which has a wide, creamy white margin. It is widely known in North America as the Harlequin Maple. Any shoots which show signs of reversion are best removed. A medium to large tree with a rounded form.

It does well on most soil types, tolerates air pollution and resists drought. It is most impressive in the spring when the variegation is at its most vivid, but summer winds can bruise the leaf margins of young trees which then scorch brown. This however is only superficial and does not affect its performance the following year.

This clone can provide vivid contrast within a garden, particularly against a dark evergreen backdrop so take care to place this tree as the results can be very rewarding. It won the Award of Merit in 1956.

7|12		
Mature height: 7-12m	Shape of mature tree	Urban trees
Variegated trees	Eco impact rating B	

ACER platanoides Emerald Queen

Selected in the USA in the late 1950s, this has a brighter green leaf colour and more regular habit than the species. It tends to keep a dominant central leader and a more regular habit. A superb cultivar and strongly recommended for street and urban plantings. Where uniformity is required, this is a far better choice than its parent, Acer platanoides.

It does well on most soil types, tolerates air pollution and resists drought. Although ascending when young, it usually gets as wide as it gets broad after about 25 years, so it is only ideal for wide verges and areas large enough to accommodate it. It is by far the most popular of the Norway Maple clones and a much safer bet than planting the seedling parent.

Mature height: 17-22m | Shape of mature tree | Urban trees | Eco impact rating: A

ACER platanoides Fairview

This tough newcomer to our range is derived from a seedling of 'Crimson King'. It thrives on poor urban soils and maintains an upright oval habit and at maturity its dimensions are approximately 15 metres tall with a diameter of 12 metres, making it a very useful urban tree.

Reddish purple foliage in the spring hardens to a deep bronze, sometimes green, by late summer. It bears green / yellow flowers from April onwards that are a lovely contrast with the dark leaves as they first emerge. Aside from Acer platanoides Crimson Sentry, this is the narrowest upright dark leaved Norway Maple we stock. It makes a striking avenue tree.

Mature height: 12-17m | Shape of mature tree | Urban trees | Red/purple foliage | Eco impact rating: B

Telephone 01353 720 748 | www.barcham.co.uk | www.barchampro.co.uk

ACER platanoides
Farlakes Green

This Swedish clone has similar characteristics to those of Emerald Queen but does not grow quite as high. This clone is preferred in Scandinavia as it is deemed hardier, resisting very low temperatures.

It does well on most soil types, tolerates air pollution and resists drought. Yellow spring flowers are replaced by crisp green foliage that turns yellow in autumn. A better clone for exposed conditions, we would recommend it more the further north you get.

- Mature height: 12-17m
- Shape of mature tree
- Urban trees
- Eco impact rating: A

ACER platanoides
Globosum

Introduced in the early 1870s, this 'lollipop' tree is top grafted onto platanoides stem to form a dense mop headed tree. A very good choice as a street tree and for urban plantings and particularly popular in Germany.

It does well on most soil types, tolerates air pollution and resists drought. The dense rounded formality of the crown makes this a delight for architects seeking contrast. Wonderful when in full foliage, it can be rather a let down in a garden after leaf fall as the crown network is small and stubby. Best for urban environments where small is beautiful. Tricky to deliver without superficial breakages to the twiggy crown, it is always best to plant when dormant and out of leaf.

- Mature height: 3-8m
- Shape of mature tree
- Urban trees
- Eco impact rating: C

ACER platanoides
Olmstead

Selected in Rochester, New York, in the mid 1950s, this cultivar is like Acer platanoides Columnare in having a columnar habit. A good choice as a street tree and where space is restricted.

It does well on most soil types, tolerates air pollution and resists drought. Generally, at maturity its height is twice its breadth making this a popular urban tree requiring little maintenance.

- Mature height: 12-17m
- Shape of mature tree
- Urban trees
- Eco impact rating: B

ACER platanoides Pacific Sunset

A cross between Acer truncatum and Acer platanoides Warrenred, this Oregon clone was selected for its autumn colour of orange and red. Its ascending but broad crown emerges with green leaves in the spring making it best suited for large gardens and urban verges. It thrives on most free draining soils and is a tougher bet than some of the Acer rubrum cultivars that have specific soil requirements and Acer freemanii types which can be prone to damage in heavy winds.

Not as long lasting for autumn colour as Liquidambar, the October / November display is nevertheless very striking, and its urban toughness makes this clone a great addition to our range of Norway maple types. We rate this variety very highly in terms of reliability and aesthetic beauty.

12|17	Shape of mature tree	Autumn colour	B Eco impact rating
Mature height: 12-17m			

ACER platanoides Princeton Gold

Also known as Prigo, this sparkling new cultivar has golden yellow spring foliage which hardens to yellow / green in summer. We recommend it for both park and street planting

Developed in the States, the foliage can tend to scorch up in hot conditions, so it is not widely used. However, our wonderfully temperate climate in the UK suits it down to the ground and the leaf colour makes it one of the best 'yellows' on the market. It does well on most soil types, tolerates air pollution and resists drought.

There are very few reliable yellow foliaged trees that thrive in the UK but in our opinion this clone rates as one that should not be overlooked. Lighter coloured leaves can provide stunning contrast to a garden with a sombre evergreen backdrop.

12|17			B
Mature height: 12-17m	Shape of mature tree	Yellow foliage	Eco impact rating

ACER platanoides Princeton Gold Upright

This new clonal variation is as it sounds, a very columnar version of Acer platanoides Princeton Gold. New foliage is a brighter yellow than old so the tree graduates from green to yellow as you work your way up the slender crown. Soil tolerances are the same as the parent, but this clone, due to its shape and size, is far better suited to restricted urban spaces and small gardens.

This spectacular tree is well used against a darker background to light up its surrounding aspect. Like all new clones brought to market, time will tell on whether it performs well through to maturity and beyond, but its attributes are so appealing that we are giving it a go!

10|15				B
Mature height: 10-15m	Shape of mature tree	Urban trees	Yellow foliage	Eco impact rating

ACER platanoides Royal Red

A large tree with a crown which is originally conical before becoming broadly round. It has dark purple leaves which turn golden yellow and orange in autumn. Attractive, bright red "keys" are an added feature. Yellow flowers in spring contrast beautifully with emerging purple foliage.

Supposedly smaller and hardier than 'Crimson King' there is an underlying suspicion that it is in fact the same tree but with a different name. I can't make my mind up either way, but I certainly wouldn't agonise over the choice for planting. It does well on most soil types, tolerates air pollution and resists drought.

12|17	Shape of mature tree	Red/purple foliage	B
Mature height: 12-17m			Eco impact rating

A

ACER pseudoplatanus
Sycamore / Celtic Maple

A native of central and southern Europe, the Sycamore has long been naturalised in Britain. Its wood has been used for making innumerable small items from violins to wooden spoons. It is a very large tree, and very fast growing for the first 20 years. It is also one of the very toughest. Many of its cultivars are smaller, but equally as durable.

It tolerates air pollution and thrives in most soils and is particularly useful for coastal sites where it can make an effective defence against strong winds and salt-laden air. Interestingly, recent work is now suggesting Sycamore is a native tree of the UK with both pollen and wood samples predating historical measures.

Native or not, the environmental impact of common Sycamore should not be understated. It makes a wonderful host to a wide range of our wildlife and provides a refuge in landscapes that do not readily support any other species.

The success of this tree gives it an unfair tag of being rather a 'weed'. It is however an incredibly versatile plant that thrives in the most difficult of circumstances so it shouldn't be overlooked. Improved clones such as 'Negenia' or 'Bruchem' are widely used on the continent as a street / verge tree as it forms a more regular crown shape at maturity.

17|22	Shape of mature tree	Urban trees	Eco impact rating
Mature height: 17-22m			A

Native or not, the environmental impact of common Sycamore should not be understated. It makes a wonderful host to a wide range of our wildlife and provides a refuge in landscapes that do not readily support any other species.

ACER pseudoplatanus Brilliantissimum

Smaller than the species and much slower growing, this top worked cultivar forms a round and dense crown. The young leaves in spring are a wonderful shell pink, hardening to light green by June. An excellent street tree and for where space is limited.

It tolerates air pollution and thrives in most soils and is particularly useful for coastal sites where it can make an effective defence against strong winds and salt-laden air. Introduced in the early 1900s, this eye-catching cultivar won the Award of Garden Merit in 2002.

- Mature height: 5-8m
- Shape of mature tree
- Garden trees
- Eco impact rating: C

ACER pseudoplatanus Leopoldii

An eye-catching cultivar first grown in the 1860s, it is a medium tree with a rounded habit. The leaves begin yellowish pink turning green later with splashed with random yellow variegation. Particularly attractive from leaf emergence in the spring to early summer. Some veer away from variegated trees but Leopoldii is out on its own as being a real stunner. It makes a wonderful contrast tree against a darker background and is both tough and reliable.

It tolerates air pollution, thrives in most soils and is particularly useful for coastal sites where it can make an effective defence against strong winds and salt-laden air. A great tree for large gardens, estates and parkland, it is not prone to the problem of reverting back to green like Acer platanoides Drummondii. Thriving on most soils, it can also tolerate a degree of wetness in winter once established.

- Mature height: 12-17m
- Shape of mature tree
- Variegated trees
- Eco impact rating: B

A

ACER pseudoplatanus Negenia

A vigorous, large and conical cultivar, it was selected in the late 1940s in the Netherlands, where it is widely used as a street tree. Negenia has dark green, red stalked leaves.

It tolerates air pollution and thrives in most soils and is particularly useful for coastal sites where it can make an effective defence against strong winds and salt-laden air. Like many clones, as it matures it represents a model shape and form of its seedling parent.

- Mature height: 17-22m
- Shape of mature tree
- Coastal sites
- Eco impact rating: A

ACER pseudoplatanus Spaethii

Also known as Acer pseudoplatanus Purpureum Spaethii and Acer pseudoplatanus Atropurpureum, this large tree is effective in exposed, windy sites as the underside of its foliage is purple. Introduced in the early 1860s.

It tolerates air pollution and thrives in most soils and is particularly useful for coastal sites where it can make an effective defence against strong winds and salt-laden air.

There are very few varieties of tree that offer an alternative leaf colour to green that can still be planted near the coast. As sea breezes are always a factor in these settings the contrast between the top and bottom sides of the leaves is constantly on display. Autumn colour is also quite dramatic so one gets an ornamental quality that can lift a drab landscape for difficult and exposed sites.

- Mature height: 12-17m
- Shape of mature tree
- Red/purple foliage
- Eco impact rating: B

ACER pseudoplatanus Worleei
Golden Sycamore

Bred in Germany in the 1890s, this is a beautiful cultivar like Corstorphinense. The leaves are primrose yellow as they open, darkening to gold before turning green in summer. A most elegant, medium sized tree.

It tolerates air pollution and thrives in most soils and is particularly useful for coastal sites where it can make an effective defence against strong winds and salt-laden air. Michael Dirr, the famous American arborist, reckons that he has come across eight different spellings of Worleei. This represents a trait of tree growers, never satisfied until they have completely baffled their customers!

- Mature height: 12-17m
- Shape of mature tree
- Yellow foliage
- Eco impact rating: B

ACER rubrum
Canadian Maple

Cultivated in Europe for its fabulous autumn colour and in America for the manufacture of furniture, this large tree has a rounded habit. The dark green leaves, slightly purple underneath, turn a brilliant scarlet in autumn.

It tolerates air pollution and wet soil. However, as a warning note, for all the attributes of this tree it is very rarely seen thriving in the UK as it is dependent on accessing the trace element manganese which it can only derive from acid soils. Please refer to Acer freemanii types if you haven't the soil to support your choice.

- Mature height: 17-22m
- Shape of mature tree
- Autumn colour
- Eco impact rating: B

A

ACER rubrum Bowhall

I first saw this tree in Portland, Oregon, growing in narrow pavements and thriving. Although its autumn colour is not as vivid as other Acer rubrum varieties we list, it still produces a fair show of yellow and orange leaves in October. Introduced in the States in 1948, this superb urban clone has never caught on in the UK and I am at a loss to understand why!

Its symmetrical ascending habit makes it an ideal subject for city planting where space is at a premium and we introduced it into our range in 2010. Its shape resembles a Lombardy Poplar as it can reach 10 metres in height with a width only of 3 metres. A low maintenance Acer that is more controlled than Acer platanoides Columnare.

Mature height: 12-17m | Shape of mature tree | Narrow trees | Eco impact rating: B

ACER rubrum October Glory

This superb female clone produces a good oval crown at maturity with an autumn display that is hard to beat. An aptly named variety, it was patented in the States in 1961 and introduced by the now closed Princeton Nursery. Widely planted, along with 'Red Sunset' and regarded as one of the best selections.

Its stunning display of vivid red and burgundy leaves in October / November is even more memorable by the length of time they are held on the tree. This clone rivals Liquidambar for its brilliant autumn display and is a great tree for parks and gardens.

Mature height: 12-17m | Shape of mature tree | Autumn colour | Eco impact rating: B

ACER rubrum Red Sunset

An American form of Red Maple, bred in the 1960s, is also known by the name "Franksred". Rated very highly by arborists for its good branch angle formation and landscape architects for its outstanding and long-lived autumn display of leaf colour.

Surely one of the most beautiful cultivars of Acer rubrum, this medium, broadly oval tree is regularly branched, and is an excellent choice for sheltered avenues. Its thick, dark, shiny foliage puts on a great display of red autumn colour. As a cautionary note, the presence of manganese in the soil is vital for Acer rubrum types to perform. Please refer to Acer freemanii types if you haven't the soil to support your choice.

Mature height: 12-17m | Shape of mature tree | Autumn colour | Eco impact rating: B

ACER rubrum Scanlon

A derivative from the North American native Acer rubrum, this wonderful urban clone produces a broadly oval crown at maturity that turns flame red in the autumn. Akin to Acer rubrum Red Sunset and October Glory, the rubrum types thrive best where the trace element manganese is present on neutral to acid soils which enhances their autumn colour. When this is in doubt, a swap to the Acer freemanii types such as Autumn Blaze or Autumn Fantasy may be a better choice to achieve a similar effect.

Acer rubrum Scanlon thrives best on free draining soils in full sun. Its iconic autumn colour is one of the chief instigators for the Eastern USA fall which attracts many a sightseer in October. Introduced in 1948 from the USA.

Mature height: 12-17m | Shape of mature tree | Autumn colour | Eco impact rating: B

A

ACER saccharinum
Silver Maple

A stately tree which grows along riverbanks in its native eastern North America, its common name is on account of the silvery underneath of its leaves, which turn golden yellow in autumn. Large and fast growing, its branches are often brittle and prone to breaking. Suitable for large and open spaces but never be tempted to shoehorn in restricted areas or you will inherit a maintenance nightmare.

It tolerates air pollution and wet soils. There are several examples that have reached over 30 metres in height in as little as 100 years so be sure to give it plenty of room at planting.

| 17\|22 Mature height: 17-22m | Shape of mature tree | Wet soils | B Eco impact rating |

ACER saccharinum
Laciniata Wieri

Discovered in 1873 by DB Wier, this large spreading tree has pendulous lower branches and deeply divided sharply toothed leaves. Its large, wide limbs make it a splendid subject for parks and other open spaces.

Like its parent plant it thrives on most soils and extreme conditions and grows with great vigour. Given enough space it can be truly dramatic but if planted for the moment rather than for the next generation you can pass on a legacy of high maintenance. Best to avoid excessively windy sites.

| 17\|22 Mature height: 17-22m | Shape of mature tree | Wet soils | B Eco impact rating |

ACER saccharinum Pyramidale

Introduced in the mid 1880s, this large, broadly pyramidal tree is best suited for parkland, open spaces and wide verges. It has heavy, ascending branches with smaller leaves than those of the species and is a good choice for verges and avenues.

Tolerating most soils and conditions it grows about half as wide as it is tall whilst often retaining its apically dominant central leader. Like other clones of Silver Maple, it is best not to manipulate by pruning as this will lead to a corrective cycle that is hard to break. Even though this could be perceived as a street form, don't be tempted as it is too vigorous and will quickly upset the pavement levels.

- Mature height: 17-22m
- Shape of mature tree
- Wet soils
- Eco impact rating: B

AESCULUS californica

The conkers we grow at Barcham were about the size of a tennis ball and orange in colour with some of the resulting seedlings getting to over six feet tall after only two growing seasons. We estimate these trees will be available for sale in 2026.

Known as the Californian Buckeye in its native land, this lovely widespreading tree is long lived but only grows to about 10 metres. It is fine on most free draining soils but would perform best in the southern half of the UK. Its sweet scented flowers are white with a tinge of pink.

- Mature height: 7-12m
- Shape of mature tree
- Parkland trees
- Flowering trees
- Bee friendly trees
- Eco impact rating: A

AESCULUS x carnea Briotii
Red Horse Chestnut

This large tree is wonderful in parks and planted in avenues. Of rounded habit, it produces dark pink, almost red, flowers in May and dates to the late 1850s. Given the Award of Garden Merit in 2002, this stately tree is a great favourite in the UK.

The fruits are smaller and less spiny, if at all, than those of the Horse Chestnut. Although they thrive in all soils and tolerate air pollution, they are most impressive in early spring when the stocky strong growth bursts into life seemingly on the first warm day in April. Having said this, trees that emerge early in the spring are often on the wane by September so don't expect a glorious autumn display.

Mature height: 17-22m | Shape of mature tree | Avenue trees | Eco impact rating: A

AESCULUS x carnea Plantierensis

Raised in France in the mid 1890s this splendid, large tree produces pale pink flowers with yellow throats in late spring. Probably the best of the carnea types it is resistant to many of the leaf afflictions that affect horse chestnuts from late summer onwards.

Raised in the famous Simon-Louis Frere nursery near Metz, it is a backcross between carnea and hippocastanum and being a triploid, it does not produce fruit. It does best in large open areas and makes a stately show when planted in avenues. It thrives in all soils and tolerates air pollution but like all the species of this type it is best in the spring and early summer.

Mature height: 17-22m | Shape of mature tree | Avenue trees | Eco impact rating: A

AESCULUS flava
Yellow Buckeye

Also known as Sweet Buckeye, this medium to large tree has creamy yellow flowers marked with red – the nearest to yellow in a horse chestnut. In its native south eastern United States, it grows on riverbanks and mountain sides, and it was once widely used to produce paper pulp. In Britain, it is a good choice for parks and open spaces.

It thrives in all soils, tolerates air pollution and, unusually for horse chestnut, has a good show of yellow autumn colour. Introduced from America in 1764, it won the Award of Garden Merit in 2002. The national champion in America is over 45 metres tall by 17 metres wide.

Mature height: 17-22m | Shape of mature tree | Flowering trees | Eco impact rating: A

AESCULUS hippocastanum
Horse Chestnut

One of the most well-known and loved of all trees! Very attractive in late spring with its white, tinged yellow then pink, candle-like flowers, followed by burnished "conkers" in their spiky casings. It originates from the borders of Greece and Albania and was introduced to Britain in the early 1600s. Wonderful in parks and open spaces.

Over recent years it has been subjected to several debilitating pests ranging from bleeding canker to leaf blotch and leaf miner so beware!

Mature height: 17-22m | Shape of mature tree | Avenue trees | Eco impact rating: A

Telephone 01353 720 748 | www.barcham.co.uk | www.barchampro.co.uk

AESCULUS hippocastanum Baumannii

This cultivar was discovered by A.N. Baumann near Geneva in 1820 and was propagated as a branch sport from the mother hippocastanum tree. It is notable for its double white flowers and the fact that it does not produce "conkers", which may be an advantage if required for large streets and avenues. The main branches are rather horizontal, so high pruning is required when used as a street tree.

It can commonly grow in excess of 30 metres and it is always amusing to see kids chucking objects at one in full foliage in anticipation of a shower of conkers as a reward, not knowing it is sterile. Particularly grand in the spring with its strong growth and flower display, it thrives in most soils and tolerates air pollution. Like all hippocastanum types however they are the first to wane in September prior to dormancy.

Like the rest of this genus, recent years have seen a wide range of debilitating pests and diseases that are making people think twice about planting this once much favoured tree. Leaf blotch, scale insect, leaf miner and bleeding canker may prove too much for this tremendous tree to withstand.

The further north you get in the UK the less the associated problems seem to be, but our advice is to stop the avenue planting and stick to specimen individuals just in case. Baumannii's flowers herald the spring and its stout growth gives it a solid appearance.

| 17|22 Mature height: 17-22m | Shape of mature tree | Avenue trees | Eco impact rating: A |

The further north you get in the UK the less the associated problems seem to be but our advise is to stop the avenue planting and stick to specimen individuals just in case. Baumannii's flowers herald the spring and its stout growth gives it a solid appearance.

AESCULUS indica
Indian Horse Chestnut

The Indian Horse Chestnut originates in the Himalayas, having been introduced to Britain in the 1850s. A majestic tall tree, well suited to parkland and large estates, it has a rounded habit.

It bears pyramidal panicles of pink flushed flowers in summer, while its foliage is bronze when young, turning glossy and dark green before changing to orange and yellow in autumn. It tolerates chalky soils well.

There has been increased incidence of what was thought to be Phytophthora bleeding canker on Horse Chestnuts, especially in the South East and Midlands of England. Research is ongoing but it is now believed the cause is a bacterium rather than a fungus, but feedback from arborists suggests Aesculus indica has immunity from the infection. However, it is not a common tree, so the jury is out on this one.

- Mature height: 17-22m
- Shape of mature tree
- Urban trees
- Flowering trees
- Eco impact rating: A

Its deeply cut leaves make it the prettiest of the Chestnut family but annoyingly it sometimes sets flower on the terminal growing bud, making it difficult to grow straight. However, this is our problem to resolve, not yours!

AILANTHUS altissima
Tree of Heaven

Introduced in 1751, this fast-growing native of Northern China was said to reach for the sky. In hot summers it is quick to naturalise and it can make fun of growing in truly inhospitable urban or rural environments.

Living up to its common name, it is certainly large and broadly columnar in habit. Although not botanically related, it produces long, ash-like foliage. Tolerant of air pollution and ideal for street plantings where space permits, it is best suited on wide verges or central reservations. It thrives in most soils.

Old Chinese medicine texts puts great faith in this tree for cures against mental illness or its ability to combat baldness. The roots, bark and leaves are still used today in the Far East to manage all sorts of ills but over here we enjoy it for its fine architectural shape.

Unfortunately this tree has been classified as an invasive species so is now illegal to trade and grow within the UK.

Mature height: 17-22m | Shape of mature tree | Urban trees | Eco impact rating: A

ALBIZIA julibrissin Rouge de Tuiliere

The Holy Grail of trees as far as Barcham is concerned, this highly ornamental tree is supposed to be the hardiest clonal selection of this group and the reward is so great that we are giving it a try for availability from 2020/21. Sometimes referred to as the Chinese / Persian Silk Tree, it is part of the mimosa family. Their arching branches support bipinnate leaves which are glorious enough but the real beauty comes from its flower clusters made up of coloured pink stamens that sit atop the tree in the summer.

Is this tree hardy enough to thrive in the UK? Time will tell on this one but there are mature examples in both Cambridge and London that we have seen over the years and this tree has such drama that it is surely worth a go! I certainly wouldn't push the boundaries anywhere but Southern England, south facing and sheltered. Once established it is fine on most free draining soils.

Mature height: 5-7m | Shape of mature tree | Flowering trees | Eco impact rating

ALBIZIA julibrissin Tropical Dream

This clonal selection is best suited to cooler climates when compared to its parent. Of all the hardiest forms of this remarkably pretty tree this has the longest flowering period with its abundant pink fluffy blossoms coming out daily between late June and August in good summers. The foliage is also captivating, making this tree a lovely addition for a south facing garden in the lower half of the UK.

Thriving on most free draining soils, this clone was selected in Belgium in 1984. It is reportedly hardy down to -25c but it is still advisable to mulch well to avoid frost getting to the roots over the winter period. Late to emerge in the spring, this really is a spectacular summer tree for both foliage and flower. Best on neutral to alkaline soils.

Mature height: 5-7m | Shape of mature tree | Flowering trees | Garden trees | Eco impact rating

Telephone 01353 720 748 | www.barcham.co.uk | www.barchampro.co.uk

ALNUS cordata
Italian Alder

Originating in southern Italy and introduced in 1820, this fast growing, medium tree has a conical habit. It's shiny, green, pear-like leaves last well into winter, particularly under street lighting. It produces notably larger fruits than other alders. Good for parks and verges, we also recommend for coastal plantings.

It thrives on all ground including dry, high ph soils but is most at home nearest water. Being highly tolerant of urban pollution it is a particularly adaptable urban tree but must be given enough room or it can outstay its welcome. Italian trials indicate that it can even tolerate acid rain. The bark is a glistening brown when young but matures to be rougher.

Once heralded by many as the perfect candidate for an urban tree, its vigour can cause the lifting of hard areas over time so I would advise planting on verges rather than paved streets where it can outplay its welcome.

| Mature height: 12-17m | Shape of mature tree | Clay soils | Bee friendly trees | Eco impact rating: B |

A

ALNUS glutinosa
Common Alder

Once used to produce clogs in northern England, this medium sized native tree has a conical growth habit and produces yellow catkins in March. Its natural habitat is boggy land and riverbanks. However, it is also very good for urban plantings as it thrives in all soils and tolerates air pollution. Available as both multi-stemmed and as a single stem.

Being a native tree, it is a wonderful host to a wide range of wildlife. It is a very useful variety to plant where the ground is liable to flood and survives many weeks with its roots underwater. There was a scare about Alder being susceptible to Phytophthora along water courses up and down the country, but this was highly overstated and Alnus glutinosa remains a vital inclusion to any native planting mix.

Mature height: 12-17m | Shape of mature tree | Multi-stem

Wet soils | Bee friendly trees | Eco impact rating: B

In its early years Common Alder can grow very quickly, sometimes putting on over two metres of growth in a single growing season when the availability of water coupled with high temperatures predominate. A great tree for use as a screen, it is often seen flanking orchards for this reason.

Telephone 01353 720 748 | www.barcham.co.uk | www.barchampro.co.uk

A

Alnus glutinosa
Imperialis

Introduced in the early 1860s this finely cut leaf tree won the Award of Garden Merit in 2002 to back up its Award of Merit in 1973. I have seen it used both in Leicester and Liverpool as a very effective street tree, but it is usually best seen planted on damp soils in parkland or gardens.

The leaves are more densely cut than Alnus glutinosa Laciniata to create a uniquely fluffy and soft foliage effect that is unrivalled by other trees in the UK. It is wonderful when planted in groups to accentuate the effect but strangely it is little used. However, once seen never forgotten and I am convinced that its popularity will grow over the coming years.

| Mature height: 12-17m | Shape of mature tree | Wet soils | Bee friendly trees | Eco impact rating: B |

Alnus glutinosa
Laciniata

Introduced from France in the 1820's, this cultivar has finely cut deep green leaves that are a joy to behold when looking up through the canopy against a rich blue sky. A tree of medium size, it has a graceful, conical habit, and is very good for broad verges and for parks.

It thrives in all soils, though prefers damp ground, and tolerates air pollution. Being a variation of a native tree, the cut leaves make this truly striking. It is particularly effective when planted as a triangle at 7 metre centres as the foliage eventually merges to magnify the effect.

| Mature height: 12-17m | Shape of mature tree | Wet soils | Bee friendly trees | Eco impact rating: B |

ALNUS incana
Grey Alder

A hardy and tough medium tree, capable of coping with cold, wet soils and exposed situations. Grey alder is a fast grower, well suited to industrial areas and street plantings. Its pointed grey leaves readily distinguish it from Alnus glutinosa.

Introduced from Europe in the 1780s it does best on calcareous soils and tolerates air pollution. In the recent past the North American tree bearing the same generic name has been changed to Alnus rugosa to avoid confusion amongst well travelled tree enthusiasts. Profuse pink / yellow catkins are produced just prior to spring.

| Mature height: 12-17m | Shape of mature tree | Wet soils | Bee friendly trees | Eco impact rating: B |

ALNUS incana Aurea

Winning the Award of Merit in 1995 and introduced in the early 1860s, this magnificent small tree is a must for any garden in need of winter interest. Unlike the species, this is a slow grower. It does best in moist soil and semi-shaded areas.

The young shoots and leaves emerge a golden yellow in spring which contrast beautifully with vivid red catkins that open to a pink / yellow. The catkins form as early as August and get better and better in colour and size throughout the winter. The bark and twiggy branches also turn orange during the winter. Good as a street tree and for parks and gardens.

As the catkins show so early this is one of the few trees, we have that can legitimately offer all year-round interest. It has always been underplayed by growers, but we have been bulking up our numbers over recent years to market it effectively. Quick to grow when juvenile, it is far more sedate in growth at maturity that its parent, Alnus incana, so is an ideal subject for a garden.

| 7|12 Mature height: 7-12m | Shape of mature tree | Bee friendly trees | B Eco impact Rating |

This lovely clone can provide wonderful contrast within a garden so care should be taken on where to site it. On frosty or even snowy winter days its vivid red catkin display can be simply stunning. Similarly its light coloured foliage can brighten a dour evergreen backdrop.

ALNUS incana Laciniata

Introduced in the early 1860s this superb cut leaf form won the First-Class Certificate in 1873. A medium tree with dissected leaves, it has a conical habit when mature and is most attractive. Equally at home in a street, park, verge or garden.

It does best in moist soil but can tolerate the vagaries of urban conditions. There is not much to choose between this variety and the cut leaf forms of Alnus glutinosa as all are remarkably striking and probably the pick of all the cut leaved trees we offer.

Mature height: 12-17m | Shape of mature tree | Bee friendly trees | Eco impact rating: B

I have seen this tree used most effectively in several towns and cities in the UK. The selections in Liverpool have outstripped expectation and must be between 12 and 15 metres tall. Their pyramidal crowns are lovely in season as the cut leaves give it a very soft and graceful appearance. Best specimens are usually found in the west as annual rainfall is higher.

ALNUS x spaethii

Of garden origin and dating from 1908, this fast growing tree of medium size has a rounded habit and is good as a park and street tree. It will also tolerate coastal conditions. The large leaves are purple tinged when young and it is at its best in spring when displaying its beautiful and numerous catkins.

It does best in moist soil, though can cope with dry soils once established, and tolerates air pollution. This variety catches many of our customers out in that it looks like a cherry when in full leaf in the summer. The leaves are vivid green and large as well as being long. The bark gives the game away but this is always a good tree to throw into a plant identification competition for the over confident!

A cross between Alnus japonica and Alnus subcordata, it is little surprise that this is a rarely seen tree but in our opinion it could and should be used more often to bring greater diversity to Alnus plantings in the UK. Its catkin display is second to none amongst the large growing Alders more regularly planted.

Mature height: 12-17m | Shape of mature tree | Bee friendly trees | Eco rating impact: B

A

AMELANCHIER
arborea Robin Hill
Serviceberry

A wonderful small tree that we consider to be by far the best tree form of Serviceberry on the market. It forms a dense, oval habit and produces its masses of spring flowers that open pink and turn white. A North American selection and as highly rated there as it is here. I have planted one outside of my office window at Barcham so I am rarely far away from this tree!

The young leaves emerge coppery red and then harden to green by late spring before they turn vivid red in autumn.

A very good choice for street plantings and residential areas as it provides plenty of interest with virtually no maintenance. Being such a small tree of ultimate size, it can be placed much closer to buildings than most trees which make it a fantastic choice for urban planting. There are very few trees that offer wonderful floral displays in the spring and glorious autumn leaf colour but this is one of them. It does best in moist, well drained, lime free soils.

- Mature height: 5-7m
- Shape of mature tree
- Bee friendly trees
- Eco impact rating: C

We latched onto this clone in the late 1990s and there are now some fine examples of how they progress at maturity. It makes a fantastic small urban tree suitable for both streets and gardens and its seasonal interest makes it one of the glamour trees of our range.

Telephone 01353 720 748 | www.barcham.co.uk | www.barchampro.co.uk

AMELANCHIER
Ballerina
Serviceberry

This small tree, with its finely toothed leaves, was selected by the Experimental Station at Boskoop in the Netherlands in the 1970s and named in 1980. It forms a broader crown than Robin Hill and is less tall making it a better choice for verges and gardens than it is for streets.

It has abundant white flowers in spring and excellent red autumn colour. It does best in moist, well drained, lime free soils and is remarkably resistant to fire blight. It won the Award of Garden Merit in 2002 and remains a great choice for any garden. Sometimes grown as a bushy shrub, we train ours to tree form with a 1.5-1.8m clear stem with a well defined central stem and rounded crown.

A hybrid of Amelanchier laevis and Amelanchier arborea, its flowers are larger than 'Robin Hill' or lamarckii making it a very showy performer in the spring. Its fruits are edible and are a particular favourite of blackbirds in my garden. Its spreading crown gives it a more rustic feel than 'Robin Hill' making it more suited to rural gardens.

AMELANCHIER
lamarckii
Serviceberry

Naturalised over much of Western Europe, it is a simply stunning sight when in full bloom with its white flowers produced in plentiful racemes. It is a small, shrubby tree with emerging copper coloured leaves turning green by late spring before they mature to a rich red as autumn progresses. The rounded fruits, red in summer before turning black in autumn, are edible.

Although we grow this both as a multi-stem and single stemmed tree please be aware that if you buy the latter form it is prone to sucker and broaden with age so requiring far more maintenance than Robin Hill if planted as a street tree. In our opinion it makes a far better subject if planted as a coppiced multi stem tree for verge or garden plantings as you maximise its flowering potential and are going with its natural habit. It does best in moist, well drained, lime free soils. Fine near buildings, I have one growing happily two metres from my front door!

| Mature height: 5-7m | Shape of mature tree | Multi-stem | Bee friendly trees | Eco impact rating (C) |

ARALIA elata
Japanese Angelica Tree

Introduced to Britain in the 1830s from its native Japan, it won the Award of Merit in 1959 and the Award of Garden Merit in 2002. A remarkably odd looking tree, wonderfully exotic in foliage which falls away in autumn to leave only a few spiky branches.

It makes a small rounded tree and is remarkable for its very large, doubly pinnate leaves, produced mainly in a "ruff" towards the tips of its stems. The foliage often gives vivid and luminous autumn colour, coinciding with its extraordinary stunning display of white panicle flowers.

Mature height: 3-5m | Multi-stem | Autumn colour | Flowering trees | Eco impact rating: D

ARAUCARIA araucana
Monkey Puzzle

Sometimes referred to as the Chile Pine it is also a native of Argentina. This ancient slow growing evergreen tree is well known for its distinctive long slender branches that are densely covered with overlapping spiked leaves. Introduced into the UK in 1795 by Archibald Menzies, the famous Navy surgeon who later turned plant collector, it won the Award of Merit in 1980. Amazingly enough, it was once a native of Britain. The fossilized wood from this tree was highly coveted by Queen Victoria. Otherwise known as Jet, it was used in the making of mourning jewellery.

Hardy in the UK, they are often planted far too close to houses so have to be removed before they get to maturity. This unusual conifer prefers a moist loamy soil and has great apical dominance drawing the tree up strongly vertical so it is very suited to crown lifting. Try not to handle the foliage unless you are well protected as the leaves are very sharp! The cones are globular, up to 20cm in length and take up to three years to mature.

Mature height: 17-22m | Shape of mature tree | Evergreen trees | Eco impact rating: B

ARBUTUS unedo
Killarney Strawberry Tree

This native of South West Ireland and the Mediterranean is, unusually for an ericaceous plant, tolerant of lime. It is a small evergreen with brown, shedding bark, and its flowers and fruits are produced together in the autumn. A good choice for exposed and coastal sites, it is also good for urban plantings.

A winner of the Award of Garden Merit in 2002 and of a First Class Certificate in 1933, it does well in most soil types, but prefers it moist. Don't be afraid to hard prune if getting untidy as if this is done in late March / April it grows back beautifully. We grow it as both a bushy shrub and a full standard tree. Young shoots are tinged red which contrasts well against the dark green leaves. Best in the West where annual rainfall is greater.

- Mature height: 5-8m
- Shape of mature tree
- Multi-stem
- Garden trees
- Eco impact rating: D

B

68 **Time for Trees** | Edition 4

BETULA albosinensis Fascination
Chinese Birch

The species from which Fascination was developed was brought back from China in 1901 by Ernest Wilson. He was very taken with it, describing it as follows: "The bark is singularly lovely, being a rich orange-red or orange-brown and peels off in sheets, each no thicker than fine tissue paper, and each successive layer is clothed with a white glaucous bloom". Further to this the catkins in the spring are amazing, up to 10cm in length, opening to a rich yellow-brown and so numerous my kids call it the 'caterpillar tree'.

Fascination is a refined clone with dark green leaves, which are large for a birch, appearing in April, along with the showy display of yellow catkins. It has outstanding stem colour – orange peeling to pink and cream and then purest white once the tree gets beyond 30cm girth. It is a medium sized tree, becoming oval as it matures, has stiffly ascending branches and the one outside my kitchen window, now over 82cm girth, is a constant joy and often commented on. A great choice for parks and verges growing well on most soils. It is listed by a few as Betula utilis Fascination but we put it firmly classified in the albosinensis group.

Mature height: 12-17m | Shape of mature tree | Bark interest | Eco impact rating: B

BETULA ermanii
Erman's Birch

This birch was originally from North East Asia and Japan and was first cultivated in the 1880s. Always the first tree to emerge with new leaf in the spring at Barcham, and one of the first to fall in autumn. Importantly it tolerates reflected heat and light very adequately so is a great urban tree that requires little maintenance.

An elegant and vigorous medium to large tree, the bright green, often heart shaped and prominently veined leaves which appear very early in spring become clear yellow in autumn. It grows well on most soils. There is a variety named Betula ermanii Holland but in my view this is synonymous with what I have described.

- Mature height: 12-17m
- Shape of mature tree
- Bark interest
- Eco impact rating: B

BETULA maximowicziana
Monarch Birch

An oddity within our Birch range, hardly looking like a member of the same family. It is a native of Japan where it can reach up to 35 metres in height but it is rare to see in the UK and reaches a more modest height of between 15-20cm. Introduced into the UK in 1893, this is one to catch someone out on a tree identification competition.

It is fast growing and has a dark brown trunk when young, maturing into greyish tinges. The large heart shaped leaves turn clear yellow in the autumn. It retains a pyramidal shape when young but this broadens at maturity. The leaves are the biggest of all the Birch family, sometimes attaining over 12cm in length.

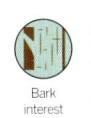

Mature height: 12-17m | Shape of mature tree | Bark interest | Garden trees | Eco impact rating: C

BETULA nigra
River Birch

Also known as the Red Birch, this is one of the very best trees for wet soils and we favour the clonal selection from the States called Heritage, selected in 1968, for its vigour and uniformity. Originally found along the river banks of the South Eastern United States, this medium sized tree makes a great show with its shaggy, flaking, cinnamon / orange bark. Mature trees are truly statuesque and broadly pyramidal in form. Foliage is soft green and diamond shaped.

Its common name of River Birch is misleading as we have seen this tree thriving in arid London tree pits. Once established, it can tolerate extreme heat in the summer, thriving in Florida as well as Kentucky in the States. This could become a good choice for the South East of the UK as temperatures continue to break records during the summer months. Available as both a standard tree and as a multi-stem.

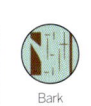

Mature height: 12-17m | Shape of mature tree | Multi-stem | Bark interest | Eco impact rating: B

BETULA papyrifera
Paper Birch

The Paper Birch is also known as the Canoe Birch in its native North America and was introduced into the UK in 1750. Until it clears 20-25cm girth the bark is a brown / red and very distinguishable from other juvenile birch but after this point the bark starts to whiten markedly. A pioneer species, particularly quick to colonise areas devastated by fire.

The waterproof qualities of its bark made it an important tree for the Native Americans who used it for making canoes and wigwam covers, as well as eating utensils. It makes a medium to large tree with a conical habit. It has white, papery bark, the colour being carried high into the canopy, and attractive yellow autumn foliage. One of the most elegant of trees for parks. It does best on moist, well drained sandy soil, but is tolerant of most conditions.

- Mature height: 12-17m
- Shape of mature tree
- Bark interest
- Eco impact rating: B

BETULA pendula
Silver Birch

The Silver Birch is also known as the "Lady of the Woods" – so called because of its slender and graceful appearance. It is a pioneer species and particularly admired in the UK. Even though it seemingly grows anywhere it is remarkably difficult to successfully transplant bare rooted but our containerised trees solve this problem. A group of three silver birches that we supplied were planted in Stamford, Lincolnshire in 2005 and have grown from 12-14cm girth to 30-35cm girth in 6 years!

A medium tree with a conical, but semi weeping habit, the bark is white with horizontal lines and large, diamond shaped cracks as the tree matures. Very good for parks and woodland, but not suitable for areas where soil becomes compacted. It grows well on most soils and we grow it as both a single stemmed tree and a multi-stemmed tree. Multi-stemmed trees are particularly useful when planted on elevated or exposed ground as they have a low centre of gravity and need no staking. Our multi-stemmed birch is grown as true single plant coppices, not three or four plants bundled together in a pot that can lead to issues further down the line.

The clonal selection 'Zwisters Glory' is reliably white stemmed and more upright in habit. It is vigorous in its younger years and may represent a better choice for the urban environment.

BETULA pendula Dalecarlica
Swedish Birch

A most elegant tree and perfect for specimen planting. For those of you that went to Writtle Agricultural College you will remember the splendid short avenue of them leading to the refectory block. Some call this clone 'Laciniata' or 'Crispa' but don't worry about it as the differences are too slight to cause a dilemma.

Found in Sweden in the 1760s, it is a medium to large tree of slender form and with a broadly columnar habit. The leaves are deeply cut and branches weep gracefully. Bark is white and peeling. Very good for parks and woodland, but not suitable for areas where soil becomes compacted or where there is too much reflected heat and light. It grows well on most soils.

It is always good to bear in mind a tree's origin to assess its physiology. Sweden has shorter day lengths than southern England so to place this clone in a paved area in London would represent extreme conditions for this tree. It is much happier planted in greener areas and further north.

Mature height: 12-17m | Shape of mature tree | Bark interest | Eco impact rating: B

BETULA pendula Fastigiata
Upright Birch

An upright form of the Silver Birch, resembling the shape of a Lombardy Poplar. It tends to spiral its way upwards giving a corkscrew effect of twiggy birch branches that hold their leaves slightly longer than most other varieties. The bark, although similar to Betula pendula is not as spectacular as the white barked clones.

This medium to large tree has stiffly ascending branches which give it a columnar habit. In cultivation since the 1870s, it makes a good street and car park tree as it requires little space. It grows well on most soils and the highest recorded specimen comes in at over 30 metres although I have never seen any at half that size.

Mature height: 7-12m | Shape of mature tree | Narrow trees | Bark interest | Eco impact rating: B

BETULA pendula Obelisk

Originating from Northern France in the mid 1950s, this densely branched tree has typical silver birch foliage and silver white trunk but grows in a very ascending fashion so doesn't exceed 3 metres diameter, making it a very useful birch for restricted areas and small gardens. I have seen this clone used to great effect on a roundabout in Oakham, Rutland, where width was at a premium.

Thriving on most free draining soils, this tough little tree is quite often growth feathered, with branches all the way down its stem. Its green leaves turn to a clear yellow for the autumn and its twiggy brown branches gives great contrast to its thicker white trunk as it matures.

- Mature height: 7-12m
- Shape of mature tree
- Bark interest
- Garden trees
- Eco impact rating: B

BETULA pendula Purpurea
Purple Birch

Introduced in the early 1870s, this slow growing and rare variety won the First Class Certificate in 1874. One of the largest specimens I have seen happens to be in my next door neighbour's garden in Rutland and has reached over 10 metres whilst retaining a slender habit.

Dark purple leaves emerge in spring soften to a dark green / purple by summer. The bark is like that of Betula pendula and the habit is similarly repeated. It will grow on most soils and is best suited for gardens and arboretums.

- Mature height: 12-17m
- Shape of mature tree
- Red/purple foliage
- Eco impact rating: B

BETULA pendula Tristis
Weeping Birch

Introduced in 1867 this outstanding cultivar won the Award of Garden Merit in 2002. It is a sight to behold in winter when its twiggy growth, supported on pendulous limbs, is shrouded in frost on a bright morning. If space is restricted, or for small gardens, Betula pendula Youngii should be chosen instead.

A most graceful and particularly beautiful tall tree, with slender, pendent branches. Although a weeping birch, it maintains a central leader, and is excellent planted as a specimen. Also good for wide verges and avenues, it grows well on most soils. The bark matures to a decent white making this, in our opinion, one of the best tall weeping trees on the market.

I think this tree is at its best when it stands still and dormant in winter with a severe frost covering its fine cascading twiggy branches.

- Mature height: 12-17m
- Shape of mature tree
- Bark interest
- Eco impact rating: B

BETULA pendula Westwood

This lovely clone of UK native Silver Birch originated from near Beverley, Yorkshire. Particularly vigorous when young, this pyramidal tree has a great form and startling bark synonymous with its genus. Birch, being a pioneer species, thrives on most free draining soils and is surface rooting.

This new introduction has enough guts about it to thrive within the urban environment and its green leaves turn to a buttercup yellow in the autumn. Its regular habit lends itself to being crown lifted over time to show off its showy silvery bark but like all birch this is best done from October through to December rather than in the Spring when it tends to weep from new pruning cuts. Formally introduced with the name 'Shaft' we use the name where the tree was found.

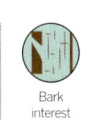

- Mature height: 12-17m
- Shape of mature tree
- Urban trees
- Bark interest
- Native trees
- Eco impact rating: B

BETULA pendula Youngii
Young's Weeping Birch

Originating in the early 1870s, this small to medium weeping birch has no defined central leader and therefore eventually forms an attractive dome shape. Sometimes produced top worked to get the initial height, we prefer to grow a structurally stronger plant from the base and draw up a leader until we have formed a 1.8-2 metre clear stem that can support the crown thereafter.

The thin branches eventually reach the ground and the serrated, triangular leaves show good autumn colour. It develops a smooth white bark and is an attractive specimen tree for lawns. It grows well on most soils and has been a great favourite in the UK for many years.

- Mature height: 5-8m
- Shape of mature tree
- Bark interest
- Garden trees
- Eco impact rating: B

BETULA pendula Zwisters Glory

This new selection originated from J van Roessel in Switzerland and was introduced into the European market in 1994. In effect it is a very uniform version of seed grown Betula pendula with a gleaming white bark so it makes an ideal choice for avenue planting. The branches grow at a 45 degree angle from the stem and remain subordinate to the main trunk to retain a graceful pyramidal crown.

This tree has great apical dominance so lends itself to crown lifting over time if needed. It is a splendid choice for the urban environment and quick to grow on most soils. The bark is nearly as good as Betula utilis Jacquemontii so we can expect to see a lot more of this clone in future years.

- Mature height: 17-22m
- Shape of mature tree
- Bark interest
- Eco impact rating: B

To vouch for its hardiness, Betula pubescens can be seen growing further north than any other broadleaf tree. It generally forms a scrubby low lying tree at this latitude and is native of both Greenland and Iceland. Its ascending branches give it a more solid appearance than Betula pendula and this makes it a tougher prospect to grow on exposed sites.

Mature height: 12-17m | Shape of mature tree | Bark interest | Native trees | Eco impact rating

BETULA pubescens
Common White Birch

The Common White Birch is also known as Downy Birch and Hairy Birch. Oil from its stem is used in the production of leather, while the bark was once used for roofing in Scandinavia. A native of both the UK and Europe, it ideally prefers damper soils than Betula pendula so is more commonly seen in the west. In our opinion it is an undervalued tree for planting in the general landscape and should be used more frequently ahead of the more popular Silver Birch.

Linnaeus classed this with Betula pendula, but it differs in not having pendulous branches and in having darker bark and downy young shoots. The white bark peels into papery layers, but does not have the characteristic diamond shaped cracks of Silver Birch. Very good for parks and verges. It grows well on most soils.

To vouch for its hardiness, Betula pubescens can be seen growing further north than any other broadleaf tree. It generally forms a scrubby low lying tree at this latitude and is native of both Greenland and Iceland. Its ascending branches give it a more solid appearance than Betula pendula and this makes it a tougher prospect to grow on exposed sites.

B

Some nurseries have tried growing this clone through micro propagation but the results at maturity are more than disappointing, with a loose and poor crown formation. We strongly recommend a budded / grafted plant as the result is proven and the mature crown structure assured.

BETULA utilis Jacquemontii / Doorenbos

There are now so many differing clones put under this banner that the trade is tying itself in knots of confusion, but suffice it to say if you are after the gleaming white barked birch under the above cultivar name from Barcham you will not be disappointed! The unsurpassed whiteness of the trunk and branches peels routinely each year and is accentuated by lenticel lines. A native of the western Himalayas, it makes a medium tree with ascending branches, and is also spectacular when grown as a multi-stem. However, beware those growers who palm off a multi-stem as three separate trees grown together as this will only lead to structural problems later on. Its oval, dark green leaves turn golden yellow in autumn. Excellent for urban plantings, it grows well on most soils.

This tree can be very effectively placed against a dark background in a garden as the white stems bounce back to you in contrast. I normally advocate a planting distance of a minimum of seven metres for any of our trees but have conceded in recent years that this clone is sensational when planted en mas at three to five metre centres. Anglesey Abbey in Cambridgeshire proves this point and a trip to this lovely National Trust garden is a must in winter.

Mature height: 12-17m | Shape of mature tree | Multi-stem | Bark interest | Eco impact rating: B

BETULA utilis
Snow Queen

This lovely white barked clone is very similar to 'Jacquemontii' but maybe a little more vigorous when younger. Its bark peels to reveal a new layer of creamy white underneath before this bleach to a pure white in the sun. Dark green leaves contrast beautifully against the white branch network in the summer and these turn to shades of yellow in the autumn.

Betula utilis types tend to broaden out when mature and can be as wide as they are tall so make sure you have the room to accommodate them. If a narrower white clone is preferred revert to Betula pendula Zwisters Glory, Betula albosinensis Fascination or Betula ermanii.

| 10\|15 Mature height: 10-15m | Shape of mature tree | Bark interest | Urban trees | Garden trees | B Eco impact rating |

BROUSSONETIA papyrifera
Paper Mulberry

Introduced in the early 18th century and now naturalised in America, fibre from the Paper Mulberry was once woven into a fine cloth in Polynesia and its bark is still processed to make paper in its native Japan. In Europe it is regarded as a highly ornamental specimen tree suitable for gardens, parks and arboretums.

A small to medium tree, it has lobed, hairy leaves, no two of which are the same shape. Male plants have pendent catkins, while the females bear orange-red fruits. The young stems are green and brown blotched giving it a somewhat unusual camouflaged effect. Tied to the same family as Morus, this is one for the plant collector. It does best on fertile, calcareous soil.

| 7\|12 Mature height: 7-12m | Shape of mature tree | Bark interest | D Eco impact rating |

CALOCEDRUS decurrens
Incense Cedar

Native to California and Oregon, this large, evergreen conifer has a columnar habit making it unmistakable. Introduced in 1853, it won the Award of Garden Merit in 2002. Resembling Thuja when young, this superb truly fastigiate conifer is often overlooked but it makes a fabulous impact in garden, verge or park with no on-going maintenance issues.

Perfect as a specimen tree or grown in avenues, it has dark green leaves crowded into fan-like sprays with oval, hanging cones. It grows well on most soils and is well suited to growing in the UK.

- Mature height: 12-17m
- Shape of mature tree
- Evergreen trees
- Eco impact rating: A

I first saw some maturing Calocedrus in the UK at the Royal Horticultural Society's garden at Harlow Carr near Harrogate and was struck by their architectural elegance. When young, they are fairly unremarkable but given time their wonderful shape makes them a fantastic asset to any landscape. As the tree matures its bark lightly cracks to produce a pleasing patchwork effect.

CAMELLIA sasanqua Rosea

Introduced in the early 1800s and a native of China and Japan, this acid loving small evergreen tree is grown at Barcham as multi-stemmed bush and often takes the form of two clonal varieties, namely 'Cleopatra' or 'Kanjiro'.

It is better planted in the south facing gardens of southern England where it thrives to make a small tree about 5 metres in height. Glossy evergreen leaves are beautifully contrasted with luscious pink fragrant flowers in both autumn and spring. Generally, the hotter the preceding summer, the better the performance. It is also best to position the plant in a sheltered spot, protecting it against cold winter winds.

CAMELLIA sasanqua Rosea 'Kanjiro'

CAMELLIA sasanqua Rosea 'Cleopatra'

Mature height: 3-8m | Multi-stem | Evergreen trees | Flowering trees | Eco impact rating: C

CARPINUS betulus
Hornbeam

The timber of the Hornbeam has traditionally been used to produce mallets, skittles and even the moving parts of pianos. Winning the Award of Garden Merit in 2002, this wonderful native tree is closely related to the hop hornbeam, Ostrya carpinifolia.

Wonderful in a parkland setting, growing in groups and ideal for pleaching, the Hornbeam is a large tree with a characteristic grey fluted trunk and ovate, ribbed and serrated leaves which turn a lovely clear yellow in autumn. This British native produces hard, finely grained timber with many uses. It grows well on most soils, including clay and chalk. A most useful tree for poor planting conditions.

Hornbeam is a super tree to fashion into different shapes. More normally it is trained into pleach panels to give architectural effect or to provide privacy above fence height.

17|22			A
Mature height: 17-22m	Shape of mature tree	Clay soils	Eco impact rating

We once had a project that required hornbeam in 8 foot letters spelling 'Welcome to Doncaster' and this can still be seen thriving on the Doncaster / Rotherham roundabout off the A1.

CARPINUS betulus Fastigiata

This Hornbeam received an Award of Garden Merit from the Royal Horticultural Society in 2002. A tree of medium size and pyramidal habit. Slender in its youth, it can often be seen growing in restricted areas despite the fact that it develops "middle age spread", reaching up to 10m wide. It is better growing in an open, parkland setting and is very effective if left feathered to the base, producing gold and orange autumn colours. It grows well on most soils, including clay and chalk. A most useful tree for poor planting conditions.

In our opinion this clone should be renamed Carpinus betulus Globosum and if care isn't taken when selecting, some are very difficult to prune and manage when older. Always look out for a straight central trunk tapering to a well defined leader because if the main stem is supplied co-dominant at a low level the tree can never be satisfactorily crown lifted at maturity and the tree gently becomes wider and wider.

For those impatient amongst you, the denser ascending branches can be used to form an instant hedge. Simply plant a four year old tree at two metre centres and hedge trim the tops to achieve immediate privacy.

- Mature height: 12-17m
- Shape of mature tree
- Clay soils
- Eco impact rating: A

CARPINUS betulus Fastigiata Frans Fontaine

This Hornbeam cultivar was selected from a street in the Netherlands in the early 1980s. A far better proposition for planting in restricted areas than Carpinus betulus Fastigiata, it retains its columnar habit, being only 3m wide after 25 years. It tolerates pollution and soil compaction, so makes an excellent street tree. It grows well on most soils, including clay and chalk. A most useful tree for poor planting conditions.

Frans Fontaine is very similar to Carpinus betulus Fastigiata when small and we often get called to describe the differences. The former sometimes has a rough fissured bark at the base of the main stem and its leaves are more crinkly than the latter.

- Mature height: 12-17m
- Shape of mature tree
- Urban trees
- Eco impact rating: A

CARPINUS betulus Lucas

This is the clonal version that looks like its habit is in between Carpinus betulus and Carpinus betulus Fastigiata. A great tree for boxing, pleaching or screening, its dense dark green foliage turns a nice yellow in the autumn before falling.

Tolerant of most free draining soils, like our native hornbeam it particularly thrives on heavier clay soils. 'Lucas' is a great addition to the hornbeam we offer with its versatility coming to the fore when screening or privacy is needed in urban gardens where space is at a premium. However, if left to its own devises it will grow to a broadly oval specimen in excess of 10 metres tall.

- Mature height: 10-15m
- Shape of mature tree
- Urban trees
- Eco impact rating: A

CARPINUS japonica
Japanese Hornbeam

Introduced from Japan in 1895, this small tree won the Award of Garden Merit in 2002. It is particularly effective when used for pleaching as the spreading horizontal branches can be easily trained and the flowering hop display along their length is a fantastic bonus compared to using native hornbeam for the same purpose.

A most beautiful and widely spreading, rounded small tree, it has heavily corrugated foliage, which is darker than the European Hornbeam, and attractive fruiting catkins which resemble hops. An excellent park tree, it has smooth, pink / grey bark. It grows well on most soils, including clay and chalk. A most useful and pretty tree for poor planting conditions.

I saw a fine specimen of this tree in Calderstones Park in Liverpool several years ago and this convinced me on its merits. Carpinus japonica needs little maintenance and combines an ornamental twist while passing for our native tree which can prove very useful in a rural garden.

- Mature height: 7-12m
- Shape of mature tree
- Garden trees
- Eco impact rating: C

CARYA cordiformis
Bitternut Hickory

The good thing about Pecan Hickory is that it produces both male and female flowers so pollination is not an issue. A large tree with Ash like leaves, it has a life expectancy of about 200 years. In its native range in North America it grows well even in boggy ground liable to flooding beside riverbanks.

Relatively rare to see in the UK, it is a nice tree to include within a parkland setting. It doesn't need a highly nutritious soil on which to thrive and you may be rewarded by some welcome nuts for your morning museli.

- Mature height: 17-22m
- Shape of mature tree
- Edible nuts
- Parkland trees
- Eco impact rating: B

CARYA Illinoinensis
Pecan

The USA champion is 35 metres tall by 48 metres wide but don't let this put you off as it will never attain this in the UK! This majestic tree has a symmetric broadly oval crown and long compound dark green leaves, regularly composed of over a dozen leaflets. It grows best on deep well drained soils that retains a good moisture content throughout the summer. Introduced in the early 1760's it never delivers the quantity of fruit that it bears in its native north America but where soil conditions allow it is a great addition for parkland and arboretum planting here in the UK.

Like Quercus petraea, it is best suited for the wetter south western half of Britain, but should be given enough room, about 20 metres, for it to thrive without competition.

Mature height: 17-22m | Shape of mature tree | Edible nuts | Parkland trees | Eco impact rating: A

There are many glorious specimens of this tree in the UK including within the fabulous parkland landscape at Burghley House, near Stamford, in Lincolnshire.

CASTANEA sativa
Sweet Chestnut

Chestnuts roasting on an open fire – or bought piping hot from a street vendor – so evocative of Christmas long ago! Believed to have been introduced by the Romans, this tree is native of Southern Europe and North Africa but has long been naturalised in the UK. It won the Award of Garden Merit in 2002. Its spiralling rough bark at maturity is lovely.

A versatile and beautiful, fast growing, large tree, which is particularly attractive in early summer when laden with its male and female catkins. Its long, glossy leaves turn gold and bronze before falling. The timber is highly prized around the Mediterranean and in Provence much furniture is made from chestnut wood. A splendid tree for grouping and quite outstanding planted as an avenue. It does best on reasonably dry, light soils, and is moderately lime tolerant.

Mature height: 17-22m | Shape of mature tree | Avenue trees | Bee friendly rating | Eco impact rating: A

CATALPA bignonioides
Indian Bean Tree

From the south eastern United States comes this magnificent, medium to large tree, which is very good as an urban subject, but not in paved areas. Introduced in 1726, this eye-catching tree won the Award of Garden Merit in 2002 and there are fine specimens in Palace Yard, Westminster.

It is late into leaf and produces exotic, orchid-like flowers in midsummer. These are followed by the "beans", which look like dark vanilla pods, in autumn. Outstanding as a specimen tree and tolerant of air pollution. It does well on most soils but avoid windy exposed sites as the large fleshy leaves can bruise.

12|17			B
Mature height: 12-17m	Shape of mature tree	Flowering trees	Eco impact rating

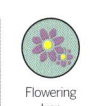

CATALPA bignonioides Aurea

This golden leaved form of the superb Indian Bean Tree was introduced in the late 1870s and won the Award of Merit in 1974. Like most yellow leaved trees, it is best placed in a south facing aspect as shade tends to dull the leaf colour to a light green. Its best floral displays come with maturity.

Its large fleshy golden yellow leaves turn to a yellow green by the time the flowers open in summer. Often top worked it forms a broadly rounded crown at maturity. It is suitable for urban plantings, does best in a sheltered position and does well on most soils. A superb tree for lighting up a garden and providing contrast against a darker background.

- Mature height: 7-12m
- Shape of mature tree
- Yellow foliage
- Flowering tree
- Eco impact rating: C

CATALPA bignonioides Bungeii

This is a wonderful top grafted adaptation of its green leaved parent, producing a very globose rounded crown at maturity. When first produced it is the shape and size of a space hopper on a stem, without the horns! Perfect for restricted places such as tight urban streets and small gardens, it requires minimal maintenance.

Catalpa is often late to emerge in the spring, but it is in full foliage by July and looks great throughout the summer into autumn. It thrives on most well drained soils but its good to keep away from exposed sites, so the huge leaves do not bruise in summer winds. Pop across the channel into France and Holland, you will see this as a regular in many gardens, but it has never taken off over here to the same extent.

- Mature height: 5-8m
- Shape of mature tree
- Garden trees
- Urban trees
- Flowering trees
- Eco impact rating: C

CEDRUS atlantica
Atlas Cedar

Introduced in the 1840s, Atlas Cedars make most imposing and stately subjects – perfect for large estates. To the untrained eye it is too similar to Cedrus libani to call and the Dutch try and clear the trade of confusion by listing it as Cedrus libani Atlantica as a catchall. We list it separately for the sake of purity!

This large, evergreen tree from the Atlas Mountains of Algeria and Morocco forms an impressive structure of wide, horizontal branches when mature. It grows rapidly in its early years and is regarded by many as a classical parkland tree. It thrives on most soils but is better equipped to withstand urban pollution compared to Cedrus libani or deodara. Cones, 5-7 cm in length, are produced along its numerous branches.

Very difficult to transplant as bare rooted or root balled, our containers solve this problem and facilitate good establishment.

- Mature height: 17-22m
- Shape of mature tree
- Evergreen trees
- Eco impact rating: B

We always think of this superb tree as an individual specimen but in their native habitat they can form imposing forests on mountainsides at an altitude of 1000 metres to 2200 metres. These forests still sustain the endangered Barbary Macaque.

As with most trees with foliage different to the normal green, it immediately draws the eye to provide marvellous contrast within a landscape.

CEDRUS atlantica Glauca
Blue Cedar

The Blue Cedar is probably the most dramatic and striking of all blue conifers. A winner of both the First-Class Certificate in 1972 and the Award of Garden Merit in 2002, it is both quick growing and sparsely furnished when young but thickens out with time.

This is another superb subject for specimen and parkland planting, where its form can be best appreciated. Its silvery blue foliage is very attractive but if it suffers stress during the establishment phase after planting, it can lose its leaves. This is alarming for an evergreen plant, but it is fairly tough and usually re-flushes the following spring. It thrives on most soils but does not appreciate waterlogged ground.

It is often seen planted too close to buildings and I think this is because it is bought my many as a tiny plant from a garden centre. Be sure not to let its initial size mislead you, it needs to be situated at least twenty metres away from a building for best long-term effect!

Mature height: 17-22m | Shape of mature tree | Urban trees | Eco impact rating: B

C

Brought from the Himalayas in the reign of George IV in 1831, this soon became a favourite planted on the lawns of large country houses and Georgian rectories.

CEDRUS deodara
Deodar Cedar

The Deodar Cedar is grown for its timber in parts of southern Europe but is grown as an ornamental in Britain. Its root system is more fibrous and compact than that of Cedrus atlantica and libani so is often used as the rootstock for these species to avoid transplantation issues. This was pioneered by Belgium growers, but they didn't account for the fact that deodara is not as long lived so we favour plants grown from seedlings.

Different from all other cedars due to its trailing leader, this large, evergreen conifer has a gently pendulous habit and soft, blue / green foliage. It thrives on most soils but does not do as well in wet ground with poor drainage.

- Mature height: 17-22m
- Shape of mature tree
- Evergreen trees
- Eco impact rating: B

CEDRUS deodara Aurea

This Deodar Cedar is most impressive for large gardens, parkland and estates. Like many yellow flushing varieties, this lovely conifer can be used as a focal point in the landscape in the spring with its yellow tipped foliage stealing the show.

It is best planted in fairly sheltered locations in full sun to bring out its vivid yellow foliage to the full. This clonal selection differs from the species in having foliage which flushes yellow before hardening to a yellow green. Like its parent it is easily identified from all the other Cedars due to its trailing leader and this large, evergreen conifer has a gently pendulous habit. It thrives on most soils though is not happy on waterlogged ground.

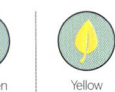

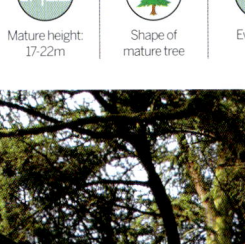

Mature height: 17-22m | Shape of mature tree | Evergreen trees | Yellow foliage | Parkland trees | Eco impact rating: B

So impressive are the trees at the Cedars Conservancy Parks in Lebanon it was put forward as a candidate for the new listing of the Seven Wonders of the World. The variety 'Brevifolia' is sometimes listed and is a native of Cyprus.

CEDRUS libani
Cedar of Lebanon

Few trees, deciduous or evergreen, can compare with the beauty and elegance of a mature Cedar of Lebanon. Some think it is its own species or that it is a geographical sub species of Cedrus atlantica but either way there is little to choose between them. It won the Award of Garden Merit in 2002.

One of the most majestic of all trees and extensively planted as part of the enduring landscape of some of our grandest stately homes and estates. It is slower growing than the Atlas Cedar, conical when young before assuming the flat topped and tiered habit of maturity. Introduced to England around the time of the Civil War in the mid 1640s, it has large, barrel shaped cones and green or grey / green foliage. It thrives on most soils though does not appreciate wet ground.

Cedar of Lebanon has been very important to many civilizations including the ancient Egyptians who used its resin for mummification. Sawdust from the tree has also been present in many of the Pharaohs tombs. However its range has been sadly depleted over time as its timber has been too highly prized by humankind and much of the original forests are no more.

Mature height: 17-22m | Shape of mature tree | Evergreen trees | Eco impact rating: A

CELTIS australis
Nettle Tree

The wood of the Nettle Tree was once used to produce charcoal. A native of Southern Europe and North Africa, it has been grown in the UK since the 16th century and is used commonly as a verge or street tree in the Mediterranean as it is tolerant of both reflected heat and salt laden air.

Related to the elms, this small to medium tree has broad, lanceolate, rough leaves. It has a broad crown and smooth trunk. It is widely planted for roadside shade in southern Europe, and the bark has been used to produce a yellow dye. Good for avenue and park plantings, where it will withstand much pollution, and is also very good close to coasts. It thrives on most soils, including very dry ones.

- Mature height: 12-17m
- Shape of mature tree
- Coastal sites
- Urban trees
- Eco impact rating: A

CELTIS occidentalis
Hackberry

Although part of the Elm family, this tree is immune to Dutch elm disease. A native of North America, it makes a medium sized tree in the UK.

It is a vigorous tree with arching stems that support large heart shaped soft green leaves. At maturity the bark becomes corky and rough and the tree produces small black fruits in profusion. A great tree for parkland and estates, it thrives on most soils. In the States on deep fertile soils they have been known to reach 35 metres in height and live for over 200 years.

- Mature height: 12-17m
- Shape of mature tree
- Parkland trees
- Eco impact rating: A

CERCIDIPHYLLUM japonicum
Katsura Tree / Candyfloss tree

The Katsura Tree was introduced from the Far East in the early 1880s and won the Award of Garden Merit in 2002. Often thought of as a small ornamental tree I stumbled across one in Rutland a few years ago that must have been over 20 metres tall. It is best grown away from frost pockets or exposed windy sites as new foliage can scorch before they harden.

Sometimes mistaken for Cercis siliquastrum, this has smaller leaves. It is sensational both in spring with emerging coppery green leaves and autumn when the foliage turns yellow or pink whilst exuding a fragrant scent reminiscent of burnt sugar. A great choice for gardens and parks, doing best on deep, fertile soils.

Mature height: 12-17m | Shape of mature tree | Multi-stem | Eco impact rating: B

CERCIS canadensis
Forest Pansy
North American Redbud

A native of South Eastern Canada and Eastern USA, it is not as free flowering as Cercis siliquastrum but this clone makes up for it by its stunning deep red / purple leaf colour. Grown and supplied as either a standard tree or multi-stemmed specimen, we rate this as one of the best purple foliaged trees on the market. It won the Award of Garden Merit in 2002. However, it is haphazard in growth and extremely difficult to grow!

It makes a small tree of rounded habit and is ideal for sunny urban gardens and courtyards. It does best in free draining soils and like Cercis siliquastrum is slow to root so we recommend stakes to be retained for the first three years after planting. Flowers are a light pink and the autumn brings a luminescent red quality to the senescing leaves. A wonderful small garden tree.

Like many trees with distinctly coloured leaves, full sun is needed to keep the leaf tone vivid. Too much shade dulls the leaf to a dark green. This tree is also keen on hot summer temperatures to encourage growth so south facing locations are a must for this clone.

Mature height: 3-8m | Shape of mature tree | Red/purple foliage | Eco impact rating: D

CERCIS Chinensis Avondale

Best grown as a multi-stem bush this Spring flowerer certainly produces a wow factor of any garden in April / May. Originating from plant propagators in New Zealand in the mid-1970s, this tree is commonly known as Redbud. Masses of deep pink flowers pop out from all along the branch networks to produce a stunning display before the leaves fully emerge in June.

The foliage is larger and a darker green than the closely related Judas Tree, Cercis siliquastrum, and this turns to shades of yellow in the autumn. It prefers a well-drained soil and a sunny aspect.

- Mature height: 5-7m
- Multi-stem
- Flowering trees
- Garden trees
- Eco impact rating: C

CERCIS siliquastrum
Judas Tree

A most beautiful tree despite its association with Judas Iscariot. Introduced in the 16th century, it won the Award of Garden Merit in 2002. It is very slow to root so is one of the few trees we recommend staking for up to three years after planting. A native of the Eastern Mediterranean, it is a must for any garden large enough to give it justice!

A stunning sight in May when clusters of rosy-lilac, pea-like flowers wreathe the wood, sometimes springing direct from mature branches and even from the trunk. These are followed by purple tinted seed pods from July onwards. It slowly forms a well-rounded tree, and is perfect for sunny urban gardens and courtyards, tolerating dry conditions well. It thrives on most soils, including very dry ones.

- Mature height: 5-8m
- Shape of mature tree
- Flowering trees
- Eco impact rating: C

CERCIS siliquastrum alba

Similar in every way to the traditional Judas Tree, but producing lovely ivory white flowers in May instead of the well-known rosy lilac. It was awarded the Royal Horticulture Society's Award of Merit from a plant grown by the Wellcome Foundation at Langley Court in Kent.

Slow to root and establish but well worth the wait, it is always wise to stake for several years after planting to give time for the roots to anchor the tree in place.

Mature height: 5-8m | Shape of mature tree | Flowering trees | Eco impact rating: C

CHAMAECYPARIS lawsoniana Columnaris Glauca

Raised in Boskoop, Holland, in the 1940s, this small and narrow conical tree has enormous garden or parkland appeal.

Densely arranged ascending branches carry flattened foliage sprays which are greenish blue and pure blue on the growing tips. Many conifer clones of this type have come and gone over the years but this one has passed the test of time and remains one of the best blue conifers around for restricted areas. It thrives best on most soils, though it is not happy on wet ground.

Mature height: 5-7m | Shape of mature tree | Evergreen trees | Eco impact rating: C

CHAMAECYPARIS lawsoniana Stardust

Introduced from Holland in the 1960s, this outstanding yellow variety won the Award of Garden Merit in 2002.

Densely arranged branches carry flattened foliage sprays which are golden yellow and bronze on the growing tips. It is columnar in habit so suitable for most gardens and parks. It tolerates most soils although, like most Chamaecyparis, soils prone to water logging should be avoided.

Mature height: 5-7m | Shape of mature tree | Evergreen trees | Yellow foliage | Eco impact rating: C

CHAMAECYPARIS lawsoniana Yvonne

I liken this to the golden equivalent of 'columnaris Glauca'. Surely one of the most stunning golden uprights on the market, this clone is ideal for gardens and parks.

Ascending branches support green / gold sprays of foliage that are luminescent gold on the growing tips. Like others of its group, it dislikes waterlogged ground and thrives on well drained sunny sites. The overall habit is columnar, so it is a great plant for restricted places.

- Mature height: 5-7m
- Shape of mature tree
- Evergreen trees
- Yellow foliage
- Eco impact rating: C

CHITALPA tashkentensis Summer Bells

A recent hybrid between Chilopsis and Catalpa. Original work on these pairings was undertaken at the Uzbek Academy of Science in Tashkent, Uzbekistan, in the 1960s before being introduced internationally in the mid 1970s.

This small hybrid with a rounded form initiates flower bud in June / July which open to produce an abundant display of frilly pink flowers with yellow throats for the rest of the summer. Best planted on well drained soils in full sun with protection from strong winds. Ideal for sheltered gardens and streets.

- Mature height: 5-7m
- Shape of mature tree
- Flowering trees
- Eco impact rating: D

CLADRASTIS kentukia
Yellow Wood

Introduced from its native South Eastern USA in 1812, this lovey tree was given the Award of Merit in 1926 by the Royal Horticultural Society. Fragrant white flowers are produced in June, hanging in drooping panicles like a Wisteria. Compound alternate leaflets can accumulate to 25cm in length on the one stalk. Flowering can be hit and miss rather than consistent every year and is usually seen only on maturing specimens.

It grows on most well drained soils, including acid and alkaline, but is better to prune, if needed, in the summer as the wounds tend to weep if pruned in the winter or spring. This makes a good urban verge tree or parkland /large garden specimen. Brown seed pods are produced in the autumn of a flowering year.

- Mature height: 7-12m
- Shape of mature tree
- Flowering trees
- Eco impact rating: D

CLERODENDRUM trichotomum

Brought from China and Japan and in cultivation since the 1880s this highly interesting tree won the Royal Horticultural Society's First-Class Certificate in 1893.

It is a small tree, but a strong grower. White, strongly fragrant flowers, enclosed in maroon calyces, appear in August and September. They are followed by bright blue berries and a glorious display of autumn foliage of luminescent reds to yellows. It thrives on most soils but is best to avoid wet and exposed sites. Although very hardy in England, it would be put to the test if subjected to colder and more northerly aspects of the UK.

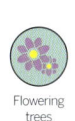

| 5|8 Mature height: 5-8m | Shape of mature tree | Flowering trees | D Eco impact rating |

CORNUS alba Sibirica
Westonbirt Dogwood

This spectacular red stemmed dog wood rose to fame in the 1960s. Winter stem colour is one of the few ways to retain vivid interest in a garden for those dreary winter months and the best way to promote this is to routinely coppice down to 5cm above ground level every March. If left to its own devices the red stem colour is restricted to the outer edges of the plant and the thicker older stems lose their lustre.

This great garden plant thrives on most soils and is particularly effective when planted in groups next to contrasting white birch varieties.

Strictly more of a shrub than a tree, we have included this as it compliments so many others!

| 1|3 Mature height: 1-3m | Multi-stem | Bark interest | D Eco impact rating |

CORNUS controversa
Wedding Cake Tree

This wonderful introduction from China and Japan has been grown in the UK since the 1880s and won the Award of Merit in 1984. One of the best specimens to look out for is at the Bath Botanic Garden. Wonderfully architectural, its striking form draws the eye through any garden.

A small to medium tree with a conical habit, its common name relates to the layered effect of its branches. Broad clusters of creamy flowers cover the branches in May. Small, black fruits develop in autumn as the foliage turns to a rich purple red. Excellent for parks and gardens, it thrives on most soils.

- Mature height: 5-7m
- Shape of mature tree
- Garden trees
- Eco impact rating: D

CORNUS controversa Variegata

Introduced in the 1890s this variegated version of the Wedding Cake Tree is a sight to behold when seen at its full potential. It is far from easy, hence the fact you hardly ever see one, but planted in a sheltered spot with plenty of care and time it is uniquely beautiful.

Layered branches take shape from an early age but are characterised by the striking white to yellow margin of the otherwise green leaves. A winner of the Award of Garden Merit in 2002 it is far more sedate than its parent listed previously but well worth the wait.

This dainty tree is best planted in dappled shade as full sun can scorch the sensitive leaves. It is particularly effective when used as an underplant beneath the open canopies of mature trees.

Mature height: 3-5m | Shape of mature tree | Variegated trees | Eco impact rating: D

CORNUS Eddie's White Wonder

This is a cross between Cornus florida and Cornus nuttallii which has won a host of awards including the First-Class Certificate, the Cory Cup, and the Award of Garden Merit. It has fallen out of favour in America, where it was raised, for not being as hardy as first thought but it is fine in the more temperate UK.

We supply this superb garden plant as a maturing bush which produces large white flower heads in the spring. It thrives on most soils, but we do not recommend planting on alkaline or waterlogged ground. It forms a compact small garden tree at maturity.

Mature height: 3-5m | Multi-stem | Garden trees | Flowering trees | Eco impact rating: D

CORNUS kousa China Girl

Introduced in the late 1970s and selected in Holland, this variety has large bracts, great autumn colour and good-sized fruits. Plants as small as 40-60cm are capable of setting flower buds making this an ideal garden tree that exhibits lots of interest.

Flowers are borne in abundance in early spring and the foliage turns vivid colours by autumn. Supplied as a maturing bushy shrub, it will eventually make a small tree. Cornus kousa types do not thrive in alkaline soils, they just linger. Best only to plant on ground with a ph less than 7 and to avoid waterlogged or compacted soils.

Mature height: 3-5m | Multi-stem | Garden trees | Flowering trees | Eco impact rating: D

CORNUS kousa Chinensis

Perhaps the most reliable of all flowering dogwoods. Bean reckoned the fruits were both sweet and edible, but I think he was getting carried away by the glamour of the plant as believe me there are better things to eat.

This small, open tree flowers in June, the white bracts turning from soft green to white to pink and lining the upper sides of almost horizontal, slender branches. It goes on to give pink, arbutus-like berries and rich bronze and crimson autumn leaves. It prefers acid and well drained soils.

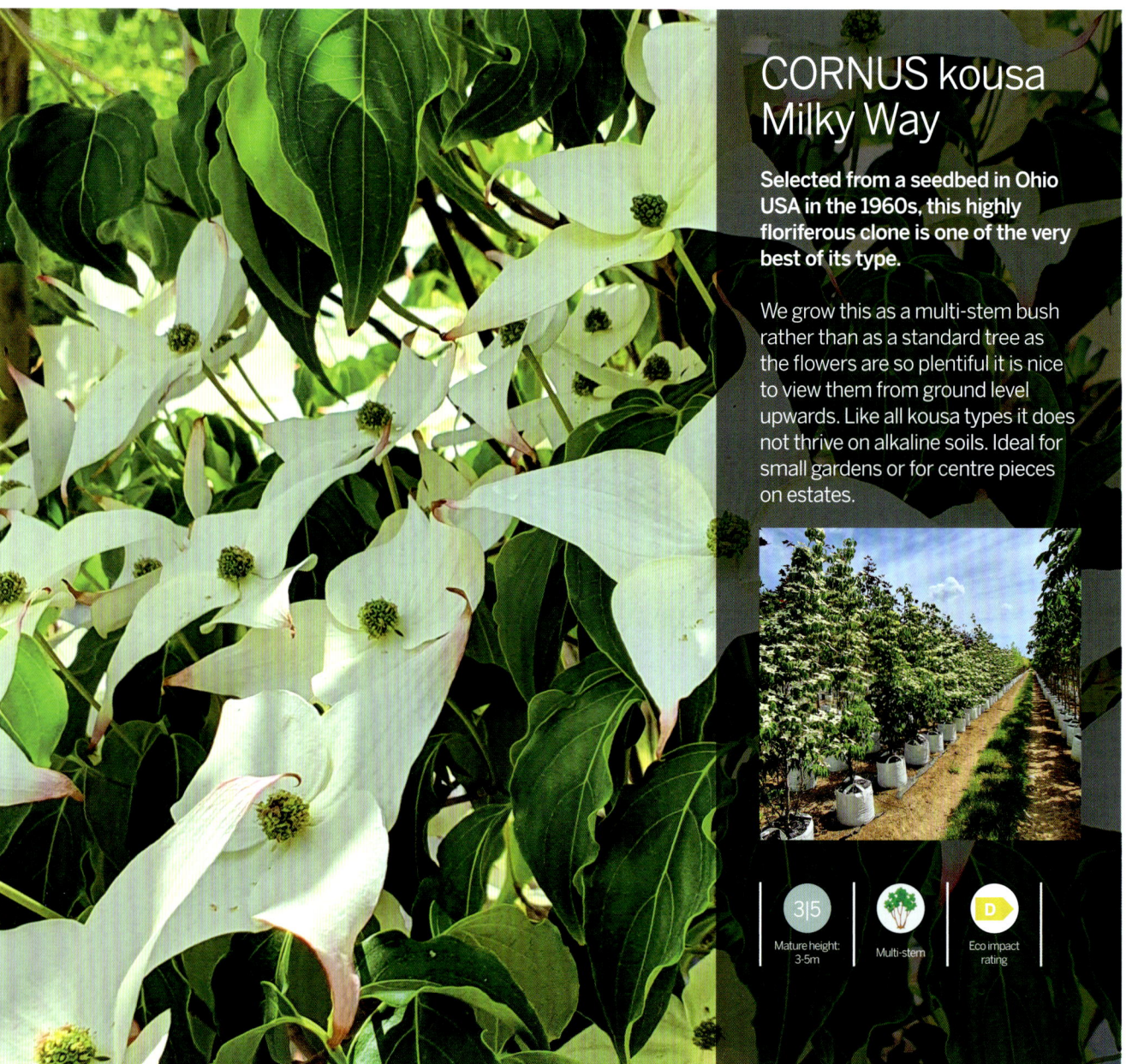

- Mature height: 5-7m
- Shape of mature tree
- Multi-stem
- Garden trees
- Eco impact rating: D

CORNUS kousa Milky Way

Selected from a seedbed in Ohio USA in the 1960s, this highly floriferous clone is one of the very best of its type.

We grow this as a multi-stem bush rather than as a standard tree as the flowers are so plentiful it is nice to view them from ground level upwards. Like all kousa types it does not thrive on alkaline soils. Ideal for small gardens or for centre pieces on estates.

- Mature height: 3-5m
- Multi-stem
- Eco impact rating: D

CORNUS kousa Stella Pink

It is not easy to grow a kousa type as a standard form, but this delightful small garden tree lends itself to be grown with a single trunk and a dominant central leader. Raised by Dr Elwin Orton at Rutgers University, New Jersey in the late 1980s for its vigour and disease resistance.

The glossy leaves of this rounded tree turn a rich crimson-bronze in autumn. Remarkable for its pink, star-shaped bracts, this stunning clone is a marvel when it is in full flow. Very good for parks and gardens but will not thrive on alkaline soils and waterlogged or compacted ground.

Mature height: 5-7m | Shape of mature tree | Garden trees | Flowering trees | Eco impact rating: D

CORNUS mas
Cornelian Cherry

Introduced in the late 1890s, the Cornelian Cherry gives a very long period of interest. A native of central and southern Europe, it won the Award of Merit in 1929.

From February onwards when the small, yellow flowers appear on the bare twigs this Cornus puts on a great display. The bright red, cherry-like fruits are edible, and the leaves turn a delightful reddish purple in autumn. Often grown as a multi-stem bush, we have managed to raise ours on a single stem to 1.8m with a well balanced and compact crown. A very good choice for parks and gardens, it thrives on most free draining soils.

Mature height: 5-8m | Shape of mature tree | Multi-stem | Flowering trees | Bee friendly trees | Eco impact rating: D

C

CORNUS sanguinea
Annie's Winter Orange

A clonal selection of our native Dogwood, this multi stemmed shrub makes a wonderful understory to our white stemmed birch varieties. Its intense stems vary from yellow / orange at their base to vivid red at the tips. Suited to most soils, it is best to routinely coppice to get the best from its stem display. Best to do this in the spring so you can enjoy its vibrant colours all winter.

Its flowers are white, and its green leaves turn a mix of yellow and reds in the autumn. I prune mine back to about 20cm from ground level once every two years for best effect.

- Mature height: 1-3m
- Multi-stem
- Autumn colour
- Bark interest
- Urban trees
- Eco impact rating: D

CORYLUS avellana
Hazel

The squirrel's favourite, also known as the cobnut or Filbert, this is our native Hazel. We supplied our neighbour with 34 plants in 2007 and this has now made a fantastic instant hedge that you can view when you visit Barcham.

A small tree with a rounded habit, it looks particularly striking in the early spring when it is adorned with its long yellow "lambs' tail" catkins. The nuts in autumn aren't bad either! A very good choice for gardens, parks and woodlands. We supply this tree as a multi-stemmed coppiced specimen that makes a great under plant for a woodland or instant infill within a hedgerow.

Quick to grow, we recommend a five-year cycle of coppicing down to only a few inches above ground level. This can be done in February / March after the catkins finish and although you will sacrifice any fruiting potential for that year, you will end up with a more bushy and vibrant plant as a result.

- Mature height: 3-8m
- Multi-stem
- Bee friendly trees
- Hedging trees
- Eco impact rating: B

CORYLUS avellana Contorta
Corkskrew Hazel

This Hazel is also known as Harry Lauder's Walking Stick, after the Scottish music hall performer who had a trademark "twisted" walking stick. At maturity it looks like a quirky bonsai and the best example of this I have seen is in my mother's garden in Surrey.

A very small and slow growing tree that has strangely twisted and contorted branches which create a dense and rounded habit. It is believed to have been discovered in a Gloucestershire hedgerow in the 1860s. A real curiosity for parks and gardens. Small twiggy branches can be sympathetically removed and used to add interest to seasonal floral displays.

- Mature height: 3-5m
- Multi-stem
- Garden trees
- Bee friendly trees
- Eco impact rating: C

CORYLUS avellana Zellernus

Also known as Red Filbert, this is a great improvement on Corylus maxima Purpurea. I have one in my garden that I coppice on a four yearly rotation to encourage the young red foliage to shine out in the spring.

This rounded and rather rare tree looks spectacular in spring when it is festooned with pink catkins set against its rich purple foliage that turns dark green by early summer. Delicious red Filbert nuts are a bonus in the autumn. It is most attractive in gardens or parks and particularly effective when randomly scattered into a hedgerow.

As with Common Hazel, coppicing every five years invigorates the plant and keeps it bushy from ground level upwards. I have seen this variety thrive within half a mile of the coast, so it is about as tough as they come!

- Mature height: 5-8m
- Multi-stem
- Edible nuts
- Eco impact rating: B

C

CORYLUS colurna
Turkish Hazel

A splendid and truly beautiful tree from South East Europe and West Asia that was introduced in 1582 and won the Award of Garden Merit in 2002. It is large, imposing and rather columnar when young before broadening to a symmetrical pyramid on maturity. Notable for its roughly textured, corky bark, it produces long, yellow catkins in early spring and clusters of fringed nuts in autumn.

Turkish Hazel is a superb choice for parkland and avenue planting, and it will tolerate paved areas. It thrives in all soils, including chalky and clay soils and is now used in cities as a substitute for Lime to combat the problem of aphid drop on cars and pavements.

- Mature height: 17-22m
- Shape of mature tree
- Avenue trees
- Eco impact rating: B

CORYLUS colurna Te-Terra Red

This unusual sport of Turkish Hazel is smaller growing than its parent but far more striking. Fresh red coloured leaves emerge in the spring that harden to a purple green by mid summer. Pink catkins are produced in February / March and the young thickening trunk has a hint of purple about it before it matures to a rough textured brown.

This relatively slow growing clone makes a fine garden tree that gives lots of year-round interest. It will grow on most well drained soils. Red husks hold the promise of pink cobnuts but this tree is rarely fertile, so they are for ornamental purposes only.

Mature height: 5-8m | Shape of mature tree | Garden trees | Bee friendly trees | Eco impact rating: C

COTINUS coggygria Royal Purple
Smoke Tree

Winning the Award of Garden Merit in 1969 this outstanding small multi stemmed tree eventually gets to about 4 metres in height but is often sold as a shrub and placed in a position it soon outgrows. Raised in Boskoop in the Netherlands, the purple oval leaves contrast beautifully with the soft 'hairy' display of random flower stalks that give the whole plant a fuzzy appearance June / July.

The summer foliage colour gives way to red in the autumn. Originating in southern and central Europe It thrives on most free draining soils but won't tolerate the most severe winters in the north of the UK. A great plant for summer garden interest.

Mature height: 3-5m | Shape of mature tree | Multi-stem | Garden trees | Bee friendly trees | Eco impact rating: D

COTONEASTER Cornubia

Raised at the famous Exbury Gardens in the early 1930s this versatile small tree won the Award of Garden Merit in 2002 and 1933 as well as the First-Class Certificate in 1936. It is a particularly useful tree for stilted semi evergreen screening in small gardens where privacy is needed.

Sometimes categorized under Cotoneaster x watereri and elsewhere said to be a cultivar of Cotoneaster frigidus, we list it as Cornubia. It is a small to medium, semi-evergreen tree which bears large red berries in abundance in the autumn. Usually grown as a shrub, we grow it as tree with a 1.8m clear stem and find it develops a nicely rounded crown at maturity. It does well in most soils.

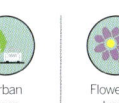

Mature height: 3-8m | Shape of mature tree | Urban trees | Flowering trees | Eco impact rating: D

CRATAEGUS laevigata Paul's Scarlet

This small hawthorn tree was a sport of Crataegus Rosea Flore Plena found in a Herefordshire garden in the 1850s. Probably the most popular of thorns on the market, it won both the First Class Certificate in 1858 and the Award of Garden Merit in 2002.

It becomes smothered in double, red flowers in May which are more stunning as the spring flowering cherries have finished their display by then. As root development can be rather slow, we recommend moderate pruning in the first few years after planting so that good anchorage is achieved. A good choice for urban and coastal planting, it is tolerant of air pollution. It does well in most soils, including very dry and wet soils.

| Mature height: 5-7m | Shape of mature tree | Garden tree | Bee friendly trees | Eco impact rating: C |

CRATAEGUS x lavallei
Hybrid Cockspur Thorn

A small hawthorn tree which produces a dense crown of thorn clad branches that give rise to its trademark rounded habit at maturity. Originating back to the 1870s this fine tree won the Award of Garden Merit in 2002 and 1924.

The large white flowers are followed by orange haws, which are retained for most of the winter. The oval, glossy, leathery leaves persist until December, colouring from red through to yellow. As it is only slightly thorny, it makes a better street tree than most other hawthorns. A good choice for urban and coastal planting, it is tolerant of air pollution. It does well in most soils, including very dry and wet soils.

| Mature height: 5-7m | Shape of mature tree | Bee friendly trees | Eco impact rating: C |

CRATAEGUS x lavallei Carrièrei

A hawthorn of garden origin, dating from around 1870, that won the Award of Garden Merit in both 1924 and 2002. This clone is particularly resistant against rust.

It makes a small, densely headed tree with glossy, deep green foliage which lasts through to December. The orange-red haws are also long lasting, often right through winter, and they contrast well with the dark foliage. A good choice for urban and coastal planting, it is also tolerant of air pollution. It does well in most soils, including very dry and wet soils. Like many clonal variations it is difficult to tell apart from its parent variety.

Mature height: 5-7m | Shape of mature tree | Urban trees | Bee friendly trees | Eco impact rating: C

CRATAEGUS monogyna
Common Hawthorn

Also known as Quickthorn or May, this small native hawthorn has many ancient associations and is most seen as hedgerow plants along the span of the UK. However, we run it up to make a standard tree for specimen planting and it is without doubt one of our prettiest native trees.

The small white, fragrant flowers which appear in May and June are followed by small red fruits in abundance during autumn, providing much needed food for wild birds. A good choice for urban and coastal planting it is also tolerant of air pollution. It does well in most soils, including very dry and wet soils.

Mature height: 5-7m | Shape of mature tree | Native tree | Bee friendly trees | Eco impact rating: C

CRATAEGUS monogyna Stricta

A tough and durable hawthorn, ideal for exposed situations. Its dark green leaves and very regular habit make this a favourite for urban planners where space is at a premium. It thinks nothing of reflected heat and light bouncing off windows and pavements making it a very versatile native variation of the traditional hedgerow parent.

Very different from other hawthorns in that it has a columnar habit with tightly ascending branches, making it a very good prospect for both streets and small gardens. It is also a good choice for coastal planting and tolerant of salt laden winds. It does well on most ground, including very dry and wet soils.

Mature height: 5-7m | Shape of mature tree | Narrow tree | Bee friendly trees | Eco impact rating: C

CRATAEGUS x prunifolia
Broad-leaved Cockspur Thorn

This small hawthorn is thornier than most others and won the Award of Garden Merit in 2002. It has wonderful autumn colour and is a winter provider for birds feasting on its profuse red fruits. Sometimes referred to as Crataegus x persimilis, it is a hybrid between Crataegus crus galli and Crataegus macracantha and originates from Eastern America.

This small, compact, round-headed tree produces long sharp thorns along the span of its branches. The burnished, oval leaves, which turn a glorious red in autumn, are accompanied by plentiful small, red fruits. A good choice for urban and coastal planting, it is also tolerant of air pollution. It does well on most ground, including very dry and wet soils.

Mature height: 5-7m | Shape of mature tree | Urban tree | Bee friendly trees | Eco impact rating: C

CRATAEGUS x prunifolia Splendens

A clonal selection of Crataegus prunifolia that is very similar to its parent in every way apart from its uniformity. Originating from Holland, it is ideal for both street verges and gardens and has all the inbuilt durability of its genera. It is a great tree for wildlife with birds especially benefitting from the abundant autumn crop of shiny red berries. Wonderful red and golden autumn foliage is a striking feature of this small tree with a regular and rounded habit at maturity. It also has characteristic white flowers and shiny, leathery, oval leaves. A good choice for park and coastal planting it is also tolerant of air pollution. It does well in most soils, including very dry and wet soils. Be sure to crown lift the stem to 2 metres over time to keep the thorns out of reach.

This much underused tree requires little maintenance after establishment and is seldom seen in Garden Centres where 'Paul Scarlet' seems to dominate. It is a small tree of ultimate size that makes a wonderful garden tree offering spring flower, lovely berry colour and great autumnal colour.

Mature height 5-7m | Deciduous broadleaf tree | Garden trees | Bee friendly trees | Eco impact rating C

CRYPTOMERIA
japonica Elegans
Japanese Cedar

Introduced by Thomas Lobb from Japan in 1854, this beautiful bushy conifer eventually makes a small tree at maturity. Its wonderful texture and feathery appearance make you want to touch it!

Evergreen feathery foliage turns bronze in winter and at this point many despair and make a phone call to us but this is all part of the annual show it performs. It tends to grow as wide as it does high but reacts well to pruning if necessary. It thrives in most soils though does not like waterlogged ground. It is such an unusual foliage plant that it provides wonderful contrast within a garden and many gardeners struggle to indentify it quite simply as it looks like nothing else!

Japanese Cedar can be prone to dry out in the first year after planting before it has time to establish. Its dense foliage can end up deflecting rainfall away from the roots so be sure to water well at planting and once per month during the dormant season before stepping this up to once a week in its first full growing season.

- Mature height: 3-8m
- Shape of mature tree
- Evergreen trees
- Eco impact rating: B

CUPRESSUS arizonica Glauca

A selection of the Smooth Arizona Cypress, this striking conifer is a native of South Eastern America. I have seen this grown as a hedging conifer in Southern France and it positively glitters when it is filmed by a morning dew.

This medium to large evergreen conifer forms a dense, pyramidal habit at maturity with very distinctive rich brown bark that peels in flakes. Its deeply fragrant blue foliage is particularly attractive, and its rounded cones swell in spring. Tolerant of air pollution, it is good for urban plantings and large gardens. It thrives on most soils.

- Mature height: 12-17m
- Shape of mature tree
- Evergreen trees
- Eco impact rating: B

CUPRESSUS macrocarpa Goldcrest

A British-bred form of the Monterey Cypress, raised by Treseder of Truro in the late 1940s, this spectacular conifer won the Award of Garden Merit in 2002. Its yellow colour is so vivid that it provides wonderful contrast to a dark landscape.

A medium size tree, and therefore much smaller than the species, Goldcrest has a narrow, columnar habit and rich yellow, feathery foliage. Certainly, one of the best of its colour, it remains dense and compact. Very good for avenues, gardens and parks. It thrives on most soils.

- Mature height: 12-17m
- Shape of mature tree
- Evergreen trees
- Yellow foliage
- Eco impact rating: B

CUPRESSUS sempervirens
Italian Cypress

The Italian Cypress is surely one of the most beautiful and evocative trees in the world! If you ever get out to Tuscany or Umbria, you will be well and truly hooked on this wonderful conifer.

The cypress of Mediterranean antiquity, and widely used in the Middle Ages to make chests because its pleasant-smelling timber helped to keep clothes sweet. In Britain it is best to avoid cold, exposed sites for this architecturally columnar beauty, but it is a splendid choice for urban plantings and courtyard gardens. It does best in rich, fertile soils.

Mature height: 12-17m | Shape of mature tree | Evergreen trees | Eco impact rating: B

CUPRESSOCYPARIS leylandii
Leyland Cypress

Love it or loathe it, the Leyland Cypress is Europe's fastest growing conifer. It is a cross between Chamaecyparis nootkatensis and Cupressus macrocarpa and is probably Britain's most well-known tree.

Unbeatable for screening, but rather too tall for most small gardens, this is a large, handsome tree with a dense, columnar habit. Single specimens and plantings in avenues show off this rather unfairly maligned conifer to best advantage. Very good for coastal plantings, where it tolerates salt laden winds. It does well in most soils, including chalk.

- Mature height: 17-22m
- Shape of mature tree
- Hedging trees
- Evergreen trees
- Eco impact rating: B

> I have a Leylandii hedge in my garden that has been kept to 2.5 metres for the last twenty years or so. The trick to taming Leylandii is to prune once per year without fail in the spring but if you miss even one year it can get away from you, so fast is its growth. Once a hedge has grown too big for its surrounds there is no going back as pruning into old wood will leave it bare and patchy. The height of your hedge is usually set by how far you want to stand on a step ladder and if done correctly a Leylandii hedge is hard to beat for year-round privacy.

CUPRESSOCYPARIS leylandii Castlewellan
Golden Leyland Cypress

The Golden Leyland Cypress is often considered more amenable than the green leaved form though in Ireland it has been so overplanted there is a lobby for making future plantings illegal! However, this is not the trees fault and it remains an excellent choice for evergreen hedging.

Slower growing and rather more useful for hedging than its green parent, it is also rather smaller, and the pale golden foliage adds to the interest of this attractive seedling, which was raised in County Down in the early 1960s. Very good for coastal plantings, where it tolerates salt laden winds. It does well in most soils, including chalk.

- Mature height: 12-17m
- Shape of mature tree
- Hedging trees
- Evergreen trees
- Eco impact rating: B

CYDONIA oblonga
Quince

This recent introduction to our range has proved very popular, especially as fruit trees are exempt from the dreaded VAT! This small genus of trees is related to the better known Chaenomeles and produces golden yellow fragrant fruit that hold on the tree for several weeks if left unpicked.

Native of south west Asia, it is fine to be grown in the UK and forms into a small rounded tree sometimes tipping 20 feet in height. Autumn leaf colour is a good and reliable yellow. It does best in south facing sheltered gardens and benefits from a free draining nutritious soil.

- Mature height: 5-7m
- Shape of mature tree
- Edible fruits
- Eco impact rating: D

DAVIDIA involucrata
Handkerchief Tree, Dove Tree

Whether known as the Handkerchief Tree or Dove Tree, it is well-named and much-loved. Discovered in China by Père David in 1869 and introduced in 1904, this is one of the great beauties of the plant world. The variety 'Vilmoriniana' is often specified but there is little or nothing to choose between this and its parent.

Its common names derive from the large white bracts which appear in May. These are followed by large, oval fruits in autumn. Foliage and habit are like those of the lime. A medium to large tree, it is very good for parks and does best in a sheltered position. On a historical note, it first flowered in England in 1911 on Vieitch's Coombe Wood Nursery. It thrives best on deep fertile soil.

From our experience of growing this tree in the Fens it thrives best on less exposed sites and is best pruned lightly in the summer rather than when it is dormant in the winter. Growing tips can frost off if subjected to icy winds and invariably the best specimens are seen nestled away in a comfy sheltered spot.

Difficult and slow to grow from a young age, it seems to thrive when beyond 8-10 feet tall. For every hundred we grow only 20 or so come through as saleable which explains its price tag!

7|12			D
Mature height: 7-12m	Shape of mature tree	Parkland trees	Eco impact rating

I first saw this tree at Kew's sister garden Wakehurst Place in Sussex. It was in full flower and even though the tree was still relatively young it was mighty impressive.

D

DIOSPYROS lotus
Date Plum / Caucasian Persimmon

This tree, rarely seen in the UK, bares fruits that taste like both date and plum. Long in cultivation accross south and east Europe, the ancient Greeks called it God Fruit. It is not fussy on where it grows in terms of soil nurtrition and type but best to avoid areas prone to laying wet.

Diospyros is at it's northern limit in the UK, not liking the severity of some of our winters so we would would recommend for Southern England only and away from frost pockets. With this in mind it performs very well and we have had some good fruiting years with it up at Barcham. Its leaves are a shiney oval and its trunk develops a rough bark earlier than most.

- Mature height: 10-15m
- Shape of mature tree
- Edible fruit
- Urban trees
- Eco impact rating: C

DIOSPYROS kaki
Chinese Persimmon

Introduced from China in 1796, this small tree has been grown in the Far East for hundreds of years for its edible tomato shaped yellow orange fruits.

In the UK it is grown more for its superb autumn colour display of its large vibrant leaves which turn orange, yellow, red and purple before they fall. Fruits are set from new season's growth but only achieve full potential in the UK in hot long summers. Flowers appear in May / June.

- Mature height: 5-7m
- Shape of mature tree
- Edible fruit
- Eco impact rating: C

EUCALYPTUS debeuzevillei
Jounama Snow Gum

One of the hardiest of all Eucalyptus, being a native of the high mountains of south east Australia, it is also one of the most dramatic. As a point of interest, grab hold of its leaves on a hot summer's day and you will immediately notice how cold they are. This is true of all Eucalyptus; they are nature's air conditioning units!

A medium sized tree of broadly pyramidal form, it has a beautiful white patchwork trunk and thick lanceolate evergreen leaves. A superb specimen for both parks and gardens, it produces stunning and unexpected dandelion clock like flowers from mid summer straight from its branches. It thrives on most soils.

This wonderfully dramatic tree has so much year-round interest that it should be considered more often for large gardens and municipal parks and verges. Its foliage provides great contrast within the landscape and always seems to draw the eye. Interestingly, Eucalyptus does not have a dormancy period and carries on growing, very slowly, even in the winter months.

Mature height: 12-17m | Shape of mature tree | Bark interest | Eco impact rating: A

E

When faced with selecting Eucalyptus never be tempted to go for the biggest and probably most pot bound. A strange physiology comes into play in that when Eucalyptus roots spiral, they tend to carry on that way and are prone to falling over through lack of anchorage over time. This is a problem exasperated by trees grown in black pots.

EUCALYPTUS gunnii
Cider Gum

This Gum is a native of the highlands of Tasmania and Australia and was introduced to the UK in the mid 1850s. A winner of the Award of Garden Merit in both 2002 and 1950, this striking tree is also well suited to being grown as a multi-stemmed coppiced specimen.

A very well-known Eucalyptus - and a very hardy one - this large, broadly pyramidal tree has smooth grey-pink to red-brown bark. The young leaves are grey-green and glaucous providing a wonderful contrast to gardens and municipal landscapes. For those florists amongst you, the foliage is particularly good to compliment cut flower arrangements. It thrives on most soils.

- Mature height: 12-17m
- Shape of mature tree
- Garden trees
- Eco impact rating: A

EUCALYPTUS niphophila
Snow Gum

A well known and lovely Eucalyptus with attractive grey, green and cream patchwork bark. A winner of the Award of Garden Merit in 2002.

Its leaves are narrow and grey-green when matured and it is well suited as a specimen tree to provide lovely soft contrast in parks and large gardens. It is slower growing than the more common Eucalyptus gunnii, but it forms such a pleasing architectural shape of superb patchwork stems it is hard to beat. If the decision were forced upon me, I would choose this as a multi-stem and Eucalyptus debeuzevillei as a single stem as they are both superb trees!

- Mature height: 12-17m
- Shape of mature tree
- Garden trees
- Eco impact rating: A

EUCOMMIA ulmoides
Rubber Tree

Introduced at the very end of the 1800s, this Chinese tree can produce rubber through very fine latex produced within their green glossy leaves. It forms a broadly pyramidal shape at maturity and will thrive on most free draining and fertile soils. This tree is quite unusual for the UK so is quite an interesting selection to throw into the mix for an arboretum as not many can identify it!

It prefers full sun but is fully hardy down to about -20 degrees Celsius once mature. Its flower and seed are hardly worthy of notice, but its lustrous leathery leaves are lovely in the summer.

- Mature height: 12-17m
- Shape of mature tree
- Parkland trees
- Eco impact rating: C

EUODIA hupehensis

A small genus and a must for any collector with an arboretum. Others list this as Tetradium daniellii but it is the same tree, caught up in a botanical debate to confuse everyone. Native of China and Korea, it was introduced into the UK in 1905 and won the First-Class Certificate in 1976.

Its compound leaves and panicles of small white flowers make this an attractive specimen tree that is excellent for shallow chalk soils. Bright red fruits are borne on female trees in the autumn. The flowers are characterised by lovely yellow anthers and are pleasingly fragrant. Autumn colour is a pale yellow.

- Mature height: 12-17m
- Shape of mature tree
- Parkland trees
- Eco impact rating: C

EUONYMUS europaeus Red Cascade
Spindle

A good choice even on chalky soils. This wonderful garden tree won the Award of Garden Merit in both 1949 and 2002. It has so much interest from September onwards that it is one of my favourite trees for a small garden. Named 'Red Caps' in America, this clone was selected by the University of Nebraska for the richness in colour of its fruits.

This small, arching tree produces an abundance of rosy red fruits which open to reveal vivid orange seed cases. The foliage display in the autumn is fantastic with green leaves turning into rich red foliage by November. It is one of the very best forms for gardens, parks and restricted areas. It thrives on most soils though avoid waterlogged ground.

Mature height: 3-8m | Shape of mature tree | Garden trees | Eco impact rating: C

EXOCHORDA
serratifolia Snow White
Pearl Tree

This little dainty is often known as a shrub but we have trained it into a small garden tree. Its flowering display rewards with a mass of pure white single flowers from late May into June. Fine on most soils, it is not a great fan of extremes, whether it be excessively wet or dry.

Originating from Korea, it does best in full sun and its oval leaves turn a pleasant yellow in autumn. It forms a round headed crown and does well to grow to over 5 metres tall so is a great addition to a small garden. Perfectly hardy for the non coastal extremities of the UK.

Mature height: 5-8m | Shape of mature tree | Flowering trees | Eco impact rating: D

FAGUS orientalis Iskander

Oriental Beech was first introduced into the UK in 1904 but 86 years later saw this fantastic new selection coming through. The leaves of Iskander are crisper, shinier and slightly larger than those of Fagus sylvatica but the defining difference is that it is far more resistant to woolly aphid, the bane of our native Beech which sucks and distorts new leaves throughout the spring and summer.

It has a great upright habit akin to Fagus sylvatica Dawyck but somehow Iskander just looks more vigorous and healthier! On its own you may not recognize that it is not our native Fagus sylvatica which is a good thing as it slips into our landscape seamlessly. The lush green leaves turn to yellow in the autumn and its dead leaves can hold for some time in the tree until the wind eventually blows them away. Great for either city verges or gardens, this new introduction is a lovely addition to our range. I estimate its mature width to be only 5 metres or so.

Mature height: 12-17m | Shape of mature tree | Garden trees | Eco impact rating: A

Beech tends to favour more temperate climates and is difficult to establish when faced with extreme heat and drought. With this in mind avoid planting in paved or tarmac areas where reflected heat and light makes Beech suffer.

FAGUS sylvatica
Common Beech

One of the most majestic of our native trees, the Common Beech can become very large with its low branched habit. My favourite specimen is in a private garden in North Luffenham, Rutland and what a beauty it is!

It has a wide range of uses – in woodland, parkland and in broad verge plantings – and few trees can surpass its rich, copper autumn foliage. Beech thrives just about anywhere other than exposed and coastal locations. As it is shallow rooted, under planting is not recommended. It does well in most reasonably fertile, well drained soils, except heavy clay or light sand.

- Mature height: 17-22m
- Shape of mature tree
- Parkland trees
- Native trees
- Hedging trees
- Eco impact rating: A

FAGUS sylvatica Asplenifolia
Cut-leaved Beech

The common name of Cut-leaved Beech comes from the deeply serrated and long leaves of this beautiful tree of medium height. Introduced in the early 1800s, this wonderful specimen tree won the Award of Garden Merit in 2002.

It is pyramidal in its early years but is eventually capable of becoming as wide as it is tall. A lovely choice for parkland where its cut leaves gives magnificent contrast. Beech thrives just about anywhere other than exposed and coastal locations. As it is shallow rooted, under planting is not recommended. It does well in most reasonably fertile, well drained soils, except heavy clay or light sand.

Sometimes referred to at Fagus sylvatica Heterophylla, it is in fact the same thing. There are few cut leaf trees that last the test of time, but this is surely one of the best. The key for planting is to give it the space it merits at maturity, a minimum 10m radius, 20m would be better!

- Mature height: 12-17m
- Shape of mature tree
- Parkland trees
- Eco impact rating: A

F

FAGUS sylvatica Black Swan

There are several Dutch clones of purple foliaged weepers but this one is the pick of them for habit and leaf colour. The leaf size is slightly larger than a rival clone, Purple Fountain, and they emerge deep red before hardening to a rich purple by mid summer. Even though this is a true weeper, this tree remains narrow so is great for gardens as well as parks.

It thrives on most free draining soils and its dark foliage and weeping branches gives excellent contrast within the landscape. Unlike other clones, there is nothing wishy washy about its foliage display which can harden to a black side of purple by late summer.

Mature height: 12-17m | Shape of mature tree | Garden trees | Red/purple foliage | Eco impact rating: B

FAGUS sylvatica Dawyck
Fastigiate Beech

The Fastigiate Beech – a rather ugly name for a rather beautiful tree! Originating in Dawyck, Scotland, in the mid 1800s, this architectural beauty won the Award of Garden Merit in 2002. There are some wonderful specimens planted by some of the university colleges in Cambridge.

This medium to large tree has a columnar habit and is a very good choice for both wide verges and specimen plantings in parks. Even when mature, it is seldom more than 3m wide. Beech thrives just about anywhere other than exposed and coastal locations. As it is shallow rooted, under planting is not recommended.

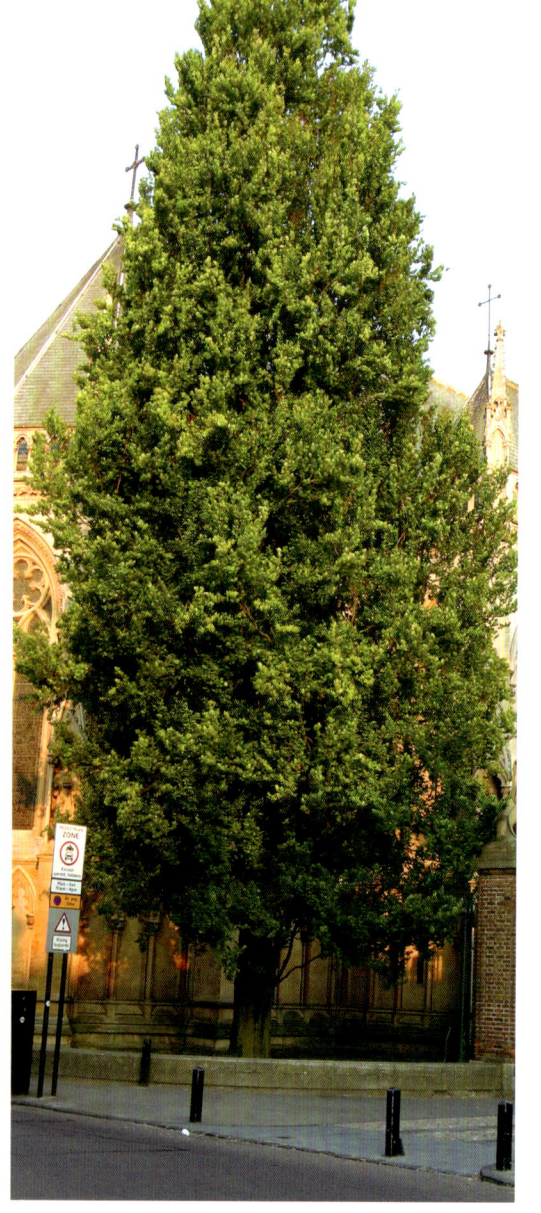

Mature height: 12-17m | Shape of mature tree | Narrow trees | Eco impact rating: B

FAGUS sylvatica Dawyck Gold

A golden-leaved form of the Fastigiate Beech. It is thought to be a seedling cross between Fagus sylvatica Dawyck and Fagus sylvatica Zlatia and was raised by JRP van Hoey-Smith in 1969. A real architectural beauty and winner of the Award of Garden Merit in 2002.

A large, columnar tree, which looks good from spring right through to autumn. In spring the leaves are golden yellow, turning pale green in summer before reverting to a golden yellow in autumn. It looks especially attractive planted against a dark background and is good as a specimen in parks and as a verge tree. Beech thrives just about anywhere other than exposed and coastal locations. As it is shallow rooted, under planting is not recommended. It does well in most reasonably fertile, well drained soils, except heavy clay or light sand.

Mature height: 12-17m | Shape of mature tree | Narrow trees | Eco impact rating: B

F

FAGUS sylvatica Dawyck Purple

A Fastigiate Beech with stunning dark foliage. Raised from the same seed source as Dawyck Gold in 1969 from a Dawyck at Trompenburg Arboretum near Rotterdam in Holland, it won the Award of Garden Merit in both 1973 and 2002. It remains a rare but stunning architectural specimen tree.

A little narrower than Dawyck Gold but not quite as dense. It makes a splendid tree for parks and verges and has striking, deep purple foliage. Beech thrives just about anywhere other than exposed and coastal locations. As it is shallow rooted, under planting is not recommended. It does well in most reasonably fertile, well drained soils, except heavy clay or light sand.

12|17			B
Mature height: 12-17m	Shape of mature tree	Narrow trees	Eco impact rating

FAGUS sylvatica Pendula
Weeping Beech

The Weeping Beech is a wonderful choice as a specimen in parks and large estates. Introduced in the mid 1830s, this stately tree won the Award of Garden Merit in 2002. Mature specimens have been known to weep to the ground and then layer up from the soil to weep again when a new trunk is formed. With this in mind they can get big over the long term!

This medium to large tree has a majestic crown with large, horizontal and pendulous branches which gives the tree a unique architectural beauty. Beech thrives just about anywhere other than exposed and coastal locations.

12|17			A
Mature height: 12-17m	Shape of mature tree	Parkland trees	Eco impact rating

FAGUS sylvatica Purpurea
Purple Beech

The Purple Beech is one of our most beautiful trees. A superb tree for creating contrast in a parkland or large garden as the darkness of the foliage draws the eye through the landscape. With this in mind it is useful to plant this on the perimeter of your area as if it is too close in view you never notice beyond it.

This large tree, somewhat pyramidal when young, matures to a broad canopy. With its dark purple leaves it is sometimes wrongly referred to as "Copper Beech", which is seed grown and variable in leaf colour. This cultivar has a much deeper purple leaf and is a tree of great beauty and majesty. It makes a magnificent subject planted as a specimen in parks and large estates. Beech thrives just about anywhere other than exposed and coastal locations. As it is shallow rooted, under planting is not recommended. It does well in most reasonably fertile, well drained soils, except heavy clay or light sand.

- Mature height: 17-22m
- Shape of mature tree
- Hedging trees
- Red/purple foliage
- Eco impact rating: A

This large, rather conical tree with its dark purple leaves is sometimes wrongly referred to as "Copper Beech", which is seed grown and variable in leaf colour. This cultivar has a much deeper purple leaf and is a tree of great beauty and majesty.

FAGUS sylvatica Rohanii

Thought to be a cross between Fagus sylvatica Quercifolia and Purpurea, this extremely pretty tree is relatively rare but highly prized. Introduced in the mid 1890s, we only ever have a few to sell every year so if you wanted one for your collection it would be best to reserve in good time!

Perhaps best described as a purple leaved form of Fagus sylvatica Asplenifolia, this slow growing, pyramidal tree is perfect for parks and large open spaces. Beech thrives just about anywhere other than exposed and coastal locations. As it is shallow rooted, under planting is not recommended. It does well in most reasonably fertile, well drained soils, except heavy clay or light sand.

Mature height: 12-17m | Shape of mature tree | Parkland trees | Eco impact rating: B

FAGUS sylvatica Roseomarginata

One of the smallest Beeches and one which does best in a sunny, rather sheltered position. Introduced in the late 1880s its availability restricts it to arboretum planting, so it is rarely seen. However, spot a good one and you will not forget it! Others list it as Fagus sylvatica Purpurea Tricolor.

The purple leaves of this small to medium, rounded tree, which only seldom reaches 15m, have attractive pink edges. The width of these margins is variable, and the foliage sometimes displays pink-white stripes. It does best in a sunny, sheltered position, and is good for parks and woodland plantings.

Taking many years to mature, this unusual tree is not for the faint hearted as it will only truly reward you many years after planting as its growth is sedate. If only we got round to planting trees in our 20's!

- Mature height: 10-15m
- Shape of mature tree
- Red/purple foliage
- Parkland trees
- Eco impact rating: B

FAGUS sylvatica Zlatia

First discovered in Serbia in 1890, this selection is rarely seen in the UK. Its claim to fame is a wonderful spring flush of yellow foliage that hardens to a yellow green by late summer before turning to yellow once again in the autumn. It forms a rounded habit at maturity and is smaller growing than Fagus sylvatica.

Thriving on most free draining soils, it gives great contrast, especially against a dark backdrop. There aren't many yellows on the market, so this is a nice addition to this range. We generally leave this clone fully branched to show off its golden leaves to the full and it is a good choice for large gardens and parkland.

- Mature height: 12-17m
- Shape of mature tree
- Parkland trees
- Eco impact rating: B

FICUS carica
Common Fig

A native of Western Asia, this well-known fruiting tree was introduced into the UK in the early 16th century. It is remarkably resistant to pest and disease and can be grown for either its foliage or fruit as both add ornamental interest to a south facing garden. We grow the variety Ficus carica 'Nero' for its lovely shape and vigour as well as its rich fruits as a half standard and Ficus carica Verdino as a full standard.

It makes a small and elegant tree with a rounded habit that does best in a warm, sheltered position, producing its green fruits by early August. Perfect for gardens or where space is restricted and often grown up against south facing walls to maximize fruiting potential.

- Mature height: 3-8m
- Shape of mature tree
- Edible fruit
- Eco impact rating: D

FRAXINUS

Sadly, this much-loved genus has fallen foul of disease imported from Europe. The Government served an importation ban on all Fraxinus in October 2012 which also restricts any movement of the genus within the UK. This was lifted in 2020 but with incidents of the disease rising it would take a brave buyer to major on this genus for the foreseeable future. We culled the last of our Fraxinus in November 2014 having once grown and sold over 6,000 per year.

Ash Die Back (Chalara fraxinea) may cause a huge shift in our treescape over the coming years as this very common tree diminishes. The important thing is that lessons are learnt to prevent this from happening again. Diversity is the key to a healthy tree population as a reliance on one genus places a massive risk once a pest takes a hold. Importing trees direct from the continent without quarantine is also asking for trouble.

The jury is out on whether Fraxinus ornus types are immune from Chalara fraxinea so we have started to reintroduce these types back, in modest quantities, into our production cycle for availability from 2021 onwards.

FRAXINUS americana Autumn Purple
Great autumn colour, selected in America in 1956.
Mature height: 12-17m

FRAXINUS angustifolia Raywood
Introduced from Australia in the mid 1920s. Superb autumn colour but prone to limb collapse when older.
Mature height: 12-17m

FRAXINUS excelsior Common Ash
Tough native tree, very free seeding which may prove its savour. Huge genetic diversity may give rise to resistance against Ash Die Back in the years to come.
Mature height: 12-17m

FRAXINUS excelsior Altena
Forestry Commission introduction in the 1940s, selected for its uniform pyramidal habit.
Mature height: 12-17m

FRAXINUS excelsior Diversifolia One-leaved Ash
Introduced in the 1780s. Tough with single rather than compound leaves.
Mature height: 12-17m

FRAXINUS excelsior Jaspidea Golden Ash
Very popular in the late 1900s and particularly susceptible to Chalara. Golden stems.
Mature height: 12-17m

FRAXINUS excelsior Pendula Weeping Ash
Introduced in the 1700s, a fine weeping tree at maturity.
Mature height: 12-17m

FRAXINUS excelsior Westhofs Glorie
Introduced in the mid 1950s and widely planted since then. As this is a clonal selection there is a high risk that Ash Die Back will take all.
Mature height: 12-17m

FRAXINUS ornus Manna Ash, Flowering Ash
Introduced before 1700. Lovely flowers in late spring.
Mature height: 12-17m

FRAXINUS ornus Arie Peters
Dutch clone, selected for its enhanced flower.
Mature height: 12-17m

FRAXINUS ornus Louisa Lady
Selected for its enhanced flower and autumn colour.
Mature height: 12-17m

FRAXINUS ornus Meczek
Introduced from Hungary in the early 1980s. Top grafted dwarfing type.
Mature height: 3-8m

FRAXINUS ornus Obelisk
Selected for its columnar habit.
Mature height: 12-17m

FRAXINUS pennsylvanica Summit
Introduced from trials in Minnesota in 1957. Fast growing and a tough urban tree.
Mature height: 12-17m

G

It is a good choice for parks and avenues, tolerating paved areas well. It has a deep root system, and curious, fan shaped leaves.

GINKGO biloba
Maidenhair Tree

Very common about 200 million years ago, this marvellous gymnosperm is making a comeback as an urban tree due to its no nonsense toughness. As it survived the radiation and devastation that wiped out 90% of all life when the comet fell to end the reign of the dinosaurs, it can cope well with traffic exhaust as well as reflected heat and light in our urban environments! Reintroduced into the UK from prehistoric times in 1754.

This large, conical tree remains relatively narrow if the central dominant leader is retained. Female plants fruit after 35 years or so and it is not possible to determine the gender until this event. Male clones such as Mayfield, Saratoga and Tremonia are disappointing in their lack of vigour. Lakeview and Princeton Sentry are the pick of the male types but remain difficult to grow, rarely come to market and command a tidy premium.

| Mature height: 17-22m | Shape of mature tree | Urban trees | Eco impact rating: B |

GINKGO biloba Blagon

This French clone originates from the 1990's and is a truely fastigaite version. Its leaf and growth habit is bushier than its parent and its autumn show of yellow foliage is truely striking. It is a great tree for a garden or urban avenue as it requires little maintenance and has the toughnes of its ancient history. Soil tolerances are the same as normal Ginkgo.

'Blagon' is a fruitless male clone but I remain sceptical until I see one several decades down the line. I remember being told that Ginkgo biloba Princeton Sentry was male but apparently the original stock plants now fruit. There is a very mature Ginkgo in the gardens by Ely cathedral that fruits profusely but I have never smelled a bad odour eminating from it. I think this 'bad smelling' Ginkgo perception is a bit of an urban myth for the UK. In warmer more humid areas where the fruit breaks down it will be an issue but over here I have never witnessed it.

| Mature height: 17-22m | Shape of mature tree | Narrow trees | Autumn colour | Garden trees | Eco impact rating: C |

GINKGO biloba
Golden Globe

This fantastic dwarfing clone forms a low spreading ball of foliage that would grace any small garden or become the centre piece of a flower bed dispaly. Its distictive maidenhair shaped leaves turn a magnificent yellow in the autumn to add to the drama.

Ginkgo leaves are supposed to have the medicinal power to aid memory retention but you have got to remember to eat one in the first place! With this clone you will never be wanting for supply as its verdant bushy habit far outstrips the leaf production of the normal Ginkgo where the leaves are out of reach anyway. It will thrive on most well drained soils and prefers a sunny aspect. As it is slow growing we only start to sell this as a maturing bush, the same age of a normal Ginkgo at 5-7m so beware, the price tag belies its stature!

| 2\|4 Mature height: 2-4m | Multi-stem | Autumn colour | Garden trees | Eco impact rating: C |

G

GINKGO biloba Lakeview

This male Scanlon introduction develops a compact pyramidal habit that is well suited for urban planting as it requires little maintenance so long as the well defined leader is left uninterrupted. There are good examples of this clone on the A47 planted on the way in and way out of Leicester.

Particularly useful for narrow city streets, this clone is well suited to deal with the reflected heat and light that bounces off pavements and buildings. It produces a great display of vivid yellow autumn colour and remains one of the best 'males' in the market.

- Mature height: 15-20m
- Shape of mature tree
- Urban trees
- Eco impact rating: B

GINKGO biloba Nanum / Globosa

Top worked on Ginkgo biloba stem at 2m this spherical dwarfing shrub form makes an ideal little tree on sites that are too restricted to accommodate a more conventional choice.

Particularly useful for narrow city streets, this clone is well suited to deal with the reflected heat and light that bounces off pavements and buildings. It also copes with urban pollution making this clone a useful addition to the Ginkgo range.

- Mature height: 3-8m
- Shape of mature tree
- Urban trees
- Eco impact rating: C

GINKGO biloba Tremonia

A superb male clone making a narrowly compact crown at maturity. Raised as a seedling in Dortmund Botanic Garden in 1930 by the late Dr G Krussmann.

Dramatic yellow autumn colour is another striking feature of this great urban clone that requires little maintenance once planted so long as its well defined leader is left uninterrupted. Superseded by 'Blagon' in recent years, this variety can be hard to find.

- Mature height: 15-20m
- Shape of mature tree
- Narrow trees
- Autumn colour
- Urban trees
- Eco impact rating: C

GINKGO biloba Princeton Sentry

Raised by the famous but now sadly out of business Princeton Nursery in New Jersey. In our opinion this is the best of the upright forms but also the most difficult to produce hence its price tag over seedling Ginkgo!

A wonderful maintenance free choice for the urban environment, the only thing holding back this male clone is its availability. Slow to grow, but the rewards are great if you persist, especially in urban settings. It is very similar to another Princeton introduction, Ginkgo biloba Magyar.

- Mature height: 17-22m
- Shape of mature tree
- Narrow trees
- Eco impact rating: C

Telephone 01353 720 748 | www.barcham.co.uk | www.barchampro.co.uk

G

GLEDITSIA triacanthos
Honey Locust

A wonderful choice for heavily polluted environments prone to vandalism. Introduced from America in 1700, its seed pods hold a sticky sweet resin from which it derives its common name.

This large, oval and rather elegant tree has leaves which resemble fronds. When mature, it looks most striking with its shiny, long seed pods. A good choice for parks and industrial areas, it does well in most soils. Be careful on handling this tree as it is very thorny!

12|17			B
Mature height: 12-17m	Shape of mature tree	Parkland trees	Eco impact rating

GLEDITSIA triacanthos Draves Street Keeper

This urban clone has been bred in the USA for its form: it grows half as wide as it does tall. Gleditzia can be a rather messy looking tree but this clone is far more suitable for the urban street scene and large garden. Mostly thornless, the leaves are darker green than Skyline and turn the same vivid yellow in the autumn.

Thriving on most soils, this tough tree was discovered just outside New York by Tom Draves who monitored it for twenty years before releasing the clone into commercial production.

Mature height: 12-17m | Shape of mature tree | Urban trees | Eco impact rating: B

GLEDITSIA triacanthos Inermis

Derived from the thorny Honey Locust, Gleditsia triacanthos, this thornless clone is a better prospect for the urban environment. Its compound green leaves go a stunning dark yellow in autumn. Suitable on most soils it will also thrive on wetter sites and is a tough tree for urban road corridors. Its habit is wide spreading so care must be taken to ensure it has enough room to develop.

Gleditsia is a native of central and North America and is now a regular throughout the UK & Europe. If you are after a narrower and more controlled thornless clone, look to Gleditsia triacanthos Draves Street Keeper.

Mature height: 15-20m | Shape of mature tree | Urban trees | Autumn colour | Eco impact rating: B

Telephone 01353 720 748 | www.barcham.co.uk | www.barchampro.co.uk

G

GLEDITSIA
triacanthos Ruby Lace

A lovely and distictive garden tree, 'Ruby Lace' is both delicate and striking. Its compound ruby coloured leaves turn to deep shades of yellow in the autumn and its irregular rounded habit gives it an architectural grace all of its own.

Gleditsia can stand a wet soil although not a waterlogged one and will thrive in the southern half of the UK. It's haphazard crown needs the committment of space so please allow for this. There are very few trees offering this leaf texture and colour and it can provide excellent contrast within a garden.

7|12			B
Mature height: 7-12m	Shape of mature tree	Autumn colour	Eco impact rating

GLEDITSIA triacanthos Skyline

One of the toughest and most reliable Honey Locusts on the market, this American clone is both thornless and near fruitless as well as being very cold tolerant. Its lime green leaves turn a remarkable showy yellow in the autumn and its pyramidal habit makes it a genuinely robust urban tree.

It is not best suited on heavier soils but thrives on well drained ones and usefully it is very tolerant of drought once established. It also copes well with reflected heat and light bouncing off pavements and buildings making it a fine prospect for inner city planting.

- Mature height: 12-17m
- Shape of mature tree
- Urban trees
- Autumn colour
- Eco impact rating: B

G

GLEDITSIA triacanthos Sunburst

Although originally from moist and even swampy areas, the Honey Locust does well in much drier and free draining soils. Introduced in the mid 1950s it won the Award of Garden Merit in 2002. It is one of the best yellow foliaged trees on the market.

This medium to large cultivar has the advantage of being thornless. It has a rounded, rather spreading form and its yellow foliage, which appears late, is retained for most of the summer. We recommend it as a very good substitute for the more brittle Robinia pseudoacacia Frisia.

| 12|17 Mature height: 12-17m | Shape of mature tree | Yellow foliage | Autumn colour | B Eco impact rating |

GYMNOCLADUS dioica
Kentucky Coffee Tree

The Kentucky Coffee Tree is surely one of the most handsome of all trees. The seeds were used as a substitute for coffee beans by the early settlers in North America but are thought to be poisonous if not roasted first. The exact introduction date is vague but it is thought to have been planted in the UK since the 1750s.

This slow growing tree of medium to large size has large, compound leaves, which are pink tinged in spring and clear yellow in autumn. The young twigs are pale grey, almost white, and particularly noticeable in winter. A wonderful choice for parks.

| 12|17 Mature height: 12-17m | Shape of mature tree | Parkland trees | C Eco impact rating |

144 Time for Trees | Edition 4

H

HALESIA monticola & carolina

Up until the early 1900s Halesia monticola and Halesia carolina were regarded as synonymous and for the sake of the general trade of this tree this is probably still the case. Monticola is larger growing with bigger leaves and flowers but it is so rarely seen in the UK as a tree that few know the difference.

Originating from the Eastern side of the USA, this pretty tree is also known as the Silverbell or Snowdrop tree on account of its profuse display of white flowers in the Spring. It produces interesting 2-3cm lime green seed pods in the autumn that give it another feature of interest. It readily grows on most free draining soils and prefers a sheltered aspect in full sun.

| Mature height: 10-15m | Shape of mature tree | Flowering trees | Bee friendly trees | Urban trees | Eco impact rating |

Telephone 01353 720 748 | www.barcham.co.uk | www.barchampro.co.uk   145

HAMAMELIS x intermedia Arnold Promise
Witch Hazel

Raised and introduced by the Arnold Arboretum in the USA, this clone is internationally recognised as being one of the best of the yellow flowering Witch Hazels. I have one in my garden since 2004 and it never fails to perform.

The original plant in the States is about 7 metres high and wide. It produces magnificent clear yellow flowers contrasting against red inners that last sometimes as long as two months without fading. It is all the more beautiful for being winter flowering.

Mature height: 3-8m | Multi-stem | Autumn colour | Eco impact rating: C

HAMAMELIS x intermedia Jelena

Unusually we grow this as a half standard rather than the more usual bush. This beautiful flowerer, coppery red towards the base, orange in the middle and yellow at the tips, is a great addition for a garden or municipal shrubbery. Early flower is so welcome when we are all longing for Spring!

Great autumn colours of yellow through to red also distinguish this Belgium introduction that was awarded the Award of Merit by the Royal Horticultural Society in 1955. It thrives on most free draining soils and I have even got one going in a sheltered coastal location.

Mature height: 3-8m | Shape of mature tree | Autumn colour | Flowering trees | Garden trees | Eco impact rating: C

HIBISCUS x Resi

We have dropped all our Hibiscus syriacus clones in preference to this one, a paramutabilis and syriacus cross selected for its early flowering and superb sized lavender coloured blossoms. As Hibiscus flowers off new season's growth, it is always worth a hard winter prune to stimulate future shoot development.

This clone is hardier, stronger, more free flowering and less nutritionally demanding than syriacus types so is perfect for a small garden or urban piazza. It flowers from late July to the end of September when most other displays have quietened down. Its maple shaped leaves turn to yellow in the autumn. In some years the flowers can mutate to white with burgundy throats and even have both pink and white flowers on the same tree at the same time. All the fun of the fair with this stunning little tree!

Mature height: 3-5m | Shape of mature tree | Eco impact rating: D

ILEX x altaclerensis Golden King

One of the very best golden variegated hollies. It was derived from a sport of Ilex x altaclerensis Hendersonii in Edinburgh in 1884. It won the First Class Certificate in 1898 and the Award of Garden Merit in 2002.

Tolerant of coastal conditions and air pollution, this medium, slow growing tree of pyramidal form has vivid golden margins to its virtually spineless leaves. Very good for gardens, female, with reddish-brown fruits.

| Mature height: 3-8m | Shape of mature tree | Variegated foliage | Evergreen trees | Eco impact rating: C |

ILEX aquifolium
Common Holly

One of the most evocative and best loved of all trees; the Common Holly is beautiful in its simplicity and brings cheer at the darkest time of year. It is very tolerant of shade and prefers well drained soils.

This native of Britain is a small, conical, evergreen tree which provides year-round interest, but is particularly attractive in autumn and winter. Great for gardens, it only retains its spiky leaves within the first ten feet of height in the tree, as after this point it suffers no predation so has no need for a thorny defence.

| Mature height: 3-8m | Shape of mature tree | Native trees | Eco impact rating: C |

ILEX aquifolium Alaska

A great clone of common Holly with spiky, dark, glossy foliage. We grow this variety as a single stemmed full standard tree ideal for either specimen planting or for spot screening. Female.

The dark evergreen foliage contrasts well with the vivid red berries that are produced in the autumn. It retains an upright pyramidal habit and is a useful tree for screening in gardens. Tolerant of shade and prefers well drained soils.

- Mature height: 3-8m
- Shape of mature tree
- Evergreen trees
- Eco impact rating: C

ILEX aquifolium Argentea Marginata
Broad-leaved Silver Holly

This lovely clone won the Award of Garden Merit in 2002. Ideal for hedging or specimen planting, it prefers free draining soils and is tolerant of shade.

It is a most dramatic small tree with spiny leaves, edged with white, and plenty of berries for winter and wildlife interest. Young growth is tinged pink. Slow growing and female.

- Mature height: 3-8m
- Shape of mature tree
- Evergreen trees
- Variegated foliage
- Eco impact rating: C

ILEX aquifolium J C Van Tol

This self pollinating Holly is in our opinion one of the best green leaved bush Hollies on the market. It won the Award of Garden Merit in 2002 and for those of you who like making up Christmas wreaths this is the clone for you!

This vigorous cultivar has very dark, shiny, almost spineless leaves and a good show of autumn berries. It remains a small tree with a good pyramidal form. Excellent for gardens, it prefers well draining soils and is tolerant of shade.

- Mature height: 3-8m
- Shape of mature tree
- Evergreen trees
- Eco impact rating: C

ILEX aquifolium Pyramidalis

This fast growing Holly has apically dominant growth and is self pollinating. A winner of the Award of Merit in 1989 and the Award of Garden Merit in 2002, it makes a great evergreen tree for gardens where space is restricted.

This clone has smooth leaves and retails a pyramidal shape if the leader is retained. Plenty of red berries in the autumn compliment its bright green evergreen leaves. It is tolerant of shade and prefers free draining soils.

- Mature height: 3-8m
- Shape of mature tree
- Evergreen trees
- Eco impact rating: C

ILEX castaneifolia
Sweet Chestnut-leaved Holly

A great favourite at Barcham, this female Holly is a vigorous grower and won the Award of Garden Merit in 2002. It is a form of Ilex x keohneana and is thought to be of French origin.

Its thick green leaves are large and resemble the shape and form of Castanea sativa from which it derives its name. Its good apical dominance produces a medium to large tree of conical habit. Red berries are produced in abundance in the autumn and it is tolerant of shade. Like all hollies it will thrive on most soils so long as they are well drained.

- Mature height: 3-8m
- Shape of mature tree
- Evergreen trees
- Privacy raised screening
- Eco impact rating: C

ILEX x Nellie Stevens

This clone was derived from a seed source collected by Ms Stevens in 1900 from the US National Arboretum. It is a hybrid between Ilex aquifolium and Ilex cornuta and is exceptional for its vigour and readiness to make a small single stemmed tree.

Smooth dark glossy leaves contrast well with the orange-red berries in autumn and we supply this clone as a feathered bush or as a clear stemmed standard at semi mature. Ideal for spot screening and it tolerates most free draining soils. Female.

- Mature height: 3-8m
- Shape of mature tree
- Evergreen trees
- Privacy raised screening
- Eco impact rating: C

It produces an abundance of nuts over a long period, but they are rather difficult to extract from their very hard shells.

JUGLANS nigra
Black Walnut

Introduced from native central and eastern America into Europe in 1629, this fast growing tree won the Award of Garden Merit in 2002. The national US champion stands at 44 metres high by 47 metres wide in Oregon so not one to be planted in restricted places.

It makes a large tree with a broadly pyramidal crown and is a very good choice for parkland settings. Rough barked from a young age so easily distinguished from the smooth barked Juglans regia. It grows on most soils but thrives on deep loam.

Mature height: 17-22m | Shape of mature tree | Edible nuts | Eco impact rating: A

J

JUGLANS regia
Common Walnut

A native of South Eastern Europe, Himalaya and China, this well known tree is highly prized for its timber. It makes a splendid and stately subject for parkland and avenue plantings, developing a broad crown at maturity and preferring full sun. Thought to have been in cultivation in the UK since Roman times.

Slow growing and of medium to large stature, this rounded Walnut has delightfully aromatic young foliage, from which a wine can be made, followed by a good crop of delicious nuts. Smooth barked when young, it thrives on most soils but does not favour waterlogged conditions.

- Mature height: 12-15m
- Shape of mature tree
- Edible nuts
- Eco impact rating: A

JUNIPERUS communis Hibernica
Irish Juniper

Introduced in the late 1830s, this is an excellent choice of small conifer, ideal for gardens and large rockeries. It won the Award of Garden Merit in 2002.

Its slender and dense form imposes a sense of architectural formality to a garden and it requires little or no maintenance. It tolerates most soils but does not thrive on waterlogged ground.

- Mature height: 3-8m
- Shape of mature tree
- Evergreen trees
- Eco impact rating: C

KOELREUTERIA paniculata
Pride of India

Also known as the Golden Rain Tree, this was introduced from China in the 1760s but it is also a native of Japan and Korea. It is a tougher tree than most credit.

A most attractive, rounded tree of medium height, it deserves to be more widely grown as it has much to recommend it. The clusters of small yellow flowers which it produces in July and August are followed by lantern shaped fruits in the autumn. It does best in dry, calcareous soils and in a reasonably sunny position.

Mature height: 5-8m | Shape of mature tree | Flowering trees | Bee friendly trees | Eco impact rating: D

I have seen this tree thriving on a narrow soil strip of central reservation in south London taking all urban pollution can throw at it. For such a pretty tree it can tolerate locations where our native trees would soon succumb to failure.

KOELREUTERIA paniculata Fastigiata

A columnar form of Pride of India. Raised by Kew Gardens from seeds received in 1888 from Shanghai, this botanical oddity is a must for plant collectors.

A good choice for restricted spaces and excellent as a specimen tree in a park. The clusters of small yellow flowers which it produces in July and August are followed by lantern shaped fruits in the autumn. It does best in dry, calcareous soils and in a reasonably sheltered position, such as an urban courtyard garden.

- Mature height: 5-8m
- Shape of mature tree
- Narrow trees
- Bee friendly trees
- Eco impact rating: D

LABURNOCYTISUS Adamii

This remarkable tree, a graft chimaera, is thought to have been fluked when a nurseryman from M Adam nurseries near Paris in 1825 turned his attention to grafting purple flowered broom after finishing with Laburnum.

Whether intentional or not the result was extraordinary! The plant looks more like laburnum than anything else until it flowers when some branches bear the anticipated yellow flowers of Laburnum while others bear dense clusters of the purple flowered Cytisus. Just to confuse matters further most branches also produce intermediate flowers of coppery pink! There is a particularly good specimen at Kew gardens. It tends to thrive on most soils though dislikes water logged conditions. As it is so rare it is best planted as an individual specimen in a tree collection.

- Mature height: 3-8m
- Shape of mature tree
- Flowering trees
- Eco impact rating: D

LABURNUM x watereri Vossii

A most floriferous cultivar that won the Award of Garden Merit in 2002. Selected in Holland late in the 19th century, it has remained very popular over the years and is readily seen in gardens up and down the UK.

This small tree produces a wealth of yellow racemes up to 50cm long in spring. All parts of the plant are highly poisonous as it contains an alkaloid called cytosine. It thrives on most soils and is particularly effective when grown as an arching avenue.

Much is made of its black seeds being fatal if eaten and rightly so, but occurrences of laburnum poisoning are extremely rare. Educating children to keep away from this genus is the key.

One of the very best examples of this is at Bodnant Gardens in North Wales where the abundant flowers droop down above you and fill the air with their fragrance.

Mature height: 5-8m | Shape of mature tree | Flowering trees | Eco impact rating: C

LAGERSTROEMIA indica Fauriei Natchez

Developed by the National Arboretum in Washington USA for its mildew resistance and fine white floral display, its clonal name honours a North American indigenous tribe. Best in full sun and freely drained moisture retentive soils, this great garden plant rewards with flowers, stem texture and great autumn colour of gold through to red.

As with all Lagerstroemia, its flowering in the UK is hit and miss depending on the intensity of the summer but the genus is so much more that its flower and I grow it for its architectual beauty. The flowers are just an incidental bonus! We grow this as a standard tree rather than a multi stem bush.

- Mature height: 5-7m
- Shape of mature tree
- Flowering trees
- Autumn colour
- Eco impact rating: C

LAGERSTROEMIA indica Rosea
Crape Myrtle

This selection of the Crape Myrtle is best grown in south facing and sheltered locations. Native of both Korea and China, it was introduced into the UK in 1759 and won the Award of Garden Merit in both 1924 and 2002.

A beautiful small tree with a rounded, somewhat flat-topped growth. The bark is most attractive, being mottled with grey and pink, while the small, dark green leaves turn flame red in autumn.

Much has been made of climate change over the last decade and I find it interesting that we have routinely been able to get our Lagerstroemia to flower in recent years. When I first started growing trees in the late 1980s this tree was treated as half hardy and flowers were not even considered!

The deep rose pink flowers, with their crimped petals, are borne late summer but are only initiated after warm summers.

- Mature height: 5-7m
- Shape of mature tree
- Flowering trees
- Eco impact rating: C

LAGERSTROEMIA indica Sarah's Favorite

We grow this Crape Myrtle as a multi stem bush with an ultimate height of about 5 metres so it is a great tree for a small garden with bark, flower and autumn colour interest. For the pruners amongst you, a lot of fun can be derived with Lagerstroemia as the flowers are borne from new season's growth so you won't miss anything when winter pruned. I routinely take off half of the previous season's growth each winter to create an architectural framework of smooth standout stems.

Its glorious white flowers can be hit and miss in the UK, only apprearing in the hottest of summers but they still seem to make a regular appearance at Barcham. Best on free draining but moist soils, try and avoid high alkalinity.

Mature height: 5-7m | Shape of mature tree | Multi-stem | Autumn colour | Flowering trees | Urban trees | Eco impact rating: C

LAGERSTROEMIA indica Tuscarora

The genus gets its name from the famous Swedish botanist Magnus Von Lagerstroem who was amongst us in the early 1700s. This upright growing multi stemmed tree gets to about 20 foot tall at maturity and is the pink flowerer within our range.

Like all Lagerstroemia in the UK, the flower is dependant on a hot and sustained summer but there is so much more to this genus in terms of stem texture, architectuarl habit and great autumn colour. Best on free draining but moisture retentive soils with a PH under 7.5. Like many trees, early growth can get burnt off by a late frost. This genus is best planted from the Midlands of England southwards in the UK to secure the climate for optimal growing.

Mature height: 5-7m | Shape of mature tree | Flowering trees | Eco impact rating: C

LAGERSTROEMIA indica Violacea

Similar in every way to the cultivar 'Rosea' this lovely small tree produces clusters of violet flowers from late August onwards so long as the summer gives enough heat. Flowers are often initiated in even the dullest summers but do not fully emerge unless we have decent weather in September and October. It is well worth taking the risk!

A beautiful small tree with a rounded, somewhat flat-topped growth. The bark is most attractive, being mottled with grey and pink, while the small, dark green leaves turn flame red in autumn.

- Mature height: 5-7m
- Shape of mature tree
- Flowering trees
- Autumn colour
- Eco impact rating: C

LARIX decidua
Common Larch

A lovely deciduous conifer and underused in amenity plantings. Being coniferous it has very good apical dominance, so retaining a lovely pyramidal habit through to maturity. Not a native tree but introduced into the UK in the early 1600s. It won the Award of Garden Merit in 2002.

Ideal for verges, as a specimen tree for parkland, or for woodlands, its crown is slender and conical when young. At maturity the older branches droop. Glorious green foliage heralds the spring and the autumn colour of yellow-orange provide good contrast. It thrives on most soils. We supplied some for the A47 coming into Leicester in 2001 and they are romping away!

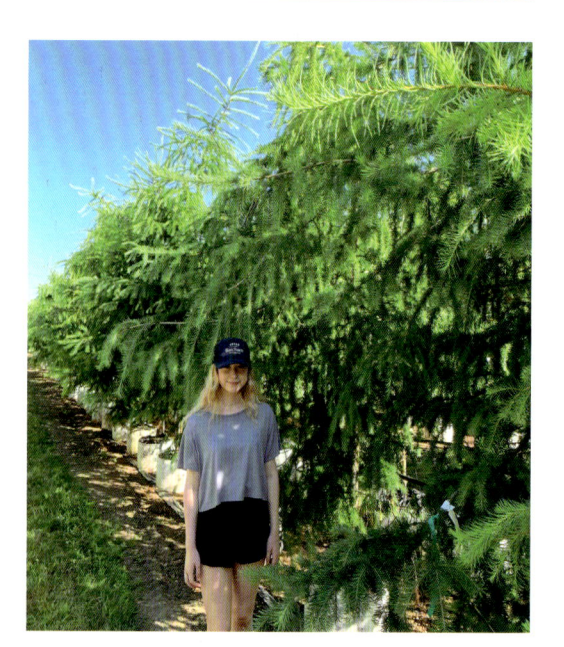

- Mature height: 17-22m
- Shape of mature tree
- Urban trees
- Eco impact rating: A

LARIX x eurolepis
Dunkeld Larch, Hybrid Larch

Discovered at Dunkeld, Perthshire, around 1904, this hybrid is particularly robust and is a cross between Larix decidua and Larix kaempferi. In truth all the Larch we grow have very similar attributes and are difficult to distinguish. I would choose this cultivar for its toughness.

It is a large and fast growing tree with good timber and amenity value. Ideal for street verges or parkland, this deciduous conifer is, in my opinion, greatly underused. There is something primeval about Larch, a wonderful relic to an age before us.

- Mature height: 17-22m
- Shape of mature tree
- Parkland trees
- Eco impact rating: A

LARIX kaempferi
Japanese Larch

This deciduous conifer was introduced from its native Japan in the early 1860s by the well known plant enthusiast JG Veitch. It thrives on most soils and is great for verges, parkland or large gardens. Unfortunately in recent years the Forestry Commission have seen huge swathes of this tree suffer a swift demise from Phytophthora ramorum, sudden oak death, so beware!

A fast growing and large tree of conical form, the bright green leaves turn yellow in autumn. Its twiggy growth is tinged red, and when seen as a plantation against a setting sun in the winter the effect of this is quite dramatic.

Mature height: 17-22m | Shape of mature tree | Parkland trees | Eco impact rating: A

LAURUS nobilis
Bay Laurel

We used to grow this as a clear stemmed full standard tree*. A native of the Mediterranean, it was introduced in the early 1560s though it's foliage probably hit these shores a lot earlier when Julius Caesar visited with a wreath of it on his head! It won the Award of Garden Merit in 2002.

Often considered as a half hardy plant when young, it proves to be tougher when mature and combats the vagaries of UK winters very well. However the harsh winter of 2010/11 accounted for many new plantings so beware! When it is used as a potted plant in a garden the soil volume may freeze in winter making it impossible for the plant to access water. Drought is the killer here, not hardiness.

Mature height: 3-8m | Shape of mature tree | Garden trees | Evergreen trees | Eco impact rating: D

*Unfortunately, this tree is a host and very susceptible to the plant killer Xylella fastidiosa which has wiped out Olive production in the south of Italy and remains a real threat to UK trees as it attacks such a broad rage of genera. In our view it is irresponsible to import this plant and we refuse to promote/grow it on this basis.

LIGUSTRUM japonicum
Japanese Tree Privet

Introduced in 1845 by PF von Siebold from its native Japan, this is often used as a stilted hedge above the fence line so is a favourite in urban gardens where privacy is needed. It can be planted very close to buildings without fear of subsidence and is compliant as such with the building regulation code. It is very useful in a small garden as its trunk below the fence line takes up little garden space.

A small semi-evergreen tree, it is generally regarded as an evergreen in the south of England. It has a rounded habit with long, pointed leaves and white flowers, which are borne in mid-summer. Very good in restricted areas and it thrives on most soils. There are some fine examples of this maturing in London, transforming winter streets with their evergreen canopy.

Like many broad-leaved evergreens this tree is at its lowest ebb in March / April as old leaves are jettisoned to make way for new. In severe winters it can look depleted in the early spring until a new flush of growth replenishes its appearance. Leaves are transitory things with their purpose to harvest sunlight to convert to energy. Over the year the environment batters them depleting their efficiency, and this is why the tree gives up on them and produces new ones to take over. Also, a tree will grow from the growing tip outwards so older leaves are shaded by newer ones making them less productive and not worthy of retention. If they are left to their own devices, they will still perform but not be as dense and still look at their most miserable in the spring until new buds emerge along the branches to fill the crown out again.

- Mature height: 5-8m
- Shape of mature tree
- Privacy raised screening
- Evergreen trees
- Eco impact rating: B

The 'before' and 'after' photos above demonstrate quite clearly how views between neighbouring properties can change in one day for the benefit of both parties!

L

To keep your Ligustrum green and vibrant for longer, a 10-20% crown reduction in March / April will give denser growth throughout the summer and following winter until this cycle of leaf renewal starts again.

LIGUSTRUM lucidum Variegata

A variegated form of Chinese Privet and a good choice for urban settings. Sometimes listed as 'Superbum', it won the Award of Garden Merit in 2002. We grow this as a full standard so it is an ideal candidate for planting close to a fence line to provide screening cover over the fence height. I saw some planted in a street in London whilst walking to our stand at the Chelsea Flower Show and they were performing admirably.

A most striking, top worked form with a rounded habit. A small semi-evergreen tree, it is generally regarded as an evergreen in the south of England. It has long, pointed gold margined leaves and white flowers, which are borne in mid to late summer. Very good in restricted areas and it thrives on most free draining soils.

Slightly more susceptible to losing leaf in severe winters than Ligustrum japonicum, the same cycle of leaf renewal applies in the spring so don't be shocked when the tree' canopy looks a bit thin in April / May. To mitigate this please refer to the advice given under Ligustrum japonicum.

- Mature height: 5-8m
- Shape of mature tree
- Urban trees
- Eco impact rating: B

LIGUSTRUM lucidum Variegata

LIGUSTRUM ovalifolium
Hedging Privet

Introduced from Japan in the late 1880s, this great hedging plant makes a fantastic evergreen screen. What is more, if it runs away through neglect a privet hedge can be absolutely butchered in March back to bare wood only to spring back into life and vigour in one season to get the screen back in order. It will lose leaves in extremely cold winters but thrives on most soils and aspects. It has almost gone out of fashion with the introduction of laurel and photinia but remains the most straightforward and easily maintained hedging plant on the market. As it is easy to grow it is also often the most economical option to buy!

Mature height: 1-3m | Hedging trees | Urban trees | Evergreen trees | Eco impact rating: D

LIQUIDAMBAR acalycina

A fast growing form of Sweet Gum introduced from China in the 1980s. Its three lobed leaves and general habit are very similar to Liquidambar formosana but it is much hardier and it grows with a tough vigour. Unlike most other Sweet Gum clones, it is better known for its spring and summer foliage effect than its autumn colour.

Of pyramidal form and medium height, it produces bronze-purple foliage that is retained with flushing new growth throughout the growing season. It turns to yellow in autumn and leaves are often retained until well into winter. Suitable for streets, avenues and parks, it does best in fertile, well drained soils. It does not thrive in chalky soils.

- Mature height: 12-17m
- Shape of mature tree
- Parkland trees
- Autumn colour
- Eco impact rating: B

LIQUIDAMBAR styraciflua
Sweet Gum

The Sweet Gum is one of the finest trees for autumn colour. Introduced from its native Eastern USA in the 17th century, it won the equivalent of the Award of Garden Merit in 1975.

Sometimes confused with maple on account of its similar leaves, this makes a large tree with a broad, pyramidal crown if its central leader is retained. Its attractive, corky bark is a feature at all times of the year, but it is at its magnificent best in autumn when it simply seems to burn with crimson and gold. Suitable for streets, avenues and parks, it does best in fertile, well drained soils. It does not thrive in chalky soils.

Mature height: 12-17m | Shape of mature tree | Avenue trees | Autumn colour | Eco impact rating: B

LIQUIDAMBAR styraciflua Gumball

This top worked tree is supplied in a number of heights but we tend to concentrate on quarter and half standards. Ideal for formal gardens, its rounded habit is thick with leaves in the summer. One stange thing we have noticed over the years is that it turns to claret in the autumn but steadfastly refuses to shed all of its leaves in the winter, unlike the rest of the genera.

Good on any free draining non alkaline soils, it can be clipped to shape in the winter to create a perfect near topiary sphere in the summer. Always plant within view of the house otherwise you will miss it!

Mature height: 1-3m | Shape of mature tree | Autumn colour | Eco impact rating: D

LIQUIDAMBAR styraciflua Lane Roberts

This sweet gum cultivar is particularly reliable in Britain and won the Award of Garden Merit in 2002. Like many of the styraciflua cultivars, the bark is smooth rather than corky. When planted en masse the autumn effect is both sensational and long lasting.

The autumn colour of the foliage is a highly dramatic dark crimson to red. A medium size tree, it has a tighter conical habit and larger leaves than the species. A good choice as a street or garden tree, it does best in fertile, well drained soils, but does not thrive in chalky soils.

Mature height: 12-17m | Shape of mature tree | Garden trees | Autumn colour | Eco impact rating: B

LIQUIDAMBAR styraciflua Rotundifolia

This distinctly different looking Liquidambar has, as its name suggests, indented but rounded leaves which turn yellow to occasioannly red in autumn. It is a tidy pyramidal tree and like all Liquidambar in the UK is very hard to find an insect pest that will predate on its leaf.

Thriving best on well drained but fertile soils, 'Rotundifolia' prefers a PH of less that 7.5. For the plant collectors amongst you, this cultivar is always good to challenge those keen to identify it as it is seldom seen in the UK.

Mature height: 15-20m | Shape of mature tree | Urban trees | Autumn colour | Eco impact rating: B

LIQUIDAMBAR styraciflua Slender Silhouette

With a leaf akin to Stella or Worplesdon, the shape of this tree is Liquidambar's equivalent of Cupressus sempervirens! Extremely columnar, it develops a ratio of height to width of 5 to 1. This American introduction also has good autumn colour with leaves turning yellow, orange and red before leaf fall.

Thriving on most free draining soils this narrow form is ideal for small gardens or restricted streets. Autumn colour is more reliable on acid soils and like many clones of Liquidambar styraciflua, its bark is smooth when young unlike its parent.

- Mature height: 7-12m
- Shape of mature tree
- Autumn colour
- Eco impact rating: B

LIQUIDAMBAR styraciflua Stella

This Sweet Gum with deeply cut star-like leaves resembles a semi dwarfing clone of Liquidambar Worplesdon. Prized for its autumn colour, this is a wonderful tree for a medium to large garden. Its bark is smooth rather than corky.

The bright green foliage of spring and summer turns from golden yellow through to crimson as autumn progresses. Stella is a medium to large tree of pyramidal habit; its leaves are similar to, but slightly smaller than, Worplesdon. Suitable for streets, avenues and parks, it does best in fertile, well drained soils. It does not thrive in chalky soils.

- Mature height: 12-17m
- Shape of mature tree
- Autumn colour
- Eco impact rating: B

LIQUIDAMBAR styraciflua Thea

This lovely Sweet Gum is broad leaved and late to colour in the autumn, starting with the top third of the tree which turns a remarkable purple. A recent introduction, selected in the Netherlands..

Thea is in many respects similar to Lane Roberts, but as a medium to large tree, is a little taller. It has a good, conical form and distinctive purple foliage in the autumn. A good choice as a street or garden tree, it does best in fertile, well drained soils, but does not thrive in chalky soils.

- Mature height: 12-17m
- Shape of mature tree
- Autumn colour
- Eco impact rating: B

LIQUIDAMBAR styraciflua Manon Variegata

This Sweet Gum is a must for those who like their variegated trees. The striking foliage is best in summer and can provide excellent contrast against a dark evergreen background.

This medium size cultivar, with its horizontal lateral branches, has a very regular, pyramidal form. It is of medium height and resistant to both pests and disease. Its blue-green foliage, with a creamy white margin, turns pink in autumn. Suitable for streets, avenues and parks, it does best in fertile, well drained soils. It does not thrive in chalky soils.

- Mature height: 7-12m
- Shape of mature tree
- Garden trees
- Variegated trees
- Eco impact rating: B

LIQUIDAMBAR styraciflua Worplesdon

Unlike most other Sweet Gums, this clone often bears fruit in British conditions. A winner of the Award of Garden Merit in both 1987 and 2002, this is our favoured clone of Liquidambar for both autumn colour and form. I have one thriving in my garden on a very thin and slightly alkaline soil. It is also the hardiest clone, thriving on our exposed Fen field unit where other clones and even the parent can fail to cope in some winters.

Its foliage is delightful and more deeply lobed than other clones and its pyramidal habit is both reliable and architecturally pleasing. However its real beauty lies in its autumn colour starting in September when some leaves turn yellow through to orange before falling but the outermost leaves gradually turn to magnificent claret red. A great tree for any urban aspect where space allows.

- Mature height: 12-17m
- Shape of mature tree
- Autumn colour
- Eco impact rating: B

L

LIQUIDAMBAR styraciflua Worplesdon

L

LIRIODENDRON tulipifera
Tulip Tree

Introduced from America in the late 1680s this stately tree is known as Whitewood in North America, where the timber is widely used in house interiors.

A large and fast growing tree, it has a broad, pyramidal crown. The tulip shaped flowers, which appear only on older trees, are produced in June and July and are yellow-green with a band of orange at the base. It is deep rooted and wind resistant, and does well on most fertile soils. A splendid subject for parks and large gardens. Apparently, excellent honey is derived from bees harvesting its flowers.

There are some tremendous specimens in the States that have grown to over 60 metres in height. As an aside, if you ever prune the young wood, take time to breathe in the sweetly fragrant sap.

17|22 Mature height: 17-22m | Shape of mature tree | Parkland trees | B Eco impact rating

LIRIODENDRON tulipifera Aureomarginatum

This form of the Tulip Tree has yellow variegation to its leaves and was introduced in the early 1900s. The British champion I have heard is in Stourhead and stands at over 25 metres tall. The foliage is at its most striking in the spring.

Growing rather smaller than the species, this is a medium tree with a pyramidal habit. The bright yellow variegation tends to turn greenish-yellow by the end of the summer. It is deep rooted and wind resistant and does well on most fertile soils. Lovely for parkland settings.

Mature height: 12-17m | Shape of mature tree | Bee friendly trees | Eco impact rating: B

LIRIODENDRON tulipifera Fastigiatum

This very upright form tends to flower earlier than its parent and we regularly see a decent floral display on 12-14cm girth crop. Like fastigiate hornbeam it can be prone to a bit of middle-aged spread so allow for a bit more room around it at planting than you think. I saw a maturing specimen in Rutland, and it was pretty much as wide as it was tall!

Its stiffly ascending branches are very effective if kept as a feathered tree, eventually competing with the leader to become a fat tear drop shape at maturity. It is best planted as a specimen tree in medium sized gardens or parks and thrives in most fertile free draining soils.

Mature height: 7-12m | Shape of mature tree | Bee friendly trees | Eco impact rating: B

MAGNOLIA x brooklynensis Elizabeth

Raised in New York by Eva Maria Sperbes in the 1970s, it is a cross between Magnolia acuminata and denudata. One of the finest yellows. The jury is still out on its ultimate shape and vigour as it is so recent an introduction.

This lovely small conical tree produces clear, pale primrose-yellow cup shaped flowers in the spring that are nicely fragrant. The flowers tend to be a deeper yellow the cooler its position, but make sure it is well placed for spring viewing as its show can be breathtaking.

Mature height: 3-8m | Shape of mature tree | Multi-stem | Garden trees | Flowering trees | Eco impact rating: C

MAGNOLIA x brooklynensis Yellow Bird

We grow this clone as a tree rather than a bush. It is a hybrid of Magnolia acuminata and was raised at the Brooklyn Botanic Garden before being introduced in 1981. The glorious flowers are yellow with a greener tinge held at the base of the outer petals and are borne in April / May.

Its leaves are nice and large to carry on the interest throughout the summer. Yellow Bird is quite a tidy looking tree with a pyramidal habit making it a good choice for medium size gardens and urban areas. It will grow on most well drained soils, preferably acid and is better without grass competition.

Mature height: 3-8m | Shape of mature tree | Multi-stem | Flowering trees | Eco impact rating: C

MAGNOLIA denudata Yellow River

A lovely addition to our deciduous Magnolia range, producing large canary yellow flowers in April and May. The flowers are beautifully fragrant, sweet melon comes to mind! It is difficult to tell apart from another yellow clone 'Yellow Lantern'.

Wonderful as a specimen plant in a garden or park, we grow this cultivar as a standard tree as well as a multi-stemmed bush. It is vigorous and has an ascending habit when young, broadening with age.

Mature height: 3-8m | Shape of mature tree | Flowering trees | Eco impact rating: C

MAGNOLIA Galaxy

This Magnolia was bred in the US National Arboretum in 1963 and is a cross between Magnolia lilliflora and Magnolia sprengeri 'Diva'. It is a seedling sister of 'Spectrum'.

Such a glamorous tree, we once supplied them in full flower to a private house in London and a day later the neighbouring property ordered some as well.

Galaxy is a medium sized tree of conical habit formed by its ascending branches that broaden at maturity. A good choice for gardens or parkland, it produces stunning, purple-pink to red, tulip-shaped flowers, which are lightly scented. Flowers emerge before the foliage. It does best on moist, but free-draining, fertile soils and in sheltered or partially shaded positions.

- Mature height: 7-12m
- Shape of mature tree
- Flowering trees
- Eco impact rating: C

MAGNOLIA grandiflora
Southern Magnolia

Introduced in 1734, this is a well known native of the USA, naturally ranging from North Carolina to Florida, Arkansas and Texas. From being associated with south facing wall plantings, this wonderful evergreen has crept into the wider landscape in southern England in recent years with the advent of warmer summers and not so punishing winters.

Capable of becoming a medium to large tree if given full sun and a sheltered position, it is a magnificent, round headed specimen. The large, cream flowers, which are delicately scented, are borne through summer and into autumn, set against dark green, almost leathery leaves. It does best in rich, fertile soil and, given this, will tolerate lime.

- Mature height: 7-12m
- Shape of mature tree
- Urban trees
- Eco impact rating: C

M

MAGNOLIA grandiflora Gallissoniensis

This Magnolia was being grown in France prior to 1750 so is more in tune with European winters. It is difficult to tell apart from its parent and is now a popular choice for urban gardens in southern Britain.

A very hardy, evergreen clone, it produces large flowers, while the large, green leaves are tinted reddish brown underneath. It is of medium stature and broadly oval habit. We offer it as a standard well-suited to urban planting.

7|12 Mature height: 7-12m | Shape of mature tree | Multi-stem | Evergreen trees | Eco impact rating

MAGNOLIA grandiflora Praecox

This evergreen Magnolia is sometimes referred to as 'Goliath'. It is hardy enough for the southern half of the UK but prefers a sheltered south facing location to keep its lush evergreen crown well furnished with its large ridged leaves that are a very distinctive dark green above and rusty brown below. Magnolia grandiflora Praecox is more floriferous at an earlier age than Magnolia grandiflora Gallissoniensis and it will flower throughout the summer and even into the early autumn when the weather is on its side.

Magnolia grandiflora types are always more open in habit than on the continent where the summers are routinely warmer. They thrive on most free draining soils from neutral to acid and its large supersized creamy white flowers are both fragrant and stunning.

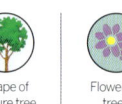

7|12 Mature height: 7-12m | Shape of mature tree | Flowering trees | Urban trees | Eco impact rating

MAGNOLIA Heaven Scent

A member of the Svelte Brunettes Group of Magnolias this lovely variety won the Award of Garden Merit in 2002. We grow it as a standard tree with an oval crown that broadens at maturity.

A superb small tree with heavily scented, rather narrow, cup shaped flowers in April. It has pale pink petals, flushed with a deeper pink towards the base, and a cerise stripe on the back. It makes an ideal tree for a medium sized garden and a showy urban tree. The conditions of the 2015 Spring gave an unrivalled flowering display that had arborists buzzing on social networks!

Mature height: 7-12m | Shape of mature tree | Multi-stem | Flowering trees | Eco impact rating: C

MAGNOLIA kobus

Introduced in 1865 from Japan, this sturdy Magnolia is both very hardy and versatile. Unlike the other magnolias we supply, this only flowers at its full potential after about 15 years but as we supply them well over five years old it isn't too long to wait! In between time you will have a decent display rather than a sensational one.

We grow this medium size, round headed tree as a full standard, and recommend it for planting on verges and in parkland. It does well in most soils, including chalky ones. The very large, white flowers are produced as early as March and can reach up to 10cm across. This is definitely the best choice for neutral to high ph soils.

Interestingly, recent research named this tree as the candidate best equipped to gobble up urban pollution so it is now being widely used in inner cities to perform this valuable service and help out all those with respiratory problems associated with exhaust fumes.

Mature height: 7-12m | Shape of mature tree | Urban trees | Eco impact rating: C

M

I planted the multi stem version of this tree in my garden in 2009 and even though it is only about 2 metres tall it produces well over 100 flower buds that furnish its limbs with bloom in March. This spectacular tree is one of the first plants in my garden to register the spring.

MAGNOLIA x loebneri Leonard Messel

A chance cross between Magnolia kobus and Magnolia stellata Rosea, originating at Colonel Messel's Nymans garden in Sussex. Often sold as a shrub, we also grow this as a single stemmed small tree that would grace any garden.

One of the prettiest and delightful Magnolias, it produces abundant dainty white-lilac flowers in spring. It only makes a small tree so is perfect for a garden and it is reasonably lime tolerant.

As many as 12 to 15 petals adorn a single glorious flower and in the spring the tree is smothered with velvety cased buds waiting to burst. In my opinion this is the pick of 'garden' Magnolias and even the oblivious register this beauty when it is in full swing.

| Mature height: 1-3m | Shape of mature tree | Multi-stem | Garden trees | Eco impact rating: C |

MAGNOLIA x loebneri Merrill

An outstanding American selection, raised at the Arnold Arboretum, Boston, in the late 1930s and the winner of more horticultural awards than you can shake a stick at! Very numerous velvety flower cases become noticeable after Christmas suggesting the promise that spring is around the corner.

This Magnolia does well in all soils- including chalky ones. Small and of rounded habit, it has large, fragrant white flowers in spring that are produced in great abundance. Very attractive in both parks, hard areas and in my garden. Normally a banker for Mothering Sunday, which gets my two out of gaol!

Mature height: 3-8m | Shape of mature tree | Flowering trees | Eco impact rating: C

MAGNOLIA x soulangeana

The most popular form of Magnolia, widely planted in parks and gardens. It has a long history, originating from Japan but was developed in France early in the 19th century. It has almost become synonymous with urban gardens in England.

Usually grown as a large shrub with a broad, round habit, the large, white, purple tinted, tulip-like flowers appear in April and May before the arrival of foliage. It tolerates heavy clay soils and is also moderately lime tolerant. Again, we buck the trend and grow this as a single stemmed tree as well as a multi-stem.

Mature height: 3-8m | Shape of mature tree | Multi-stem | Flowering trees | Eco impact rating: C

Telephone 01353 720 748 | www.barcham.co.uk | www.barchampro.co.uk

M

MAGNOLIA Spectrum

This Magnolia was bred in the US National Arboretum in 1963 and is a cross between Magnolia lilliflora and Magnolia sprengeri 'Diva'.

A medium sized tree of conical habit formed by its ascending branches that broadens at maturity. A great choice for gardens or parks, it produces most attractive, dark purple, tulip-shaped flowers, which are lightly scented. Flowers emerge before the foliage. It does best on moist, but free-draining, fertile soils and in sheltered or partially shaded positions.

It is a seedling sister of 'Galaxy' and one of our customers routinely sends us an emailed photo of his every spring when it is in full flower.

- 7|12 Mature height: 7-12m
- Shape of mature tree
- C Eco impact rating

MAGNOLIA Susan

A lovely small deciduous tree that tolerates alkaline soils. One of the so called 'Little Girl Hybrids' developed between 1955 and 1956 at the US National Arboretum, it is renowned for its profuse floral display.

Abundant deep pink-purple flowers are produced in April-June and its erect habit makes this clone a lovely addition for a small garden. We grow this variety as a tree rather than as a bush and although growth is slow the flowers never fail to disappoint. I've recently placed one within view of the coast in Cornwall but within shelter of a conifer to protect it against the strongest winds and it's romping away.

- 3|8 Mature height: 3-8m
- Shape of mature tree
- Garden trees
- C Eco impact rating

MALUS baccata Street Parade

This is a cultivar of the Siberian crab which is widely distributed throughout Southern Asia and was introduced into the UK in 1784.

This small crab has a tight, columnar habit and is a good choice for small gardens, street plantings or where space is limited. Plentiful, single, white flowers emerge from salmon pink buds. Shiny, purple-red fruits are produced from August onwards. Street Parade has the added advantage of being scab and mildew resistant.

Mature height: 5-8m | Shape of mature tree | Garden trees | Eco impact rating: C

MALUS Bramley Seedling

A superb and well known cooking apple that produces large green fruits. It has been in cultivation for over 200 years and many a house buyer inherits one with their new purchase as it had been widely planted during this period.

The original tree resides in Nottinghamshire. The white, pink blushed, flowers in spring provide a lovely display and like other Malus, this variety is best suited to heavier but well drained soils. The abundant fruit crop can be harvested by autumn and when combined with blackberries makes my favourite fruit pie.

Mature height: 5-8m | Shape of mature tree | Edible fruits | Flowering trees | Bee friendly trees | Eco impact rating: C

MALUS Butterball

This lovely crab apple sets a prolific amount of decorative creamy yellow fruits for the early autumn. Held in clusters, this display is hard to match. White flowers are produced in spring and like all the crab apples, this variety is best on heavier land and is more tolerant to wetness than Prunus.

It's spring floral display is stunning with profuse white flowers, flushed pink in bud, all over its rounded and slighty arching branches. Best for gardens and parks, we do not recommend this variety for hard surface areas as the fruit will make a mess of your paving / pavements. It responds well to pruning in winter but beware, it flowers on previous season wood so the display will be comprimised if too much material is removed.

- Mature height: 5-8m
- Shape of mature tree
- Flowering trees
- Bee friendly trees
- Urban trees
- Clay soils
- Eco impact rating: C

MALUS Cox's Orange Pippin

The nation's favourite eating apple, available from us as a clear stemmed full standard and grown on the robust M16 rootstock. An ideal spring blossom specimen for any garden with the added bonus of autumn fruit.

Profuse white flowers lead to good sized eating apples by late summer. A round headed tree that thrives on most soils, including clay, and a must for any garden orchard. Autumn colour of yellow tinged with red, is an attractive ornamental attribute.

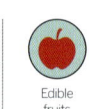

- Mature height: 5-8m
- Shape of mature tree
- Edible fruits
- Bee friendly trees
- Eco impact rating: C

MALUS Director Moerland

A round headed variety notable for its distinctive large red / purple maple like leaves. It was bred as a disease resistant form of Malus Profusion.

Slightly fragrant wine red flowers are borne profusely in spring which complements emerging red leaves making this a stunning little tree for the first few growing months of the year. Best suited for gardens and parks and tolerant of most soils and conditions.

Mature height: 5-8m | Shape of mature tree | Flowering trees | Bee friendly trees | Eco impact rating: C

MALUS Discovery

Introduced from Essex in 1949, this rosy red tinged fruiting desert apple is a firm favourite with its agreeable sharp flavour. If no other Malus is around it is best to include a crab apple such as Malus John Downie or Evereste as pollinator.

It will thrive on most soils including heavy clay but will benefit from keeping competition at bay around it, especially grass, to fulfil fruiting size potential. Lovely white flowers are borne in the spring and these produce the lush fruit for use in August / September which can be stored with success.

Mature height: 5-8m | Shape of mature tree | Flowering trees | Edible fruits | Bee friendly trees | Eco impact rating: C

MALUS Donald Wyman

A tried and tested performer raised by the late Donald Wyman at the Arnold Arboretum in the USA. Satisfactorily resistant to both apple scab and mildew it develops a rounded habit at maturity and is ideal for parks and gardens.

The spring flower is red to pink in bud, opening to white when in full glory. The fruit matures to a glossy vivid red and can be profuse so it is best to plant away from paved areas to avoid cleaning up. The leaves are dark green by summer.

5|8			C
Mature height: 5-8m	Shape of mature tree	Bee friendly trees	Eco impact rating

MALUS Egremont Russett

First recorded in 1872, this lovely eating apple is thought to have originated in Sussex. It rose to popularity in Victorian times and is still a favourite today, only behind Cox's Pippin and Bramley Seedling in terms of commercial production acreage. The yellow / green russet apples are sweet with a hint of pear flavour and can store well.

Where no other Malus is in the vicinity it is always worth planting with a Malus John Downie or Evereste to pollinate. It is a tough tree, thriving on most soil types, light and heavy, as well as taking on more northerly aspects of the UK with ease. Pink tinged flower buds open to white in the spring and apples can be harvested from August onwards.

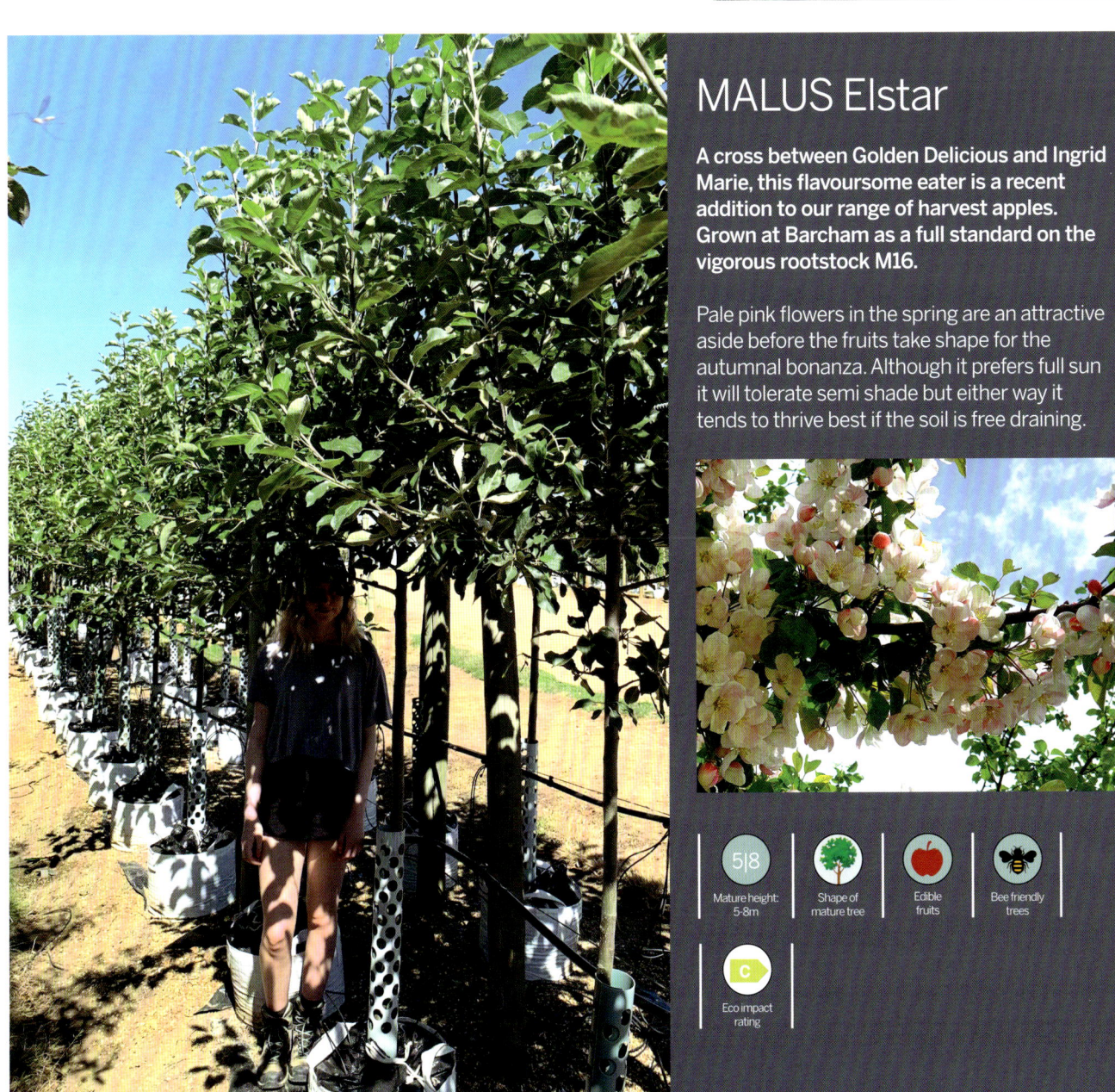

- Mature height: 5-8m
- Shape of mature tree
- Edible fruits
- Bee friendly trees
- Eco impact rating: C

MALUS Elstar

A cross between Golden Delicious and Ingrid Marie, this flavoursome eater is a recent addition to our range of harvest apples. Grown at Barcham as a full standard on the vigorous rootstock M16.

Pale pink flowers in the spring are an attractive aside before the fruits take shape for the autumnal bonanza. Although it prefers full sun it will tolerate semi shade but either way it tends to thrive best if the soil is free draining.

- Mature height: 5-8m
- Shape of mature tree
- Edible fruits
- Bee friendly trees
- Eco impact rating: C

MALUS Evereste

We recommend three crab apples in particular, one white, one red and one upright and this is one of them! A winner of the Award of Garden Merit in 2002, it was introduced in the early 1980s.

This rounded tree of medium height has flowers that are red in bud before turning white – and the blossom is borne in profusion. The small fruits look like miniature 'Gala' and are held onto until they are taken off by birds after Christmas. On the continent they are used in displays as the little fruits hold their form so well. The orange-yellow autumn foliage also holds well. Good for gardens, parks and verges.

| Mature height: 5-8m | Shape of mature tree | Flowering trees | Eco impact rating: C |

MALUS floribunda
Japanese Crab

A most elegant crab, introduced from Japan in the early 1860s, but prone to suffer badly from Apple Scab after flowering rendering the crown to look rather threadbare from June onwards. This popular variety has been superseded by more disease resistant clones such as Malus Rudolph and Evereste in recent years so as a result it is seen less and less in commercial production.

Very early to flower, the crimson buds open to reveal white or pale blush blossom, making this one of the most attractive crabs. The plentiful and long-lasting fruits are greenish-yellow with a hint of red to them. Good for gardens, verges and parks.

- Mature height: 5-8m
- Shape of mature tree
- Flowering trees
- Eco impact rating: C

MALUS Golden Delicious

Always derided by the purists as a tasteless French import, getting anything green and organic down my kids is a godsend in my book! Crunchy and sweet is the main criteria for my two and Golden Delicious fits the bill.

Grown at Barcham on M16 vigorous rootstock and as a full standard, my old Writtle fruit lecturer would not be amused to hear we were growing this clone! The abundant autumnal fruit is best eaten straight off the tree as it doesn't store too well.

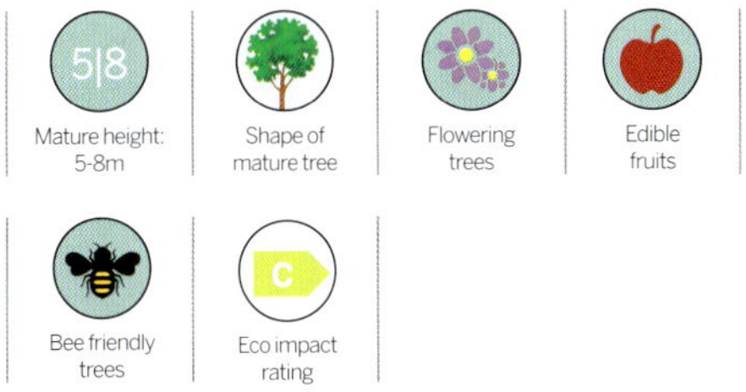

- Mature height: 5-8m
- Shape of mature tree
- Flowering trees
- Edible fruits
- Bee friendly trees
- Eco impact rating: C

MALUS Golden Hornet

This well-known garden crab has been in cultivation since the 1940s and is highly regarded for its profuse display of yellow marble sized fruits. A winner of numerous awards including the First-Class Certificate in 1961.

A small tree which produces white blossom and yellow fruits, which are retained for many weeks. It has a good, oval habit and is a reliable "all-rounder", well suited to parks, verges and gardens.

| Mature height: 5-8m | Shape of mature tree | Flowering trees | Eco impact rating |

MALUS Howgate Wonder

This rosy tinged cooking apple has been eclipsed in popularity by Bramley Seeding but should not be overlooked! For those of you who can take a sharp taste, this apple can be enjoyed straight from the tree as well as being the basis for pies, crumbles and juices.

Introduced in the early 1900s, this apple is best planted with a Malus John Downie or Evereste to enhance pollination if no other Malus are within sight. It thrives on most soils and produces a lovely floral display in the spring. The apples are generally ready from August onwards and are suitable to store.

| Mature height: 5-8m | Shape of mature tree | Flowering trees | Edible fruits | Bee friendly trees | Eco impact rating |

MALUS hupehensis

A lovely crab introduced to Britain from the Far East by Ernest Wilson in 1900. Rarely planted but never forgotten if seen in full cry in the late spring. It is quite susceptible to cold springs when propagated so is always hit and miss when it comes to availability further on down the line.

A fine choice for gardens and parkland plantings, the ascending branches of this small tree give it a broadly columnar appearance. The fragrant flowers are pale pink while in bud, opening to white, while the small fruits are generally dark red.

Mature height: 5-8m | Shape of mature tree | Flowering trees | Eco impact rating: C

MALUS James Grieve

A classic addition to our eating apple range and one that is particularly popular with our despatch lads in the autumn!

Pale pink flowers in spring are followed by sweet edible fruits in late autumn to early winter. It prefers a fertile and moist free draining soil in full sun or partial shade. For best fruiting results keep the ground fallow a metre radius from the trunk and top dress this area with bark mulch. This cuts down weed competition which in turn increases fruit size.

Mature height: 5-8m | Shape of mature tree | Edible fruits | Bee friendly trees | Eco impact rating: C

MALUS John Downie

Raised in 1875, this is thought by many to be the best fruiting crab. It won the updated Award of Garden Merit from the Royal Horticultural Society in 2002.

A small tree with an irregular, oval crown, it makes a splendid tree for gardens with limited space. The white flowers are followed by relatively large, conical orange-red fruits, which have a good flavour if required for preserves or jelly. Like all crab apples, it thrives on most soils.

Mature height: 5-8m | Shape of mature tree | Flowering trees | Bee friendly trees | Eco impact rating: C

M

MALUS Jonagold

This American apple is a cross between Jonathon and Golden Delicious. Grown on the tough M16 rootstock its white flowers in spring are attractive in their own right. Not the best on its own for pollination, it is always recommended to plant this within a varied mix of Malus to aid fertilization.

A vigorous small tree with a rounded habit, it bears an excellent crop of crisp, juicy fruits, which are full of flavour. The apples are large, greenish-yellow, lightly flushed with red, can be picked from mid October and will store well until the following spring.

| Mature height: 5-8m | Shape of mature tree | Edible fruits | Eco impact rating: C |

MALUS Laxton's Superb

This late fruiting sweet tasting eater is an old English original dating back to 1897. Developed by the famous Victorian Laxton brothers in Bedford it is a cross between Malus Cox's Orange Pippin and Malus Wyken Pippin.

Lovely pink tinged white apple blossom in the spring gives way to young fruits swelling to maturity by October. Like all Malus, Laxton's Superb prefers a heavier soil and can tolerate a degree of being wet. It is always best to keep the ground free of grass within a two-metre radius around its trunk to promote fruit size.

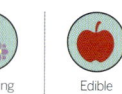

| Mature height: 5-8m | Shape of mature tree | Flowering trees | Edible fruits | Urban trees | Clay soils | Eco impact rating: C |

MALUS Mokum

A beautiful crab for small gardens, parks and verges that is often overlooked by people favouring the more well-known varieties.

The leaves of this small, oval headed tree are an eye-catching dark red and its rosy-red flowers emerge by late spring. The autumn fruits are also red giving this clone a very long season of interest. Like most crab apples, it thrives on most ground including heavier clay soils.

- Mature height: 5-8m
- Shape of mature tree
- Flowering trees
- Eco impact rating: C

MALUS Profusion

A fast growing and well-known crab from the late 1930s. It can occasionally get clobbered by both apple scab and mildew in the summer so it is best to avoid if replacing other Malus that may carry these pathogens.

This lovely cultivar is just about the best of those with wine red flowers. It is a small tree with a rounded crown, well suited to gardens and parks. The young, copper-crimson foliage turns bronze-green at maturity, while the rich, purple flowers, which are lightly fragrant, turn pink as the season progresses. Its fruits are small and blood red in colour.

- Mature height: 5-8m
- Shape of mature tree
- Bee friendly trees
- Eco impact rating: C

Telephone 01353 720 748 | www.barcham.co.uk | www.barchampro.co.uk

MALUS Red Sentinel

Brought into cultivation in 1959, this profusely fruiting crab is a favourite for gardeners who are looking for winter interest. In some years the fruits are so numerous that the branches can weigh too heavily with them so that the crown loses its shape.

The red leaves of this small, round headed tree contrast well with its white flowers. These are followed in autumn by clusters of dark red crabs that often stay on the tree right through the winter. Good for gardens and parks.

- Mature height: 5-8m
- Shape of mature tree
- Bee friendly trees
- Eco impact rating: C

MALUS Royalty

An upright crab bred in Canada in the early 1950s. The foliage is so dark it is always canny not to overdo the numbers on this one. A dark foliaged tree always focuses the eye in a landscape so too many can make a garden quite dark.

Its ascending branches give Royalty a broadly columnar form. A small tree, it has shiny, rich purple foliage, which turns a vivid red in autumn. Large, purple-crimson flowers give rise to dark red fruits. Like most crabs, this is suitable for parks and gardens.

Mature height: 5-8m | Shape of mature tree | Flowering trees | Bee friendly trees | Eco impact rating: C

MALUS Rudolph

Another Canadian crab developed in the 1950s. I have mentioned before that we recommend one white, one pink and one upright apple, well this is the pink. The autumn colour of clear yellow is an added bonus but the main reasons we rate it so highly is its resistance to pest and disease as well as its glorious floral display.

A tree of medium size, it is rather columnar when young, but the crown becomes rounded at maturity. The leaves gradually turn from copper-red to bronze-green, and rose pink flowers are followed by numerous elongated fruits, which last well. Rudolph is resistant to scab, and is particularly good as both a garden tree and for urban verge plantings.

Mature height: 5-8m | Shape of mature tree | Bee friendly trees | Eco impact rating: C

MALUS sylvestris

Arguably one of our prettiest native trees, this small crab apple provides profuse white, tinged pink in bud, flowers in the spring and a good yellow autumn colour. Yellow / green and occasionally red flushed fruits are a favourite for birds in the autumn.

Most suited to heavy and clay soils, this small tree is rarely seen above twenty feet in height and is the parent of numerous crab and eating apple varieties. Ideal for native mixed planting or shelterbelts that provide great low cover for wildlife.

- Mature height: 5-8m
- Shape of mature tree
- Native trees
- Bee friendly trees
- Eco impact rating: C

MALUS toringo

A delightful little dainty Japanese crab that is rarely seen but never forgotten. Its leaves are attractively lobed and it is otherwise known as Malus sieboldii, a Japanese type introduced in 1856.

This semi-weeping, very small tree has flowers that are pink in bud, fading to white and small red or yellow fruits. Perfect for even the smallest gardens and thrives on most soils, its distinctive growth habit makes it easily identifiable even during dormancy. Like all crabs, it thrives on even heavy soils so it is a useful inclusion for inhospitable gardens where space is restricted.

- Mature height: 5-8m
- Shape of mature tree
- Flowering trees
- Bee friendly trees
- Eco impact rating: C

MALUS toringo Brouwers Beauty

This stunning little crab apple produces a mass of single white flowers in the Spring that are pink tinged in bud. We pleached a batch of these bespoke for a customer and the result was superb. Its light green small, indented leaves are decorative in their own right. Rounded in habit, 'Brouwers Beauty' is a more uniform version of normal Malus toringo.

Suitable of heavier soils this small garden tree is also a good pollinator for any fruiting varieties.

- Mature height: 5-8m
- Shape of mature tree
- Flowering trees
- Clay soils
- Urban trees
- Bee friendly trees
- Eco impact rating: C

MALUS toringo Scarlet Brouwers Beauty

Beauty by name and nature! This glorious new introduction looks like a cross between Malus toringo and Malus Director Moerland with purple / red foliage and pink to faded pink / white flowers in the spring giving way to small dark red fruits in late summer.

A great tree for giving contrast within a garden, it thrives on most soils, light and heavy, and is one of the last crab apples to lose its leaves on the nursery in the autumn. Malus toringo has such a pretty leaf and this also shows through in this variety. It is a good pollinator for culinary apples whilst providing stunning interest in its own right.

- Mature height: 5-8m
- Shape of mature tree
- Flowering trees
- Eco impact rating: C

M

MALUS trilobata

A rather rare crab from the Mediterranean, so distinct it is sometimes classed as a separate genus, Eriolobus. We doggedly keep it under the Malus section and it is our recommended upright form for restricted spaces. It is a wonderfully symmetrical tree and gives a formal structure to any garden or street.

A medium size tree with an upright habit, this is a good choice for parks and gardens. Its deeply lobed leaves are maple-like and take on attractive burgundy tints in autumn. It produces large, white flowers and green fruits, which are sometimes flushed red. The fruits only usually appear following hot summers.

Mature height: 5-8m | Shape of mature tree | Flowering trees | Bee friendly trees | Eco impact rating: C

MESPILUS germanica
Medlar

The Medlar has been in cultivation since early times, having been grown in the Emperor Charlemagne's garden. The small brown fruits it produces are only edible when "bletted" or left to turn half-rotten.

A small, gnarled, wide spreading tree which is at home in a garden, where it produces a rounded form. It has large, hairy leaves, which turn a russet brown in autumn, and large, white flowers borne in May and June. There are some particularly interesting specimens in the Kitchen Garden at Grimsthorpe Castle in Lincolnshire that are mushroom shaped and well worth a visit in the summer.

- Mature height: 5-8m
- Shape of mature tree
- Edible fruits
- Eco impact rating: C

M

It has spongy, shaggy bark, and its pale green, feathery foliage turns brown in autumn. The Dawn Redwood is tolerant of air pollution, but needs a moist soil in its first year to establish successfully.

METASEQUOIA glyptostroboides
Dawn Redwood

This Redwood is of great botanical interest. It was discovered in China in the 1940s, before which the genus consisted only of fossilised forms. A deciduous conifer, it has rapidly established itself as a huge urban and rural favourite. Often confused with Taxodium, it is quite different if they are seen together at close quarters.

Very large and statuesquely pyramidal, it makes a grand park or specimen tree, but is also good for streets and avenues with a clear stem.

- Mature height: 17-22m
- Shape of mature tree
- Avenue trees
- Eco impact rating: A

METASEQUOIA glyptostroboides Goldrush

I first saw this as a maturing specimen at Uppingham School arboretum in Rutland and its golden foliage bounced back against a barker backdrop. It is smaller growing than the green Dawn Redwood but apart from its yellow foliage is similar in every other way.

Importantly, its delicate yellow foliage doesn't seem to scotch under the intense summer sun but this tree does thrive best in damp soils like its parent. Its lovely pyramidal habit makes it suitable for medium gardens and parkland alike. There aren't many yellow deciduous trees on the market and this one is one of the best for intensity of colour that is sustained all summer long.

- Mature height: 12-17m
- Shape of mature tree
- Yellow foliage
- Eco impact rating: B

M

MORUS alba
White Mulberry

In our experience, whether a black or white Mulberry is requested, a white one is usually supplied within the trade. Both are nice but they are also quite different so be careful what you are getting! Smooth leaf and smooth stems for Morus alba, rough leaf and rough trunk for Morus nigra.

This is a most beautiful, small, architectural tree, perfect for parks and gardens, with a rounded habit. The white fruits, from which it takes its name, can turn pink or red – and they are both sweet and edible. The leaves of the White Mulberry are the main food of the silkworm.

| 5\|8 Mature height: 5-8m | Shape of mature tree | Edible fruits | C Eco impact rating |

MORUS alba Fruitless

This male clone has maple like foliage and is an ideal form to pleach or 'roof top' where a flat frame is installed above head height for the foliage to colonize and provide a green umbrella to shade patios of urban piazzas. Its tough leaves make it a good tree to take windy conditions and I have seen this plant thriving within view of the coast but not as the first line of defence.

It thrives on most free draining soils and enjoys full sun and reflected heat bouncing up from surrounding hard areas such as paving or adjacent buildings. Its lustrous foliage display gives it a healthy disposition.

| 5\|8 Mature height: 5-8m | Shape of mature tree | Garden trees | C Eco impact rating |

MORUS alba Pendula

Awarded with several accolades over the years from the Royal Horticultural Society, this weeping tree is ideal for a medium sized garden. This fruiting clone has cascading branches that mushrooms as it matures to form a dense dome of lush foliage in the summer. The leaves turn to yellow in the autumn.

It thrives on most free daring soils and prefers full sun. There aren't many weepers like this to go at in the tree world as most are contrived man made affairs that structurally implode over time but this tree is the real ticket!

| 3\|5 Mature height: 3-5m | Shape of mature tree | Garden trees | C Eco impact rating |

MORUS nigra
Black Mulberry

Brought to Britain by the Romans and widely planted by James I, who wished to establish a silk industry – only to find that silkworms feed exclusively on the White Mulberry! People commonly mistake white and black mulberry and they are not defined by the colour of their fruit. Rough stems and rough leaves for black, smooth stems and smooth leaves for white!

A medium tree of great dignity and beauty, it has a gnarled, rugged trunk and most attractive, heart shaped leaves. The deep purple fruits, which look like large loganberries are tasty and have a variety of culinary uses. It has a domed, rounded habit, giving it a most architectural appeal. Very long-lived, but not as slow growing as is often supposed.

- Mature height: 5-8m
- Shape of mature tree
- Edible fruits
- Eco impact rating: C

N

NOTHOFAGUS antarctica
Antarctic Beech

A native of Chile and introduced to Britain in the early 1830s, this beech is a fast grower. Many see this in leaf and take it for an evergreen tree but it is deciduous.
Its bark is dark and covered with attractive white lenticels.

Of rounded habit and medium to large size, this has small, heart shaped leaves which turn yellow as the year progresses. Very good for parks and public spaces, it does best in a sunny position and fairly fertile soil. It will not tolerate planting in calcareous soils.

| 12|17 | Shape of | Parkland | A |
| Mature height: 12-17m | mature tree | trees | Eco impact rating |

NYSSA sylvatica

Introduced from America in 1750, this is widely regarded as the most attractive of all the native trees from the States. It won the Award of Garden Merit in 2002.

Pyramidal when young it can resemble Quercus palustris in shape and habit, and certainly rivals it for autumn colour when its foliage turns magnificent reds, oranges and yellows. The dark glossy green leaves are narrowly oval and can reach 15cm in length. They do not tolerate lime soils so please bear this in mind if you choose one.

| 12|17 | Shape of | Autumn | B |
| Mature height: 12-17m | mature tree | colour | Eco impact rating |

OLEA europaea
Olive

Surely the quintessential tree of the Mediterranean and cultivated virtually since the beginning of time, the Olive is only hardy in the milder areas of Britain. I have one thriving in my garden in Rutland, but I have yet to reap a harvest. However, times have changed and sadly this tree is best not to plant in the UK anymore.

In 2013 a deadly plant disease called Xylella fastidiosa swept through Southern Italy and wiped out Olive oil production. Xylella attacks a broad spectrum of plant genus including trees like Quercus and Acer as well as shrubs like Lavender and Rosemary. As one of the chief hosts to this disease in our view it is morally reprehensible to import and trade Olive within the UK as importing Xylella into the country would have far reaching adverse impacts on British plant life. Sadly, it is still being specified by the unknowing and supplied by 'white van man' and a few nurseries even though DEFRA are making imports of this genus very difficult to do legally.

Please do not buy this plant!

| Mature height: 3-5m | Shape of mature tree | Edible fruits | Eco impact rating: B |

OSMANTHUS armatus

Native of Western China and introduced into the UK back in 1902, this evergreen tree produces fragrant flowers in the autumn. Its thick dark evergreen leaves are excellent for screening and it grows happily in shade or sun.

It thrives in most free draining soils and as it is such a small tree it can be planted very close to a house without any worry about disturbing foundations or compromising building regulations. Although hardy enough for Southern and middle England, winters in the rest of the UK may prove too much for it to endure.

| Mature height: 3-5m | Shape of mature tree | Privacy raised screening | Evergreen trees | Eco impact rating: D |

OSMANTHUS burkwoodii

Strictly speaking this develops as a large shrub but its attributes are so appealing we like to include it within our range as a small bushy tree. Dark evergreen leaves make this a good screening plant which grows on most soils. Its main attribute is in the early summer when its highly scented tubular white flowers are in full swing.

The sweet scent of Osmanthus can be enjoyed even at a distance when this is planted as a hedge. Although hardy enough for the UK, it will take a bit of a battering if faced with cold east winds over winter. Free draining but fertile soils see it thrive the best.

Mature height: 3-5m | Multi-stem | Flowering trees | Evergreen trees | Bee friendly trees | Eco impact rating: D

OSMANTHUS fortunei aquifolium

This dense evergreen shrub will make a small tree if left alone. Mostly grown for screen hedging, its glossy leaves have a semblance to Holly. Like many within the Osmanthus group, its tubular white flowers are richly fragrant and this can be well appreciated if it is used as a hedge.

Free draining and fertile soils provide the best conditions for it to thrive and although hardy, it may succomb to the coldest of winters so best to avoid very exposed areas. It is a cross between Osmanthus heterophyllus and Osmanthus fragrans.

Mature height: 3-5m | Multi-stem | Flowering trees | Evergreen trees | Eco impact rating: D

OSTRYA carpinifolia
Hop Hornbeam

The Hop Hornbeam is so-called because it looks like a Hornbeam and its creamy white flowers resemble hops. Introduced in 1724 from Southern Europe and Western Asia it won the Award of Merit in the hot summer of 1976.

It is worth considering this variety for pleaching in place of the more traditional choice of Carpinus betulus as the hops can create quite a show when grown in this way. Think of it as hornbeam with flowers!

The wood produced by Ostrya carpinifolia is extremely hard and its name is derived from the Greek word 'ostrua' which literally means 'like bone'. It is also dense and heavy so bare this in mind if you are ever considering some for your log burner for the winter! Typically growing to less than 20 metres, this lovely tree is often overlooked for UK planting but thrives on most free draining soils so is worthy of being far more widespread.

Mature height: 12-17m | Shape of mature tree | Clay soils | Eco impact rating: B

This medium to large tree is good for parkland settings, verges and many urban locations. It looks particularly good in spring with its display of yellow-green catkins. A really tough tree, which will tolerate most conditions.

PARROTIA persica
Persian Ironwood

Persian Ironwood is usually grown as a large shrub and was formerly classified as a species of Hamamelis. It takes its name from the well-known German horticulturalist, FW Parrot and is a native of Iran. There are some particularly nice specimens at the Westonbirt Arboretum near Stroud.

A beautiful, small, rounded tree with grey-brown bark which becomes attractively mottled with yellow. This really is one of the finest small trees for autumn colour, giving a display of crimson, purple, red and gold. A splendid choice for gardens and parks, it does well on most soils, including chalk.

| Mature height: 7-12m | Shape of mature tree | Autumn colour | Eco impact rating: C |

PARROTIA persica Vanessa

Vanessa has a more tree-like form than the species and was selected as a seedling in the Netherlands in the mid 1970s. A great favourite at Barcham, it produces small but vivid red flowers at maturity.

A small tree with a broad, oval crown. Vanessa gives a stunning display of autumn colour and is ideal for specimen planting in a park or large garden. Prior to that, it displays red shoots and bronze edges to its deep green leaves. It does well on most soils and will tolerate chalk.

| 7|12 Mature height: 7-12m | Shape of mature tree | Autumn colour | Eco impact rating: C |

PAULOWNIA tomentosa
Foxglove Tree

One of the most spectacular of ornamental flowering trees, the Foxglove Tree takes its name from the foxglove-like flowers, which are formed in autumn, but do not open until the following spring. Introduced from China in 1834, its wood is much prized in Japan for furniture making.

It is so quick to grow in its younger years that its growth rings have been recorded at three every inch. However, our more temperate climate slows it down and any growth under pencil thickness generally succumbs to winter frosts which contribute to its overall broadness. The flower cases are formed in the autumn so if the temperature dips below 5 degrees Celsius for too long, no flower will develop the following spring.

A fast growing, medium to large, round headed tree. It does best in a sunny, reasonably sheltered site, where it will produce a breathtaking display of violet-blue and yellow flowers in May once it is established. Its large, hairy leaves can reach 30cm or more across.

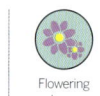

Mature height: 12-17m | Shape of mature tree | Flowering trees | Eco impact rating: C

Amazingly, a mature tree in its native environment can produce up to 20 million seeds per year which converts to over 85,000 seeds per ounce. The tree was named after Anna Pavlovna, daughter of Czar Paul 1 and wife of Prince Willem II of the Netherlands.

PHELLODENDRON amurense
Amur Cork Tree

A small genus from East Asia, resembling Ailanthus that was introduced into the UK in 1885. It is more suited to rural rather than urban settings but is rarely seen in Britain.

Large leaves, over 25cm in length, and silver, hairy winter buds distinguish this tree from others, but it is the corky bark of mature trees that is its most impressive feature. An unusual tree for arboricultural collectors.

- Mature height: 12-17m
- Shape of mature tree
- Parkland trees
- Eco impact rating: B

PHOTINIA x fraseri
Red Robin

This beautiful clone was bred in New Zealand and won the Award of Garden Merit in 2002. Much is made of its foliage, but more mature plants give a profuse display of white flower in the spring that contrasts magnificently with emerging red leaves.

This small, evergreen tree is often grown as a shrub. As a tree, it develops a rounded crown; its new leaves open to red before hardening to green as they age. Frequent pruning encourages glorious red foliage and makes it every bit as beautiful as Pieris formosa. Lovely in gardens and parks. It is mostly grown as a shrub but we grow it as a standard tree, mainly for stilted screening.

- Mature height: 3-8m
- Shape of mature tree
- Privacy raised screening
- Eco impact rating: D

PHYLLOSTACHYS aurea
Golden Bamboo

In the Far East the canes of this Bamboo are used for walking sticks and umbrella handles, while in America they are turned into fishing rods. Introduced from China in the 1870s it won the Award of Garden Merit in 2002.

This Bamboo forms clumps of canes which are bright green at first and then mature to a pale creamy yellow. The young shoots, which it produces in spring, are edible but beware, this plant is not for the faint hearted as it is extremely vigorous! If it ever gets out of hand you can decimate it to an inch or two above ground level and it will sucker up good as new. Being evergreen, it is a very useful plant to achieve dense screening from ground level to fence height.

- Mature height: 3-5m
- Multi-stem
- Evergreen trees
- Eco impact rating

PHYLLOSTACHYS nigra
Black Bamboo

Black Bamboo is surely the most dramatic of all. It is less vigorous than the golden equivalent but that didn't stop me reducing mine to 5cm off ground level in the Spring to stimulate a fresh display only three months later.

This stylish Bamboo has a gracefully arching habit and does best in a sunny position. The canes begin as green before becoming mottled with brown and then black. The shoots which it produces in spring are edible.

- Mature height: 3-5m
- Multi-stem
- Evergreen trees
- Eco impact rating

PICEA abies
Norway Spruce

Introduced into the UK in about 1500, this well known spruce is common over most of Northern and Central Europe. For many of us its fragrance is very familiar as it was the Christmas tree of choice when we were kids and its foliage litter over carpets up and down the country before Twelfth Night must have clogged up many a vacuum cleaner. Non-needle dropping varieties like the Nordman Fir have since balanced its numbers but it still remains one of the most common conifers around.

Quick to grow and thriving on most free draining soils its stiff ascending branches are clothed with 2cm dark green needles. It is a pyramidal tree producing brown cones when older and it can outgrow a small garden as many have found out after trying to rescue their Christmas tree in January.

- Mature height: 17-22m
- Shape of mature tree
- Evergreen trees
- Eco impact rating: A

PICEA omorika
Serbian Spruce

The Serbian Spruce was widely distributed through much of Europe before the onset of the Ice Age. It was not, however, introduced to Britain until the late 1880s. Similar in looks to a traditional Christmas tree when young, its branches adopt a graceful pendulous habit when mature.

Certainly, one of the most beautiful of Spruces, this is a medium to large, slender columnar tree which grows quickly. It tolerates air pollution, calcareous soils and is good as an evergreen street or avenue subject. If planting in a public area my advice is to install after Christmas and not before!

- Mature height: 17-22m
- Shape of mature tree
- Evergreen trees
- Eco impact rating: C

PICEA pungens Hoopsii (Edith)

This form of Colorado blue spruce is slow growing but highly ornamental. Introduced in the mid 1950s it won the Award of Garden Merit in 2002 and like most conifers it prefers free draining soils.

Vividly glaucous blue leaves and dense conical habit make this small tree a real contrast in a garden or parkland setting. It is so slow to grow that it is perceived as expensive for its size supplied but it offers a unique colour to a garden.

3|8 — Mature height: 3-8m | Shape of mature tree | Evergreen trees | D — Eco impact rating

PINUS nigra austriaca
Austrian Pine

Sometimes referred to as 'Black Pine' or 'Pinus nigra nigra' this tough two needled evergreen was introduced in the mid 1830s. Its needles are much greener and longer than Scots Pine and its growth more solid giving it a denser habit than our native pine. Stand behind a maturing Austrian Pine on a windy day and be amazed how the wind is diffused by the needles to calm the air flow.

A first-rate choice for coastal areas and exposed, windswept sites, it thrives even in very chalky soils. This large evergreen has a pyramidal form, but retains its bushy, juvenile appearance much longer than Scots Pine. It is from ancient genera, so its toughness is based on a very solid track record.

| Mature height: 17-22m | Shape of mature tree | Evergreen trees | Eco impact rating: B |

PINUS nigra maritima
Corsican Pine

Introduced way back in 1759 from Southern Italy, this large tree is a great wind diffuser for coastal sites. Its long green needles are distinctive, and it is generally a little quicker to grow than the Austrian Pine, sometimes throwing up a 60cm whorl of new growth in early summer.

Thriving on most free draining soils, this large broadly pyramidal tree can be too big for a small garden but is ideal for parkland and southern coastal sites where shelter is needed to get other species in play.

PINUS mugo Mops
Swiss Mountain Pine, Mugo Pine

Introduced in the early 1950s, this clone of the dwarf shrub pine is considered by many to be the finest. Pinus mugo can be very variable in size and habit with recorded mature heights of between 1 metre and 15 metres but 'Mops' rarely gets larger than 1.5 metres.

This is a new addition to our range and should be online in containers by September 2012. It is a very versatile garden or landscape plant, mimicking a bonsai effect of traditional pine and requiring minimal maintenance. It is tough and is suited to most soil types including shallow chalk.

PINUS peuce
Macedonian / Balkan Pine

We added this tree to our field range in 2016 and they have now come through to graduate to our container unit for sale. Related to the White Pine group, its needles are soft and in clusters. A native of the alpine regions of Northern Greece, Bulgaria, Albania, Serbia and Montenegro where it can grow up to 40 metres tall with trunks approaching two metres across.

Like most evergreens, a well draining soil is a must but otherwise this tree is pretty tolerant of most conditions. This Pine is prized for its durable wood which is used widely in the construction industry. Its cones are between 6 and 10 cm in length. A nice addition for parkland and woodland schemes.

PINUS pinaster
Bournemouth Pine, Maritime Pine

A highly useful introduction from the Western Mediterranean. Introduced in the 16th century it thrives on light sandy soils and tolerates coastal conditions. It won the Award of Garden Merit in 2002. Commonly planted on England's South coast from which it derives its common name.

Sparsely branched, it can get quite large and develops a dark reddish-brown patchwork bark at maturity. Shiny brown cones are produced about 18cm long which compliment the long leaves that are grown in pairs. It is very important in Western France where it supplies industry with large quantities of turpentine and resin. Also referred to as Pinus maritima.

- Mature height: 12-17m
- Shape of mature tree
- Evergreen trees
- Eco impact rating: B

PINUS pinea
Italian Stone Pine

The Stone Pine is sometimes also known as the Umbrella Pine. Its seeds, which when roasted, are an essential ingredient of the well known Italian pesto sauce. Unlike other Pines we grow, this one is produced as a half standard or standard tree with a well developed rounded crown.

A distinct and rather picturesque medium tree, this Pine does well in coastal locations and on light, sandy soils. Its bark is gorgeously craggy, flaking off easily when disturbed. A native of the Mediterranean, it won the Award of Garden Merit in 2002.

- Mature height: 12-17m
- Shape of mature tree
- Evergreen trees
- Eco impact rating: B

PINUS radiata
Monterey Pine

This makes a large tree with a deeply fissured bark and a dense crown of branches supporting needles in threes up to 15cm in length. Introduced in 1833 by David Douglas from California, it won the Award of Garden Merit in 2002.

Cones are borne in whorls along the branches and often remain intact for several years. A very useful subject for coastal areas as it is quick to grow and able to withstand strong salt laden winds.

Mature height: 17-22m | Shape of mature tree | Evergreen trees | Eco impact rating: B

PINUS strobus
Weymouth Pine, Eastern White Pine

Introduced from Eastern North America in the early 1600s, when I first saw this Pine in a nursery setting, I mistook it for Pinus Wallichiana as it had similar long, soft and slightly glaucous needles.

The leaves are in 5's and last for two seasons before falling. It is a very touchy-feely plant and incredibly graceful, especially when young when its pyramidal habit flows beautifully in the breeze. Thriving on most well drained soils it makes a wonderful specimen parkland tree. It is not for urban planting as it is not tolerant of pollution and especially salt so it is best placed in our countryside.

Mature height: 17-22m | Shape of mature tree | Evergreen trees | Eco impact rating: B

Telephone 01353 720 748 | www.barcham.co.uk | www.barchampro.co.uk

PINUS sylvestris
Scots Pine

The Scots Pine is the only Pine native to Britain. A familiar sight in bleak and inhospitable landscapes, it can be grown as a tall stemmed or a low, spreading subject. Its paired needles can be very variable in colour from green to almost blue, especially when juvenile. It is very quick to develop a symbiotic relationship with mycorrhiza which helps sustain vigorous growth.

This large evergreen tree is distinctive by its tall, bare trunk and broadly pyramidal crown. It is best suited in parks, gardens, heath land and woodlands. It is tolerant of most soils but never reaches its true potential in areas prone to flooding.
As a cautionary note, it is worth sticking with Austrian Pine for coastal conditions as Scots Pine rarely seems to thrive near the coast.

- Mature height: 17-22m
- Shape of mature tree
- Evergreen trees
- Native trees
- Eco impact rating: B

PINUS sylvestris Fastigiata
Sentinel Pine

A wonderfully columnar form of Scots Pine, so tight in habit that one has to get quite close to indentify it. There are some nicely maturing specimens in the conifer garden at the Harlow Carr arboretum. The needles appear almost blue when young giving it a highly ornamental feel.

Introduced circa 1856, it is naturally occurring in Europe. It can reach over 10 metres tall if it isn't hampered by snow and ice build up which can cause it to fracture. However, there are no such problems in the UK making this a fabulous choice for many aspects.

- 7|12 — Mature height: 7-12m
- Shape of mature tree
- Narrow trees
- B — Eco impact rating

PINUS wallichiana
Bhutan Pine

A native of the Himalayas, this wonderfully attractive soft needled pine was introduced to Britain in the early 1820s and is also known by many as Pinus griffithii. A winner of the Award of Garden Merit in 2002 and the Award of Merit in 1979, it is a worthy subject for any large garden.

Elegant and most ornamental, this large, rather conical tree has blue-green foliage and pendent cones which become covered in resin. It is moderately lime tolerant but shallow chalk soils should be avoided. It offers a unique softness to a large garden and so easily draws the eye.

- Mature height: 17-22m
- Shape of mature tree
- Evergreen trees
- Eco impact rating: B

Reputedly the oldest Plane tree in England is in the Bishops Palace Garden at Ely. Planted by Bishop Gunning more than 300 years ago it is one of the most impressive trees in Britain, and just a stones throw from Barcham.

PLATANUS x hispanica (acerifolia)
London Plane

First recorded in the early 1660s, the London Plane was extensively planted as a street tree in the capital due to its tolerance of air pollution and of pruning. It is believed that it was significantly responsible for clearing up the smog laden air resulting from the industrial revolution.

A large, fast growing tree with a broadly oval crown. One of its main features is the trunk, which flakes to reveal a patchwork of green, white and cream. The leaves are large, deeply lobed and palmate. The rounded fruit clusters, produced in strings, resemble little baubles, which hang from the branches for much of the year. Still a good choice for urban plantings, it is also great for parkland.

- Mature height: 17-22m
- Shape of mature tree
- Urban trees
- Eco impact rating: A

PLATANUS orientalis Digitata

One of the most striking of Planes, it is also known as the Chinar Tree, and often provides shaded meeting places in southern European villages. There is a wonderful example of its parent, Platanus orientalis, in the Bishops Palace garden in Ely not too far from Barcham.

This has similar, attractively flaking bark to the London Plane, but has deeply cut five lobed leaves. A large tree with a generally rounded habit, it can attain a very great age. Magnificent in parkland and large estates as well as gracing the main arterial roads of central London.

Mature height: 17-22m

Shape of mature tree

Eco impact rating: B

PLATANUS orientalis Minaret

Similar to 'Digitata' this clone was planted along the pavement avenues of O'Connell Street in Dublin to great effect. Very neat in habit when young, it develops a broad crown much the same as its parent, Platanus orientalis, when maturing.

Lovely cut leaves and a good pyramidal habit makes this a good choice for urban streets and parkland. Reputed to have good resistance to anthracnose, but I have not seen it for long enough to make judgement.

Mature height: 17-22m | Shape of mature tree | Urban trees | Eco impact rating: B

POPULUS alba
White Poplar

The fast-growing White Poplar is ideal for exposed and coastal plantings. Long naturalised in the UK, it was first introduced from South Eastern Europe. Its vivid foliage is most spectacular on a bright sunny day against a cloudless sky.

Ultimately a large tree of fairly rounded form, it has green leaves, the undersides of which are silver-white, turning yellow in autumn. It is a tough tree, but it needs to be given plenty of space for its extensive root system to develop. A good choice for calcareous soils.

- Mature height: 17-22m
- Shape of mature tree
- Eco impact rating: B

POPULUS alba Raket

This cultivar of White Poplar was raised in Holland in the 1950s for urban use. It is a particularly useful choice for coastal settings where the sea breezes constantly flicker the silver white leaves to provide splendid contrast.

It is notable for its columnar and slender habit when young, but it still makes a formidable tree when mature so care should be taken to give it enough space to colonise. It thrives on most soils and is quick to grow.

- Mature height: 17-22m
- Shape of mature tree
- Coastal sites
- Eco impact rating: B

POPULUS balsamifera

This tough Poplar is a native of North America and gets its name from the sweet-smelling fragrance emanating from its sticky buds.

Suitable for wet and exposed sites this tree is very useful for land that periodically floods in winter. Its lush green summer leaves produce a good canopy and they can turn a glorious yellow in the autumn. Not a long-lived tree, the oldest recorded are about 200 years old.

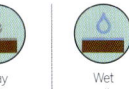

- Mature height: 17-22m
- Shape of mature tree
- Clay soils
- Wet soils
- Parkland trees
- Eco impact rating: B

POPULUS x candicans Aurora

Given the Award of Merit in 1954, this highly showy tree is both vigorous and instantly recognisable. Universally used as a substitute by the trade for Populus serotina Aurea, which is totally different, so beware!

The leaves are randomly variegated, especially when young, with coloured creamy white leaves that are also often tinged pink. Older leaves turn green and mysteriously newly transplanted trees show no sign of variegation either until they settle down in the second year. For best results, hard prune the shoots in winter and you will be rewarded by a magnificent display the following growing season.

- Mature height: 12-17m
- Shape of mature tree
- Variegated trees
- Eco impact rating: B

POPULUS nigra
Black Poplar

The Black Poplar, a native of Europe and Western Asia, is rarely found these days. We propagate native Black Poplar trees, originally from parent trees in Thurrock, Essex, so can supply the true type instead of relying on hybrid lookalikes from continental imports.

Very good for parks and woodland, this tough tree is also great for getting trees going in exposed areas by giving much needed shelter.

Cultivated for a long time and prized for its timber, this makes a large, rounded and heavy-branched tree, characterised by its burred trunk and glabrous twigs.

- Mature height: 17-22m
- Shape of mature tree
- Native trees
- Eco impact rating: B

POPULUS nigra Italica
Lombardy Poplar

The Lombardy poplar is a male clone, propagated from cuttings taken in Lombardy in the 1700s. It is a particularly tough tree even coping with coastal exposure. Introduced to the UK in 1758 it won the Award of Garden Merit in 2002.

These are the trees that line mile after mile (or should that be kilometre after kilometre?) of French roads. Very tall, tightly columnar and of uniform habit, they make a fine windbreak or screen, and are also good for specimen planting in parks. One of the very best for verges and avenues.

Mature height: 17-22m | Shape of mature tree | Narrow trees | Eco impact rating: B

POPULUS serotina Aurea
Golden Poplar

Derived from a sport taken at Van Geert's nursery in Ghent in 1871, this won the Award of Garden Merit in 2002.

Large and fast growing, this tree is also known as Populus x canadensis serotina Aurea. It sometimes produces a rather uneven crown so it is best for parkland. Its leaves, coppery red when young, are late to show and its catkins have conspicuous red anthers. Like all Poplars, it thrives on most soils.

Mature height: 12-17m | Shape of mature tree | Parkland trees | Eco impact rating: B

POPULUS tremula
Aspen

The shimmering of Aspen leaves, set in motion on even the most gentle of breezes, provides a wonderful rustling sound in the landscape reminiscent of slow cascading water. Thriving on most soils, light or heavy, this tough tree can also cope with wet land so is an ideal candidate for exposed and difficult sites.

Grey catkins appear in early spring, while the serrated leaves turn clear yellow in autumn and often remain on the tree for many weeks. The Aspen is a medium to large tree with a rounded habit. Well suited to verges and parkland.

- Mature height: 17-22m
- Shape of mature tree
- Parkland trees
- Native trees
- Eco impact rating: B

POPULUS tremula Erecta

Widely used as a street tree in the USA this underused tree was first discovered in a Swedish woodland and still bears the name 'Swedish Upright'. Similar in shape and habit to the Lombardy poplar it offers far more ornamental interest with bronze foliage emerging in April once the long catkins have finished.

We rate this highly as a tightly columnar tree that is very suitable for planting within an urban environment. The trembling leaves turn a lovely orange yellow in the autumn and this clone requires very little maintenance. The architectural shape of this tree is very striking within a landscape and tends to draw the eye with its symmetry. In Italy they have the evergreen pencil cedar to define their rolling Tuscan hills but we are restricted to this deciduous version in the UK to achieve a similar effect. Usefully, this variety is also suited to coastal planting, though not as the first line of defence.

- Mature height: 17-22m
- Shape of mature tree
- Narrow trees
- Autumn colour
- Eco impact rating: B

PRUNUS Accolade

This Flowering Cherry is a cross between Prunus sargentii and Prunus x subhirtella and so inherits the best features of both, namely profuse pink flowers in spring as well as a smattering in the winter. This great clone is well proven, winning the First-Class Certificate in 1954, the Award of Merit in 1952 and the updated Award of Garden Merit in 2002.

An outstandingly fine small tree with a rounded and spreading habit, its semi-double pink blossoms are hard to rival. Tolerant of most soils, including calcareous ones, this is a good choice for streets, parks and gardens.

5|8	Shape of mature tree	Bee friendly trees	C
Mature height: 5-8m			Eco impact rating

PRUNUS Amanogawa

This late April and early May blossoming Japanese Cherry is also known as Prunus serrulata Erecta Miyoshi. A well used and recognised variety, it won the Award of Garden Merit in 2002.

Perfect as a street tree or garden tree where space is at a premium, this tightly columnar cultivar is often grown as a feathered tree to maximise the number of semi-double, shell pink flowers it produces. The young leaves are a copper-bronze. Tolerant of most free draining soils.

5|8	Shape of mature tree	Bee friendly trees	Eco impact rating
Mature height: 5-8m			C

PRUNUS avium
Wild Cherry

The red-brown wood of the Wild Cherry is used in cabinet making and for musical instruments and pipes. Although its own fruits tend to be bitter, it is one of the parents of most European cultivated Cherries.

One of the most attractive of our native, woodland trees, this becomes a medium to large tree with a broadly rounded form. Its white flowers in spring are followed by foliage which often shows good autumn colouring of red and gold. A good tree for parks and woodlands that thrives on most free draining soils.

12|17	Shape of mature tree	Native trees	Flowering trees	Bee friendly trees	Eco impact rating
Mature height: 12-17m					B

PRUNUS avium Kordia

For fresh cherries straight off the tree this one is hard to beat! Lush black fruits are produced by August and their tough shiny skins make them resistant to splitting when growing with summer rain. White flowers in the spring add to the garden interest.

It will thrive on most free draining soils but benefits greatly from a fertilizer in the spring and a one metre mulch strip around the stem to keep other plant completion at bay. With no VAT on edible fruit trees, if you like cherries look no further! Combine with Prunus Early Rivers to get early and late fruit.

| Mature height: 5-8m | Shape of mature tree | Flowering trees | Edible fruits | Bee friendly trees | Eco impact rating: C |

PRUNUS avium Plena

This wonderful double flowering version of our native Wild Cherry has been in cultivation since the early 1700s and is still a favourite today. Its mass of double white flowers are absolutely superb when in full swing.

Although it is best suited to parkland / woodland planting it is also a very useful urban tree, coping well with reflected heat and light bouncing back from hard surfaces. It often retains a strong apically dominant leader making the trunk easy to crown lift over time. Given the right conditions the autumn foliage can also be glorious, and like most cherries it thrives on most free draining soils. If it is grown on avium rootstock it may cause damage to hard areas, so it is safer to plant trees that have been budded onto colt.

Being a native derivative, it is easily placed within the UK landscape and is probably one of our prettiest indigenous clones.

| Mature height: 12-17m | Shape of mature tree | Flowering trees | Urban trees | Bee friendly trees | Eco impact rating: B |

PRUNUS cerasifera Nigra
Purple Leaved Plum

Introduced in the early 1900s this form of the Cherry Plum (or Myrobolan) usually sets only a few red fruits. A popular tree, often planted in city streets or verges, it is easy to maintain in a garden as it reacts well to very severe winter pruning. I once decimated an overgrown specimen in a friend's garden by reducing the crown by about 60%. They were pretty sceptical but now always comment on its regrowth and apply the same treatment every five years of so!

A small tree with a rounded form, it is most notable for its purple leaves and stems. Early pink spring flowers fade to white before the leaves take full effect. This is a robust performer, thriving on most free draining soils.

- Mature height: 5-8m
- Shape of mature tree
- Red/purple foliage
- Eco impact rating
- Eco impact rating: C

P

PRUNUS Cheals Weeping

This well-known garden tree has been oversold by garden centres for years but still represents one of the best weeping cherry cultivars in production. It requires very little maintenance, thrives in most free draining soils and never fails to perform.

Rather similar to Prunus Kiku-shidare Sakura, this has a more steeply weeping habit. It is a small tree and is stunning in spring when it bears double pink flowers. An excellent choice for gardens where space is limited.

| 3|5 Mature height: 3-5m | Shape of mature tree | Bee friendly trees | C Eco impact rating |

PRUNUS domestica Early Rivers

Bred by the well-known Rivers Nursery in Hertfordshire in the 1860s, this edible cherry produces dark red fruits by July. Buying cherries from the supermarket can be so expensive to getting them from your own tree may be a better option. Classified as fruit, this tree has no VAT attributed to it.

White flowers in the spring add to the generl interest and this round headed tree thrives in most free draining soils. It is always beneficial to keep competition away from its base and to top dress with a general-purpose fertilizer each spring to enhance fruiting.

| 5|8 Mature height: 5-8m | Shape of mature tree | Garden trees | Edible fruits | Bee friendly trees | C Eco impact rating |

PRUNUS domestica Hauszwetsche

This dark blue damson / plum has green tinged flesh and is great eaten straight from the tree or as the ingredient for a crumble or pie. As it is classified by the Government as food, there is no VAT when buying this tree which makes it even more palatable!

Thriving on most free draining soils, its fruit size and flavour can me enhanced by keeping completion, especially grass, at bay within a metre radius of its trunk. Attractive white flowers in the spring should not be forgotten as a reason to include this round headed tree into a garden.

Mature height: 5-8m | Shape of mature tree | Garden trees | Edible fruits | Bee friendly trees | Eco impact rating

PRUNUS domestica Reine-Claude d'oullins
Greengage

Raised in France, greengages are less common than plums in the UK but I think that means we have missed out! Green plum-like fruits mature to green / yellow when ripe and are sweet and juicy eaten straight from the tree. They are also a fantastic ingredient for a crumble or pie.

There is no VAT on this tree making it even better tasting! Thriving on most free draining soils a spring fertilizer is recommended to power fruit size and flavour. Keeping grass competition away from the base of the trunk is also beneficial, based on many a commercial fruit trail. White flowers in the spring and good autumn colour also add interest for the garden.

Mature height: 5-8m | Shape of mature tree | Garden trees | Edible fruits | Eco impact rating

PRUNUS domestica Victoria
Victoria Plum

The nation's favourite eating plum, grown on a colt rootstock here at Barcham as a full standard. The small white flowers that emerge in the spring are superseded by good sized red blushed fruits that beckon to us, birds and insects alike.

Our despatch teams tend to gorge themselves with the plums prior to autumn delivery so don't be surprised to take delivery of barren plants! Nutritious free draining soils free from grass competition within a metre radius from the trunk provide best results for your fruiting harvest.

| Mature height: 5-8m | Shape of mature tree | Bee friendly trees | Eco impact rating: C |

PRUNUS dulcis
Common Almond

I was shown a lovely painting of Hampstead Garden Suburb depicting a Victorian tree-lined avenue of Almonds but alas this is from a bygone age. It is fraught with difficulty as they tend to attract every insect pest and fungal mildew under the sun so beware!!

The reason for listing this tree is to make you aware that it is a key host for Xylella fastidiosa so should be avoided to prevent this nasty disease from coming into the UK from the continent. We no longer grow this tree for sale with this in mind.

| Mature height: 5-8m | Shape of mature tree | Edible nuts | Bee friendly trees | Eco impact rating: D |

PRUNUS fruticosa Globosa

This man-made tree has its uses in urban environments where space is limited. Small white flowers in spring are replaced by a dense canopy of small vivid green leaves that turn a glorious orange / red in the autumn.

A top worked, dwarfing clone which forms a compact and rounded crown. Budded onto Colt rootstock, Prunus avium is used as the inter-stock, with fruticosa Globosa top grafted to form the crown. The avium inter-stock gives the height, while the Colt rootstock prevents pavement heave. It requires virtually no maintenance and is an admirable urban tree.

- Mature height: 5-8m
- Shape of mature tree
- Urban trees
- Bee friendly trees
- Eco impact rating: D

PRUNUS x gondouinii Schnee

A most attractive form of Duke Cherry with lustrous and large green leaves that give a good autumnal display of gold and orange. It is a cross between Prunus avium and Prunus cerasus and although not commonly planted it has considerable merit.

This small, rounded tree is perfect for gardens, parks and street plantings. The large, white, single flowers are borne in late April and early May. It thrives best in free draining soils and there is a historic avenue of them in Battersea Park, London.

- Mature height: 5-8m
- Shape of mature tree
- Garden trees
- Bee friendly trees
- Eco impact rating: C

PRUNUS x hillieri Spire

A cross between Prunus sargentii and Prunus yedoensis raised in the late 1920s. The original tree now stands at 10 metres high and its autumn colour can be a joy to behold. It has had many accolades over the years and won the Award of Garden Merit in 2002.

This ranks as one of the finest of small street trees, and it is also excellent in gardens and parks. With its tight, upright habit and profusion of pink flowers, it is ideal for most sites where space is limited. Rather slow growing and not suited to the north of Scotland where the winters are too wet and cold.

- 5|8 Mature height: 5-8m
- Shape of mature tree
- Bee friendly trees
- D Eco impact rating

PRUNUS Kanzan

A very widely planted and most popular Flowering Cherry. Introduced in the early 1900s, it has won numerous awards culminating in the Award of Garden Merit in 2002. Its large green leaves can turn to a glorious display in the autumn but first emerge a coppery red. It is more vigorous but otherwise similar to 'Pink Perfection'.

This cherry has stiffly ascending branched forming a columnar crown when young before becoming more rounded at maturity.

It is of medium height and reliably produces plenty of very showy, dark pink flowers in the spring. Sometimes rather too vigorous for paved areas, it is, nevertheless, good in parks.

- Mature height: 5-8m
- Shape of mature tree
- Bee friendly trees
- Eco impact rating: C

PRUNUS laurocerasus Caucasica

One of the few laurel types that lends itself to growing as a small tree, making it a very useful addition for stilted screening above fence height. A tough and hardy tree but like most evergreens its achillies heel is sitting in waterlogged ground over winter. Evergreens are harder to read than deciduous ones as when they show stress it can be too late to provide a remedy. A cut off Christmas tree looks fine in your lounge in December even though it's dead.

Free draining land is the key as they are still dependant on decent waterings in the summer after planting to establish. Given all this it makes a fine evergreen tree, perfect for screening off neighbouring gardens.

- Mature height: 5-8m
- Shape of mature tree
- Evergreen trees
- Garden trees
- Privacy raised screening
- Eco impact rating: D

This clone of laurel has thinner leaves than that of Prunus Rotundifolia and also runs up as a standard plant so the screening is effective beyond the fence line without encroaching into valuable garden space at ground level.

PRUNUS laurocerasus Novita

A tree form of laurel, grown as a standard. White flowers in the spring and year round evergreen leaves marks this clone as very useful for those requiring privacy. Another clone, Novita, is also an option but too similar to merit a separate listing!

Hedging laurel often takes as much horizontal space as vertical space in a garden, and with small areas this can be problematic.

- Mature height: 5-8m
- Shape of mature tree
- Privacy raised screening
- Eco impact rating: D

PRUNUS laurocerasus Rotundifolia
Cherry Laurel

Cherry laurel was introduced from its native Eastern Europe in 1576 and is now naturalised over much of the UK. It relies on the trace element magnesium so if your hedge is yellowing you now know what to apply! It does not thrive on shallow chalky soils.

A particularly bushy, rounded form, this cultivar is ideal for hedging and screening. It is a very versatile plant as it can be savagely pruned back to bare wood and still only takes a few months to regain its screening use.

Mature height: 5-8m | Multi-stem | Hedging trees | Eco impact rating: D

PRUNUS lusitanica Angustifolia
Portugal Laurel

Portugal Laurel is widely used for hedging, but also makes a fine, specimen tree if required. It is prettier than common laurel with red stems and narrower leaves, but it is just as durable. White flowers in the spring are a bonus.

We offer them as half-standards. Grown as a tree, it remains small and has a good rounded habit, and it does well on most soils, including shallow chalk. Very attractive as a hedge, giving year-round interest and cover to many small birds. Ideal for gardens and parks.

Mature height: 5-8m | Shape of mature tree | Privacy raised screening | Hedging trees | Bee friendly trees | Eco impact rating: D

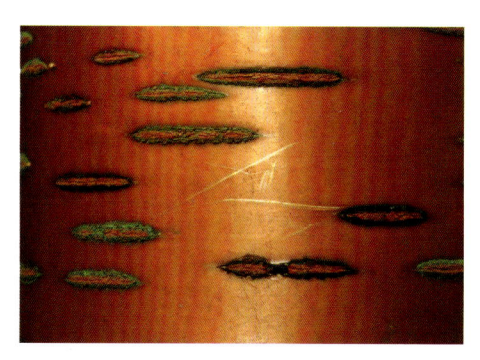

PRUNUS maackii Amber Beauty

A Dutch selection of the Manchurian Cherry. Thriving on most free draining soils the white flowers in spring are more akin to Bird Cherry than anything else and their effect is lovely against a clear blue sky.

Stunning in winter with its smoothly polished, golden stems, this cultivar of medium height and rounded form is early into leaf in spring. It is a stout and vigorous grower tolerating the harsher aspects of our urban environments.

- Mature height: 5-8m
- Shape of mature tree
- Bark interest
- Eco impact rating: D

I have seen this clone planted as a street tree in Portsmouth and it makes a fantastically stocky tree with a rounded crown as it drifts into maturity.

PRUNUS Okame

This very pretty cherry is derived from Prunus incisa and was raised by Captain Collingwood Ingram in the 1940s. A winner of the Award of Garden Merit in 2002, its dainty foliage produces a great autumnal display of orange and reds.

A small rounded tree, Okame produces a mass of profuse rich pink flowers in late March and early April. It is a splendid choice for gardens and parks. Like most of its type it is not suited to waterlogged soils.

Mature height: 5-8m | Shape of mature tree | Garden trees | Bee friendly trees | Eco impact rating: C

PRUNUS padus
Bird Cherry

The Bird Cherry, a native of Britain as well as the rest of Europe, is a relatively late flowerer. It is a tough tree, withstanding the rigours of the urban environment but like other cherries does not thrive on waterlogged ground.

The white flowers of the Bird Cherry are produced in May in hanging racemes. The black fruits in late summer are edible but rather bitter. Luscious and large green leaves turn yellow to bronze in autumn. This is a rounded tree of medium height, and is good in parks, gardens and woodlands.

Mature height: 7-12m | Shape of mature tree | Bee friendly trees | Eco impact rating: C

PRUNUS padus Albertii

This clone of Bird Cherry has been cultivated since the 1900s and is probably the best clone for urban plantings where space is more restricted. The crown is very ascending when young before developing into an oval to rounded shape at maturity.

A rather good choice for garden, street and verge planting, this very free flowering form has an excellent track record for requiring little maintenance. It thrives on most soils but is best suited to free draining sites.

| 7|12 Mature height: 7-12m | Shape of mature tree | Urban trees | C Eco impact rating |

PRUNUS padus Watereri

Sometimes referred to as Prunus padus Grandiflora, this clone of Bird Cherry was introduced slightly after 'Albertii' in the early 1900s. It won the Award of Garden Merit in 2002 and is a popular choice for amenity planting.

Remarkable for its long white racemes – up to 20cm long – this cultivar is of medium height and with a rounded, rather spreading habit. A good selection for parks and other open spaces but is too vigorous for streets. Quick to grow in the first few years it tolerates most soils.

| 7|12 Mature height: 7-12m | Shape of mature tree | Parkland trees | Bee friendly trees | C Eco impact rating |

Pandora makes only a small tree, but its ascending branches, which give its broadly columnar habit, become smothered by pale pink blossom in March and early April.

PRUNUS Pandora

This wonderful Prunus yedoensis cross is a great choice for an urban garden or street. It won the Award of Merit in 1939 and the updated Award of Garden Merit in 2002. It has relatively small leaves for a cherry and requires very little maintenance for so much ornamental interest.

The bronze-red leaves in autumn also provide a wonderful show. It thrives best on free draining sites.

| 5\|8 Mature height: 5-8m | Shape of mature tree | Flowering trees | Bee friendly trees | C Eco impact rating |

PRUNUS Pink Perfection

A British-bred form of flowering cherry that started its commercial origins in about 1935 and won the Award of Garden Merit in 2002. It prefers free draining soils and will generally suffer if waterlogged.

Similar in some ways to Kanzan, which we believe to be one of its parents, Pink Perfection is less vigorous. Its double flowers, dark pink in bud, opening slightly paler, are borne in long clusters. It has a broadly oval crown and is of medium to large form. Suitable for verges, broad streets and parks.

- Mature height: 5-8m
- Shape of mature tree
- Flowering trees
- Bee friendly trees
- Eco impact rating: C

P

Its double, shell pink flowers are set against beautiful, wine-red foliage to create an eye-catching effect. Lovely in parks and gardens but like most cherries it prefers a free draining soil.

PRUNUS Royal Burgundy

This Flowering Cherry is rather like a purple-leaved equivalent of the well known Prunus Kanzan. Fairly new to our range, it gives wonderful contrast to a garden with its spectacular foliage and flower display. Historically Prunus cerasifera Nigra is thought of as the choice for purple leaf interest but this clone provides real competition.

A small tree with ascending branches, it forms an oval to rounded crown at maturity.

5|8	Shape of mature tree	Multi-stem	Bee friendly trees	C
Mature height: 5-8m				Eco impact rating

PRUNUS sargentii

Introduced from its native Japan in 1890 this is widely regarded as one of the loveliest of flowering cherries – and with the advantage of its blossom usually being ignored by bullfinches. A winner of numerous accolades culminating in the Award of Garden Merit in 2002.

A superb, small tree of rounded habit, and a great choice for gardens, parks and streets. It bears abundant, single, pink flowers in March and April, and is one of the first to take on its autumn tints of orange and crimson, which complement its chestnut-brown bark so effectively.

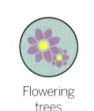

Mature height: 5-8m | Shape of mature tree | Flowering trees | Bee friendly trees | Eco impact rating: C

PRUNUS sargentii Rancho

Sometimes too close to call from straight forward Prunus sargentii, this flowering cherry was raised in the USA in the 1950s and came across to be grown by European nurseries shortly afterwards.

A broadly columnar form of the species, it is of similarly low height, and is just the job where space is rather restricted. It bears abundant, single, pink flowers in March and April, and is one of the first to take on its autumn tints of orange and crimson. Its bark is noticeably darker than most cherries and it thrives best on free draining soils.

Mature height: 5-8m | Shape of mature tree | Flowering trees | Bee friendly trees | Eco impact rating: C

PRUNUS x schmittii

This Prunus avium cross originates back to 1923 and can grow more than 15 metres given suitable conditions. Sometimes too vigorous for streets, it is better placed on green verges or gardens where it needs little or no maintenance.

It is most remarkable for its polished, red-brown bark that improves with every passing year. Fairly quick growing, it's stiffly ascending branches form a narrow but large conical crown even at maturity. It shows fine autumn colours and thrives best on free draining soils.

Mature height: 5-8m | Shape of mature tree | Bark interest | Bee friendly trees | Eco impact rating: C

PRUNUS serrula Tibetica
Tibetan Cherry

This lovely cherry was introduced from Western China in 1908 by Ernest Wilson and is surely one of the best trees available for bark interest.

Available as single stemmed or multi-stemmed this wonderfully dramatic tree can provide great contrast within a garden or urban environment. Its many horticultural honours culminated in the Award of Garden Merit in 2002. Like most cherries it thrives best on free draining soils.

A fast growing, but small tree of rounded form. It has really shiny, mahogany-brown bark that just keeps on getting better and more sensational with age which makes it worth growing for this reason alone. It has narrow, willow-like leaves and small, white flowers, which are produced in April.

Mature height: 5-8m	Shape of mature tree	Multi-stem	Bark interest	Bee friendly trees	Eco impact rating
5|8					C

Telephone 01353 720 748 | www.barcham.co.uk | www.barchampro.co.uk

P

PRUNUS Shimidsu Sakura

This dainty Japanese Cherry introduced very early in the 1900s is also known as Shôgetsu. It is remarkably pretty in flower and in my opinion the most attractive flowering cherry on the market although Prunus Shirofugen comes a close second! A First-Class Certificate winner in 1989 it also won the Award of Garden Merit.

A small tree with a broad, rounded habit, this is one of the most outstanding Japanese Cherries, and one we strongly recommend for verges, parks and gardens. The pink buds open to reveal large, white, petals sharply toothed at the fringe, which clothe the branches in long stalked clusters.

| Mature height: 5-8m | Shape of mature tree | Flowering trees | Bee friendly trees | Eco impact rating: C |

PRUNUS Shirotae

This cherry is sometimes referred to as Mount Fuji and was introduced to Britain in the early 1900s. Like most weeping varieties it gets better with age and at maturity it can be overwhelmingly stunning when seen in full flower against a blue spring sky. It won the Award of Garden Merit in 2002.

Gently weeping is perhaps the best way to describe the habit of this small, but vigorous tree. Green fringed foliage is followed by very large single and semi-double pure white flowers. Very good for verges, parks and gardens.

| Mature height: 5-8m | Shape of mature tree | Flowering trees | Bee friendly trees | Eco impact rating: C |

PRUNUS Shirofugen

A late and long-lasting flowerer introduced in the very early 1900s by Ernest Wilson that won the Award of Garden Merit in 2002. Considered by many as the best flowering cherry on the market, it is hard to disagree with them. A superb garden tree, it also thrives within an urban environment.

A rather spreading tree with a rounded crown, Shirofugen remains small. Its large, double, white flowers finish pink, contrasting well with the young, copper coloured foliage. Excellent for verges, parks and gardens it is a wonderful sight when in full flow. It thrives best on free draining soils. Its floral display is incredibly long lasting.

- Mature height: 5-8m
- Shape of mature tree
- Flowering trees
- Bee friendly trees
- Eco impact rating: C

P

PRUNUS x subhirtella Autumnalis
Autumn Cherry

The Autumn Cherry brings cheer at the darkest time of year. Introduced in 1894 it won the Award of Merit in 1930 and remains a favourite for planting in the UK. Often top grafted on the continent, we strongly recommend base grafted trees for structural longevity.

This small, rounded tree produces its semi-double, white flowers intermittently from November through to March – a welcome sight on a bleak, winter's day. Autumn foliage is orange yellow. A lovely tree for streets, parks and gardens that thrives best on well drained soils.

- Mature height: 5-8m
- Shape of mature tree
- Flowering trees
- Bee friendly trees
- Eco impact rating: C

PRUNUS x subhirtella Autumnalis
Rosea

An alternative form of the beautiful Autumn Cherry that won the Award of Garden Merit in 2002 after it received the Award of Merit in 1960. Prized by inventive flower arrangers in winter for its woody flowering stems.

This small, rounded tree produces its semi-double, pink flowers sporadically from November through to March – a welcome sight in the dark, winter months. Autumn foliage is orange yellow. Ideal for streets, parks or gardens but it does not care for waterlogged ground.

- Mature height: 5-8m
- Shape of mature tree
- Flowering trees
- Bee friendly trees
- Eco impact rating: C

PRUNUS Sunset Boulevard

This relatively new introduction was bred at the Arboretum Kalmthout, Belgium, in the late 1980s for urban use. Many states it is extremely columnar but we reckon broadly oval would be more appropriate a description.

Its young coppery foliage turns green in summer and golden yellow in autumn and its large, white, single flowers are edged with pink. This durable tree is very good for parks and street plantings and thrives best on free draining soils. The more I have seen of this tree the more I like it and once it develops a good crown the floral display is lovely, especially against a blue sky. I think this may become an urban favourite for its durability and aesthetics.

- Mature height: 5-8m
- Shape of mature tree
- Flowering trees
- Bee friendly trees
- Eco impact rating: C

PRUNUS Tai haku
Great White Cherry

The Great White Cherry makes a magnificent specimen. The famous cherry enthusiast, Captain Collingwood Ingram, reintroduced this fine tree back to its native Japan in 1932 after he found a specimen growing in a Sussex garden. A winner of numerous awards including the First Class Certificate in 1944, the Award of Merit in 1931 and the Award of Garden Merit in 2002.

One of the finest of all Cherries, and probably the best of the "whites", it bears its large, single flowers profusely, contrasting beautifully with its young, copper coloured foliage. Very good for urban plantings, streets, parks and gardens, but in our experience, it does not thrive in very wet soils. It is of medium height and rounded habit.

Like many flowering cherries its best moments are demonstrated mainly in the spring and early summer, but this relatively short display still makes planting this clone well worth the endeavour. Its foliage can turn to a beautiful yellow / orange in the autumn. Never accept a top grafted plant as they are prone to a shorter life expectancy.

Mature height: 5-8m	Shape of mature tree	Bee friendly trees	Eco impact rating
5|8			C

PRUNUS Ukon

Introduced in the early 1900s this unusual cherry won the Award of Garden Merit in 2002. Sometimes imported as top grafted from the continent. This is a false economy in the long term, as the top can outgrow the bottom. We would advise base grafted trees.

A vigorous, rounded, medium size tree with a rather spreading crown, it has unusual pale yellow flowers, tinged with green and occasionally flushed with pink. They are semi-double and work well with the young bronze foliage. Its large green leaves produce a great autumn display of red and purple.

- Mature height: 5-8m
- Shape of mature tree
- Flowering trees
- Bee friendly trees
- Eco impact rating: C

PRUNUS Umineko

This Flowering Cherry is a cross between Prunus incisa and Prunus speciosa. Sometimes also referred to as 'Snow Goose' it won the Award of Merit in 1928 and represents a very good tree for the urban environment.

Umineko has a narrow, columnar form, which broadens with age and is a very good choice for streets, parks, gardens and other restricted areas. It makes a medium size tree, and its white, single flowers are produced in April, along with the foliage, which colours very well in autumn. It is a robust and vigorous tree that thrives best on free draining soils.

- Mature height: 5-8m
- Shape of mature tree
- Flowering trees
- Bee friendly trees
- Eco impact rating: C

PRUNUS x yedoensis
Yoshino Cherry

The Yoshino Cherry is a cross between Prunus speciosa and Prunus x subhirtella. It came from Japan around 1902 and won the Award of Garden Merit in 2002. This superbly pretty tree is hard to beat when in full flow and there is a particularly nice specimen to behold at Kew Gardens.

A broad, flat crowned tree, its arching branches create an almost weeping effect. It is of medium height and puts on a wonderful display of almond-scented, blush-white blossom in late March and early April. The fruits are dark red, almost black. Lovely as a park tree and very good on broad verges.

- Mature height 5-8m
- Shape of mature tree
- Flowering trees
- Bee friendly trees
- Eco impact rating: C

PTEROCARYA fraxinifolia
Wing Nut

The Wing Nut, a relative of the Walnut originating from Iran, was introduced into the UK way back in 1782. It is a brute of a tree with some specimens reaching over 38 metres high with a crown diameter of 35 metres so be sure to give it enough room!

A fast growing, large and broadly oval tree, which does well in most fertile, moisture-retentive soils, but is especially good for use close to rivers and lakes in parkland setting. It has deeply furrowed bark and very long summer catkins, which produce two-winged nut fruits. Its deciduous dark green leaves can be up to 60cm in length and separated by numerous toothed leaflets.

17|22	Shape of mature tree	Parkland trees	Eco impact rating
Mature height: 17-22m			A

PYRUS Beurre Hardy

A strong growing pear, grown at Barcham as a full standard and a vigorous cropper that is particularly valued by our staff in September!

This small, rounded tree does best in a warm, sunny, sheltered position, such as a courtyard garden. The large fruits, greenish yellow flushed with red, are juicy and have a distinctive flavour. They are best picked while still hard and allowed to ripen in store. The foliage turns bright red in autumn.

5|8	Shape of mature tree	Edible fruits	Bee friendly trees	Eco impact rating
Mature height: 5-8m				D

PYRUS calleryana Chanticleer

This Ornamental Pear was selected in the USA and named after the cockerel in Chaucer's Canterbury Tales. Bred by Edward Scanlon and patented in the States in 1965, it is often referred to as the 'Bradford Pear' which is in fact slightly broader, denser and unlike Chanticleer is prone to crown collapse at maturity. It won the Award of Garden Merit in 2002 and as its green lush foliage is so early to appear in spring and so late to fall in autumn it has excellent screening uses.

It is one of the very best Ornamental Pears with much to recommend it. It is of medium height, generally rather columnar, becoming more oval when mature.

- Mature height: 12-17m
- Shape of mature tree
- Urban trees
- Privacy raised screening
- Bee friendly trees
- Eco impact rating: C

Abundant blossom is produced as early as March, followed by glossy foliage, which is late to fall in autumn, when it turns orange and red and even golden. It has rapidly established itself as a fine street tree, and is tolerant of air pollution and even salty, coastal winds. An excellent choice for the urban or rural environments

PYRUS calleryana Redspire

Patented by Princeton Nursery in America in 1975, this seedling of Bradford Pear is happily less vigorous than its parent which has been known to break apart when older due to tight branch angles. As the foliage is so late to fall in autumn it is also great for screening.

Similar in many ways to Chanticleer, but Redspire has rather better autumn colour. It is of medium height, generally rather columnar, becoming more oval when mature. Profuse white blossom is produced in spring, followed by glossy foliage which becomes orange and red. An excellent choice for urban conditions and very good in streets and gardens.

12|17	Shape of mature tree	Autumn colour	C
Mature height: 12-17m			Eco impact rating

PYRUS communis Beech Hill

Many nurseries describe this as a splendid upright variety requiring little maintenance but most fail to mention the volume of fruit produced by late summer that weigh the stiffly ascending branches down. The small fruits are not edible and very hard so not ideal for urban plantings.

This medium size tree has a columnar form when young, but opens out as it matures. It provides good spring interest with its white flowers and shiny green leaves that turn to attractive shades of orange and red in autumn. Best suited to gardens.

7|12	Shape of mature tree	Garden trees	Bee friendly trees	D
Mature height: 7-12m				Eco impact rating

P

PYRUS communis Conference
Conference Pear

First introduced in 1885, this well-known eating pear variety won the Award of Garden Merit in 2002. Grown at Barcham as a full standard tree for garden planting.

Juicy and sweet green / yellow fruits are generally ready October through to November. This cultivar partially self pollinates and is a good pollinator of other varieties. It tolerates most soil conditions and is still the nation's favoured edible pear.

- Mature height: 5-8m
- Shape of mature tree
- Edible fruits
- Bee friendly trees
- Eco impact rating: D

PYRUS communis Gieser Wildeman

What first attracted me to this variety was its summer foliage which is a vibrant grey green. White spring flower is replaced with good sized russet pears in the late summer that are great for stewing and cooking. So if you like your crumbles, this is a must for the garden!

Free draining but moisture retentive soils produce the best rewards and it is always good to keep up a one metre mulch ring around its base to limit grass completion which will promote fruit size. This pear has the functionality of producing a good crop but also looking nice at the same time. So if you get a late frost or the wasps get to the fruit before you do, not all is lost.

- Mature height: 5-8m
- Shape of mature tree
- Edible fruits
- Eco impact rating: D

PYRUS Doyenne du Comice
Comice Pear

Introduced from France in 1849 this tasty pear requires a pollinator and produces yellow / green rotund fruits that can be harvested from late September.

Not as well cultivated as Conference, it has more flavour but less storage longevity. It won the Award of Garden Merit in 2002 and is worth planting alongside Pyrus communis Beech Hill which can act as the pollinator. Like most fruit trees we recommend a metre radius mulch ring round each tree to promote fruit size and to avoid planting in soils with poor drainage.

- Mature height: 5-8m
- Shape of mature tree
- Edible fruits
- Bee friendly trees
- Eco impact rating: D

PYRUS salicifolia Pendula
Willow-Leaved Pear

This very popular garden tree won the Award of Garden Merit in 2002. Its dainty foliage can provide lovely contrast and the tree is very adaptable in that I have seen it pruned in a variety of shapes and sizes.

This small, weeping and rather broad tree produces its creamy white flowers and willow-like silvery grey foliage at the same time in spring. Its weeping branches are silver grey, giving good winter interest. A very good subject for parks and gardens tolerating urban conditions well. It reacts well to severe pruning in the early spring, just before the leaves emerge to prevent the crown getting too woody.

- Mature height: 5-8m
- Shape of mature tree
- Garden trees
- Bee friendly trees
- Eco impact rating: D

Q

QUERCUS castaneifolia
Chestnut-Leaved Oak

The Chestnut-leaved Oak was introduced from the Caucasus and Iran in the mid 1840s but is rarely seen in the UK. A must for any plant collector who has the space to plant one.

Similar to Quercus cerris in appearance, this medium to large, oval shaped tree has oblong leaves, tapered at both ends. It is a magnificent tree for parks, arboretums and woodlands where there is space for its superb crown to mature.

Mature height: 17-22m | Shape of mature tree | Parkland trees | Eco impact rating: A

QUERCUS cerris
Turkey Oak

The highly durable Turkey Oak was introduced into the UK in 1735. A magnificent specimen can be seen at the National Trust's Knightshayes Garden in Devon, where it imposes itself on the field in which it stands.

This large, rounded tree is probably the fastest growing Oak grown in Britain. It does well even in chalky soils and in coastal areas. The dark green, lobed leaves are resistant to mildew, which affects some others of the genus. A tough tree, good for wide verges and parks, but also a host of the Knopper Gall Wasp which can migrate to Quercus robur and distort the acorn.

Mature height: 17-22m | Shape of mature tree | Parkland trees | Eco impact rating: A

Q

QUERCUS coccinea
Scarlet Oak

This superb autumn colourer was introduced from its native South Eastern Canada and Eastern USA in 1691. The USA national champion in Kentucky is over 40 metres tall by 31 metres wide but trees of this stature are only seen on dry sandy soils which suits it best. It requires a slightly acidic soil to perform at its best so select the more robust Quercus palustris if in doubt. The overall effect is very similar.

A large and impressive subject, with a broad and rounded habit. The summer's dark, glossy, green leaves turn, branch by branch, to a flaming scarlet as autumn progresses. Its acorns are carried in shallow cups. A magnificent specimen for planting in parkland but it is often confused in the UK with Quercus palustris.

12|17	Shape of	Parkland	Autumn	B
Mature height: 12-17m	mature tree	trees	colour	Eco impact rating

QUERCUS frainetto
Hungarian Oak

This stately tree was introduced from South East Europe in the late 1830s. There are some magnificent specimens at the National Trust's Anglesey Abbey in Cambridgeshire which coincidentally is a garden not to be missed if you are in the vicinity!

This is a large tree with a broad, rounded crown. Its fissured bark and large, dark green leaves, which are boldly cut and regularly lobed, makes this a most striking subject for parks and woodlands. We also recommend it as an avenue tree. It does best on moist soils, but will tolerate chalky ones. The clone "Trump" retains a slightly improved shape at maturity.

- Mature height: 17-22m
- Shape of mature tree
- Parkland trees
- Eco impact rating: A

QUERCUS x hispanica Wageningen

This rarely seen tree is thought to be a hybrid between Quercus cerris and Quercus suber and is furnished with green glossy leaves that are beyond 10cm in length and 5cm across.

An interesting addition to parkland planting as this clone generally hangs onto its leaves until the spring. It has an upright habit when young and broadens with age to develop into a large tree with a rough bark at maturity. It thrives on most fertile soils.

- Mature height: 12-17m
- Shape of mature tree
- Parkland trees
- Eco impact rating: A

QUERCUS ilex
Holm Oak

The Holm Oak is a native of Mediterranean countries, but it has been grown in Britain since the 1500s, and is now thought to be a native of Southern Ireland. The timber is hard and long-lasting, used for joinery, vine-props and for charcoal. It won the Award of Garden Merit in 2002 and is surely one of the most majestic of evergreen trees grown in the UK. They seem to be more intensely silver on the coast and can quickly be mistaken for Olive when the tree is juvenile.

If left to its own devices it forms a large tree with a densely rounded habit, fine examples of which can be seen within the Holkham Hall Estate on the North Norfolk coast. The avenue there is so impressive that I obtained permission to harvest acorns for our production. Many thanks to the Estate for this.

Quercus ilex is surprisingly versatile, being suitable for coastal planting, hedging, topiary and stilted screening. It also tolerates shade and air pollution. Suitable for parks and gardens but thriving best on free draining soils.

Mature height: 17-22m | Shape of mature tree | Evergreen trees | Coastal sites | Eco impact rating: A

QUERCUS imbricaria
Shingle Oak

The Shingle Oak was introduced from North America in the 1780s. Its name derives from its use for roof tiles "shingles" in its native land. The USA national champion is in Ohio and stands at over 35 metres in height with a crown at over 23 metres across, so it is not for the faint-hearted!

A medium to large vigorous tree, it has a pyramidal habit, and shiny dark green leaves, which turn golden in the autumn. Splendid for parks or estates, it thrives best on moist but well drained deep fertile acid soils and prefers full sun.

- Mature height: 17-22m
- Shape of mature tree
- Parkland trees
- Eco impact rating: A

QUERCUS palustris
Pin Oak

More pyramidal at maturity than the similar Quercus coccinea, this magnificent tree was introduced into the UK from its native North America in 1800. It is a relatively tough tree and can withstand limited periods of water logging even though it prefers free draining slightly acidic soils. The USA national champion is in Tennessee and stands at 37 metres tall and broad. It won the Award of Garden Merit in 2002.

This large, pyramidal tree is one of the most graceful of Oaks, with its slender branches gently drooping at their tips. Its autumn colour is simply stunning.

- Mature height: 17-22m
- Shape of mature tree
- Parkland trees
- Autumn colour
- Eco impact rating: A

Q

QUERCUS palustris Green Dwarf

This topped worked dwarfing clone is ideal where space is at a premium. It's rounded habit is pretty much maintenance free and its decorative autumn colour is a superb inclusion for restricted spaces or tree lined streets. Happy on moisture retentive soils, avoid soils prone to waterlogging and ground with a PH of more than 7.5.

Summer foliage is a tight ball of green that gives way to oranges and reds in the autumn. We grow this variety on a 1.8-2m stem so the mature height will only get to about 5 metres which is pretty small for an oak. Its leaves are indented, glossy and distinctive.

Mature height: 4-6m	Shape of mature tree	Autumn colour	Parkland trees	Eco impact rating
4|6				C

Oak update

In 2019 DEFRA imposed importation restrictions on the Quercus genera to combat the threat of Oak Processionary Moth. The caterpillars have a defence mechanism in play when they are threatened, projecting tiny hairs on their bodies which are highly toxic if inhaled or fall on unprotected skin, resulting in nasty rashes or breathing difficulties in the most serious cases. This pest is a huge problem on mainland Europe and unfortunately way too many imported Quercus were coming to the UK with this pest hitching a ride.

The nursery trade has become dependant on importing Oaks to satisfy demand so when this practice was stopped via government intervention, the few UK nurseries who actually grow our national tree from acorns were suddenly overwhelmed by demand. This resulted in very few Oak being available in the marketplace, especially those that thrive best in slightly acidic soils such as Quercus palustris and Quercus rubra as these soils are a rarity for UK tree growers to exploit.

Our British providence grown Quercus take about 8 years before they get to harvestable size from acorns. We are taking forward orders for Quercus but please be mindful that numbers are limited as we can't grow them quick enough to satisfy the demand.

This again highlights the importance of biosecurity and buying trees with approved 'Plant Healthy' status, a new national kitemark which only gives accreditation to growers who have robust biosecurity procedures in play. Dutch Elm Disease, Ash Die Back, Oak Processionary Moth and now the threat of Xylella fastidiosa, all could be countered by buying British grown trees.

A single moth can lay up to 300 eggs which hatch as caterpillars that predate on Oak tree leaves.

QUERCUS palustris Green Pillar

An introduction from the USA, where it is referred to as 'Pringreen'. It is an exceptional tree with ascending branches forming a very columnar crown, akin to our Quercus robur Fastigiata. Its leaves are lustrous and shiny, particularly pleasing in the summer when the sun shines on them. However, its real glory is in its autumn colour which can turn to vivid scarlet when supported by a free draining soil without alkalinity.

Great for urban areas where space is restricted, this clone is also a good choice for medium sized gardens. This clone was spotted within a seedling bed in New Jersey in the 1990s and was raised by a nurseryman working for the famous Princeton Nursery. A good find! We are sure this clone will be used more in the UK in the years to come as it ticks amny of the boxes for urban planners.

Mature height: 12-17m | Shape of mature tree | Urban trees | Autumn colour | Eco impact rating: A

Quercus palustris Helmond

The first time I saw this variety I thought it was my ideal urban Quercus palustris, not knowing it was a clonal variation. Large shiny leaves and a very regular ascending habit that forms a symmetrical broadly oval crown, this tree also has a stunning autumn display of reds and scarlet.

Like its parent, it can take wet soil but those soils prone to waterlogging should be avoided. The best autumn colour comes from trees planted in neutral to acid land. Best in full sun it can also toerate partial shade. An ideal urban tree where space allows but also great for a large garden.

Mature height: 12-17m | Shape of mature tree | Parkland trees | Autumn colour | Eco impact rating: A

QUERCUS petraea
Sessile Oak

One of our two native Oaks, the Sessile Oak is long-lived and was extensively used in shipbuilding. A winner of the Award of Garden Merit in 2002 it is more often seen on the west side of the UK where rainfall is higher.

A good choice for coastal locations, this large, oval shaped tree will also tolerate acid soils. Similar in many respects to Quercus robur, it tends to have a greater degree of apical dominance so developing a more pyramidal crown. A wonderful choice for wildlife, this tree supports a host of animals.

- Mature height: 17-22m
- Shape of mature tree
- Parkland trees
- Native trees
- Eco impact rating: A

QUERCUS phellos
Willow leaved Oak

Introduced from the Eastern USA in 1723, this distinctive oak has willow shaped leaves and is best grown on neutral to acid free draining soils even though it can tolerate wetter soils once established. It forms a broad crown at maturity so is best suited to parkland and estates to show off its autumn tints of orange and yellow.

Its slender green leaves make it difficult for the uninitiated to identify but autumn acorns that mature in their second year give it away. A great tree for plant collectors, this tree remains rare in the UK and is often restricted to arboretums.

- Mature height: 12-17m
- Shape of mature tree
- Parkland trees
- Eco impact rating: A

QUERCUS Regal Prince

Selected from acorns in 1974 from a mother plant in Illinois, this magnificent clone is thought to be a Quercus robur Fastigiata x Quercus bicolor cross. Its upright habit makes it a great urban tree but its resistance to powdery mildews gives its leaves a lustrous and clean look that makes Quercus robur Fastigiata look positively dowdy! Its leaves are two toned, dark green above and silvery green beneath and the tree has great hybrid vigour.

Thriving on most free draining soils, its wonderful summer foliage display turns to yellow and orange in the autumn. Not as fastigiate as 'Koster' it is nevertheless still very narrow and even through I haven't seen one at full maturity I expect it to grow to be a quarter of its width to height and this view is supported by the ongoing evidence from 30 year old plants in the States.

- Mature height: 12-17m
- Shape of mature tree
- Urban trees
- Eco impact rating: A

Q

QUERCUS robur
English Oak

Perhaps the most majestic of our native trees, the English or Common Oak was once the predominant species in English lowland forests, and has become virtually a national emblem. Very long-lived, its hard timber has been used to produce the finest furniture, from ships through to coffins. Many superb specimens exist in our countryside but perhaps the most famous is the Major Oak in Sherwood Forest which is estimated to be some 1000 years old and weigh over 23 tonnes. Whether Robin Hood actually took refuge in it is of debate!

A large, imposing, broadly oval tree, heavy-limbed and long-lived. Its deeply grained bark gives year-round appeal, and its expansive root system does best on deep, heavy soils. A wonderful choice for parkland and large estates, it is also good in avenues and wide verges. It is a great host for supporting wildlife and its acorns are hidden and distributed by forgetful Jays. Given the right conditions one can expect between three and four summer flushes of growth.

It is a great host for supporting wildlife and its acorns are hidden and distributed by forgetful Jays. Given the right conditions one can expect between three and four summer flushes of growth.

Mature height: 17-22m | Shape of mature tree | Native trees | Eco impact rating: A

Q

Q

QUERCUS robur Fastigiata (Koster)
Cypress Oak

The Cypress Oak used to be seed grown, which resulted in variability in its form, so now the industry standard is the uniformly narrow clone 'Koster' which is grafted onto Quercus robur rootstock. It won the Award of Garden Merit in 2002.

Common Oak is such a wonderful tree for wildlife, that for restricted areas this clone makes it possible to plant one. It thrives best in more rural environments where soil volumes are greater to support its growth.

- Mature height: 12-17m
- Shape of mature tree
- Narrow trees
- Eco impact rating: A

QUERCUS rubra
Red Oak

Introduced from its native North America in 1724, this well known stately tree won the Award of Merit in 1971 and the updated Award of Garden Merit in 2002. The bark of the Red Oak is rich in tannin – essential for tanning leather.

This large, broadly oval tree does best in deep fertile soils, but tolerates most others. It is a fast grower and seems to tolerate polluted air well. Young growth emerges almost yellow in the spring before expanding into large broad green and lobed leaves by May. These in turn go a wonderful red in autumn before turning a red / brown and falling. Best suited for planting in parks and large gardens.

- Mature height: 17-22m
- Shape of mature tree
- Parkland trees
- Autumn colour
- Eco impact rating: A

QUERCUS suber
Cork Oak

Introduced in the late 1690s, the Cork Oak is a native of southern Europe and North Africa so in the UK it is best suited to the warmer south. Until it gets beyond semi-mature it is often buoyed up by a thick bamboo cane by nurseries to support the weak stem.

However, this is academic as Quercus suber is another host to the dangerous plant disease Xylella fastidiosa so should be avoided in terms of specifying and planting in the UK at all costs for fear of spreading this dangerous disease.

Widely grown in Spain and Portugal for the wine industry it is resistant to British frosts. It is a short stemmed, wide, rounded, evergreen tree. Its thick and craggy bark can provide outstanding interest in a garden and it tends to thrive better on free draining soils.

- Mature height: 7-12m
- Shape of mature tree
- Garden trees
- Eco impact rating: A

QUERCUS x turneri Pseudoturneri
Turners Oak

Raised by Spencer Turner of Essex way back in the 18th century, this rare collector's item is a must for any specialist arboretum. Thriving on most calcareous soils, this semi evergreen tree slowly develops into a broad headed medium sized tree with distinct dark green leaves.

During very severe winters the tree sometimes defoliates completely before new leaves emerge in April and May. Sheltered gardens in southern England generally sees it keep most of its leaves through the winter period. It prefers free draining soils and will not tolerate waterlogged ground.

- Mature height: 7-12m
- Shape of mature tree
- Garden trees
- Eco impact rating: A

RHUS typhina
Stag's Horn Sumach

Stag's Horn Sumach can be grown as a small tree or as a shrub. A native of North America, it was introduced into the UK in the late 1620s and won the Award of Garden Merit in 2002. It may surprise you that the national champion in the States is over 20 metres tall but I have not seen one much over 5 metres over here.

This small tree has an irregular wide spreading and rather architectural habit. It provides superb autumn colour, and the conical red fruit clusters last for much of the winter. Very good for gardens and parks. It can be prone to suckering so allow for this when planning its position.

- Mature height: 3-8m
- Multi-stem
- Garden trees
- Eco impact rating

ROBINIA pseudoacacia
False Acacia

The False Acacia was introduced to France from America in 1601, and is now naturalised through much of Europe. It produces large epicormic thorns and can be prone to suckering so it can be used as a stout defence against unwelcome visitors.

A large irregular crowned tree with soft, green, pinnate leaves that emerge early May. Racemes of sweetly scented white flowers in June are replaced by purple tinged seed pods in autumn. It thrives on any soil, and tolerates urban pollution, but is not good in windy, exposed locations due to its rather brittle branches.

- Mature height: 12-17m
- Shape of mature tree
- Parkland trees
- Eco impact rating: A

ROBINIA pseudoacacia Bessoniana

This thornless clone, in cultivation since the 1870s, can be seen at its mature dimensions in the Royal Horticultural Garden at Wisley. It seldom flowers and its foliage is a paler but more vibrant green that its parent.

Of only medium height, this clone is probably the best Robinia cultivar for street planting. It has a compact, rounded crown of virtually thorn-free branches and pale green leaves. It thrives on any soil, and tolerates urban pollution, but its brittle and twiggy growth is not suited to windy sites. Robinia and its clones are generally high maintenance but this clone is without doubt the pick of them. Its soft green spring growth is particularly attractive.

- Mature height: 7-12m
- Shape of mature tree
- Urban trees
- Eco impact rating: B

ROBINIA pseudoacacia Casque Rouge

This delightful cultivar of False Acacia makes a particularly fine garden, verge or parkland tree as its profuse flowers emerge in June after the Cherries, Crab Apples and Thorns have all finished.

This tree of medium height and broadly rounded habit, it is greatly prized for its showy and highly ornamental lilac-pink flowers that are richly appreciated by all those who notice. It thrives on any soil, and tolerates urban pollution, but is not good in windy, exposed locations due to its rather brittle branches. It should be noted that its scruffy form makes it a highly unsatisfactory urban tree.

- Mature height: 7-12m
- Shape of mature tree
- Flowering trees
- Eco impact rating: B

ROBINIA pseudoacacia Frisia

This superb yellow clone has been very popular over the past 25 years and can now be seen in most urban areas in the UK. It is tolerant of dry conditions and is well suited to cope with reflected heat and light from buildings and pavements. It won the Award of Garden Merit in 2002. Beware however, in recent years it has proven to be very susceptible to disease and decline.

Raised in the Netherlands in the mid 1930s, this medium tree of rounded habit only rarely flowers, but displays its beautiful golden yellow foliage from spring through to autumn. It thrives on any soil, and tolerates urban pollution.

- Mature height: 7-12m
- Shape of mature tree
- Garden trees
- Yellow foliage
- Eco impact rating: B

ROBINIA pseudoacacia Umbraculifera

In cultivation since the early 1800s this top grafted clone forms a rounded and compact crown ideal for urban piazzas and town gardens. It is more regularly seen in French and German cities than here in the UK.

This small, mop-headed tree seldom flowers and requires very little maintenance. The largest tree of this clone I have heard of is about 6 metres in diameter. It is best to have them top grafted between 1.8-2 metres from ground level so they can easily be walked under. It thrives on most soils and is tolerant of urban conditions. Almost impossible to deliver without superficial breakages as the twiggy growth is so brittle, it is best to take delivery when dormant without leaf.

- Mature height: 5-8m
- Shape of mature tree
- Garden trees
- Eco impact rating: B

S

SALIX alba
White Willow

Our native White Willow is a lovely subject for water-side plantings. Very prominent in our fenland landscape surrounding the nursery, it reacts well to regular pollarding where size becomes an issue.

A fast growing, large, broad canopy tree with slender branches which droop at the tips. The leaves give a characteristically silver appearance from a distance. Catkins are borne in spring. Although it is good in wet soils and will tolerate temporary flooding, it thrives in most soils, and is a fine choice for coastal areas.

17|22			B
Mature height 17-22m	Shape of mature tree	Native trees	Eco impact rating

SALIX alba Chermesina
Scarlet Willow

This clone is also known by the cultivar name of Britzensis. A winner of the Award of Garden Merit in 2002, it has been known to extend over 3 metres of growth in a single growing season from a coppice.

A medium to large tree with a rather pyramidal crown, its young branches are a brilliant orange red in winter, especially if severely pruned every other year to produce a multi-stemmed tree. It makes a very good park tree and thrives on most soils including those prone to flooding.

- Mature height: 17-22m
- Shape of mature tree
- Multi-stem
- Eco impact rating: B

SALIX alba Liempde

This male clone has been planted extensively in the Netherlands, where it was selected in the late 1960s. As with all willows it reacts well to pruning if its ultimate size is too much to handle and this work is best undertaken in the winter months.

This vigorous tree has upright branches which form a narrow, conical tree. The slender, silvery green leaves turn clear yellow in autumn. It does particularly well in wet soils, and is suited to coastal areas.

- Mature height: 17-22m
- Shape of mature tree
- Wet soils
- Eco impact rating: B

It is a large, weeping and wide spreading tree, often seen close to water as it does so well in wet soils. The narrow, pale green leaves are early to flush in the spring and slow to fall in the autumn.

SALIX alba Tristis
(x sepulcralis Chrysocoma)
Golden Weeping Willow

The beautiful and much-admired Weeping Willow has several botanical names including Salix babylonica and Salix vitellina Pendula but in fact is a hybrid of the two with a bit of Salix alba thrown in for good measure. A winner of the Award of Garden Merit in 2002 this is surely one of the most graceful weeping trees grown in the UK.

A fast grower well suited to parks. It reacts well to severe crown pruning sending the glorious golden stems and light green foliage plunging towards the ground.

Mature height: 17-22m | Shape of mature tree | Wet soils | Eco impact rating: B

SALIX caprea
Pussy Willow

The Pussy Willow has been loved by generations of children and is often associated with Easter. Sometimes referred to as Goat Willow, it is a tough prospect for industrial areas that need rapid greening.

One of our native Willows, this makes a small, rounded tree and is often found by rivers and streams, as it thrives in damp soil. It is particularly noted for its silver-white, furry catkins, which open to yellow in spring

- Mature height: 3-8m
- Shape of mature tree
- Wet soils
- Eco impact rating: B

SALIX caprea Pendula
Kilmarnock Willow

The weeping form of Pussy Willow that is top grafted onto a Salix caprea stem. It was discovered by the side of the River Ayr in Scotland in the mid 1850s and was granted the Award of Merit in 1977.

This small male weeping tree, which does best on moist soils, is perfect for gardens, producing the ultimate shape resembling an umbrella. Its yellow shoots are followed in spring by attractive, grey catkins.

- Mature height: 3-5m
- Shape of mature tree
- Garden trees
- Eco impact rating: D

SALIX daphnoides
Violet Willow

Native to Northern Europe, Central Asia and the Himalayas, this lovely tree was introduced into the UK in the late 1820s and won the Award of Merit in 1957. The Violet Willow is an excellent choice for coppicing to show off its sensational purple-violet shoots overlaid with a white bloom.

Catkins are an attractive feature in spring. This is a medium, fast growing tree with a rounded habit that thrives on most soils including wet ones. The male clone 'Aglaia' is often grown by nurseries for ease of propagation but its properties are the same.

- Mature height: 7-12m
- Shape of mature tree
- Wet soils
- Eco impact rating: C

Very early to leaf in spring, this vigorous tree can outgrow a small garden so beware! Its contorted branches can cost a fortune from florists so it is always nice to harvest your own when the need arises.

SALIX matsudana Tortuosa
Dragon's Claw Willow

Introduced from its native China in 1905, the fondly known 'Wiggerly Willow' is otherwise known as Salix babylonica Pekinensis, the Pekin Willow.

A weird and wonderful sight in winter when its framework of contorted and twisted branches can be best appreciated. It is a fast growing, medium to large tree with a rounded habit. Good for parks, garden and for waterside plantings, it is also prized by flower arrangers and by my wife to hang Easter decorations.

- 10|15 Mature height: 10-15m
- Shape of mature tree
- Garden trees
- C Eco impact rating

SALIX pentandra
Bay Willow

The native Bay Willow is sometimes found growing wild in northern areas of Britain and developed its name from the Norwegians who use it as a substitute for tender Laurus nobilis as its foliage is pleasantly aromatic when crushed.

A most beautiful, medium size tree with a rounded crown at maturity. Catkins are produced at the same time as the leaves in late spring. Very good for parks and wetland areas, it is both vigorous and vibrant. It is often overlooked by specifiers but is a lovely native tree that could be used more often. This tree is always a good one to throw into the mix on a plant identification competition as it tends to catch a lot of people out.

- Mature height: 7-12m
- Shape of mature tree
- Wet soils
- Native trees
- Eco impact rating: D

SAMBUCUS nigra Black Lace

Even though many wouldn't classify this as a tree we have chosen to refute this so we can include it in our listing. Given time this wonderful multi-stem shrub can grow to over three metres making it a tree and giving us a perfect excuse to grow it. Fantastic fern like dark purple to black leaves contrast beautifully with the clusters pink/white elder flowers in June.

Growing well on most free draining soils, this tough plant provides superb summer contrast within a garden or municipal border. It can be vigorously pruned each winter or left alone to become a small tree. It grows well in full sun but it doesn't perform so well in exposed windy locations.

- Mature height: 3-5m
- Multi-stem
- Garden trees
- Eco impact rating: C

SEQUOIADENDRON giganteum
Wellingtonia

The Wellingtonia is a native of California, where it grows incredibly tall on the western slopes of the Sierra Nevada and can live for more than 3000 years. It holds the distinction of being the largest living thing on Earth. Introduced into the UK in the early 1890s, it is quick to grow and there are a number of fine examples growing today including the collection at Wakehurst Place in Sussex. The USA national champion is in Sequoia National Park and stands at a staggering 92 metres tall by 36 metres wide.

Its deeply furrowed, red-brown bark is another of the hallmarks of this magnificent specimen, which is suited to large country estates and parklands. It thrives on most soils and romps away when young given enough water.

A large, evergreen conifer, it has a densely branched, conical habit while young, but the branches become more widely spaced and distinctly down swept as it ages.

Mature height: 17-22m | Shape of mature tree | Evergreen trees | Eco impact rating: A

SEQUOIADENDRON giganteum Glauca

First introduced in the early 1860s this stunning clone is narrower and generally smaller that it's green parent. Sequoias can grow very quickly when young and this blue clone is no exception. Its lovely foliage is a subtle blue and really stands out when compared to a green equivalent nearby.

It thrives on most free draining soils but needs plenty of moisture to get it established. Lifting Sequoia from the field to transplant them is a very hit and miss affair but once they are established in their containers they are much more straight forward. Best planted in either large gardens or parkland, this majestic conifer forms a symmetrical pyramidal shape at maturity.

| Mature height: 12-17m | Shape of mature tree | Evergreen trees | Eco impact rating: B |

SEQUOIA sempervirens
Coastal Redwood

The Coastal Redwood first came to Europe (St Petersburg) from California in 1840. You cannot help but be touched by the majesty of these trees as you head through California to Oregon on the coastal road into the Valley of the Giants. Even my young children were awestruck at the beauty and sheer magnitude of these trees!

A large, conical evergreen, it has a thick, fibrous, red-brown outer bark, which is soft and spongy to the touch. The slightly drooping branches bear two-ranked, linear-oblong leaves. A wonderful choice for large areas of parkland, they prefer the cleaner air of rural sites and plenty of water to get them going.

| Mature height: 17-22m | Shape of mature tree | Evergreen trees | Eco impact rating: A |

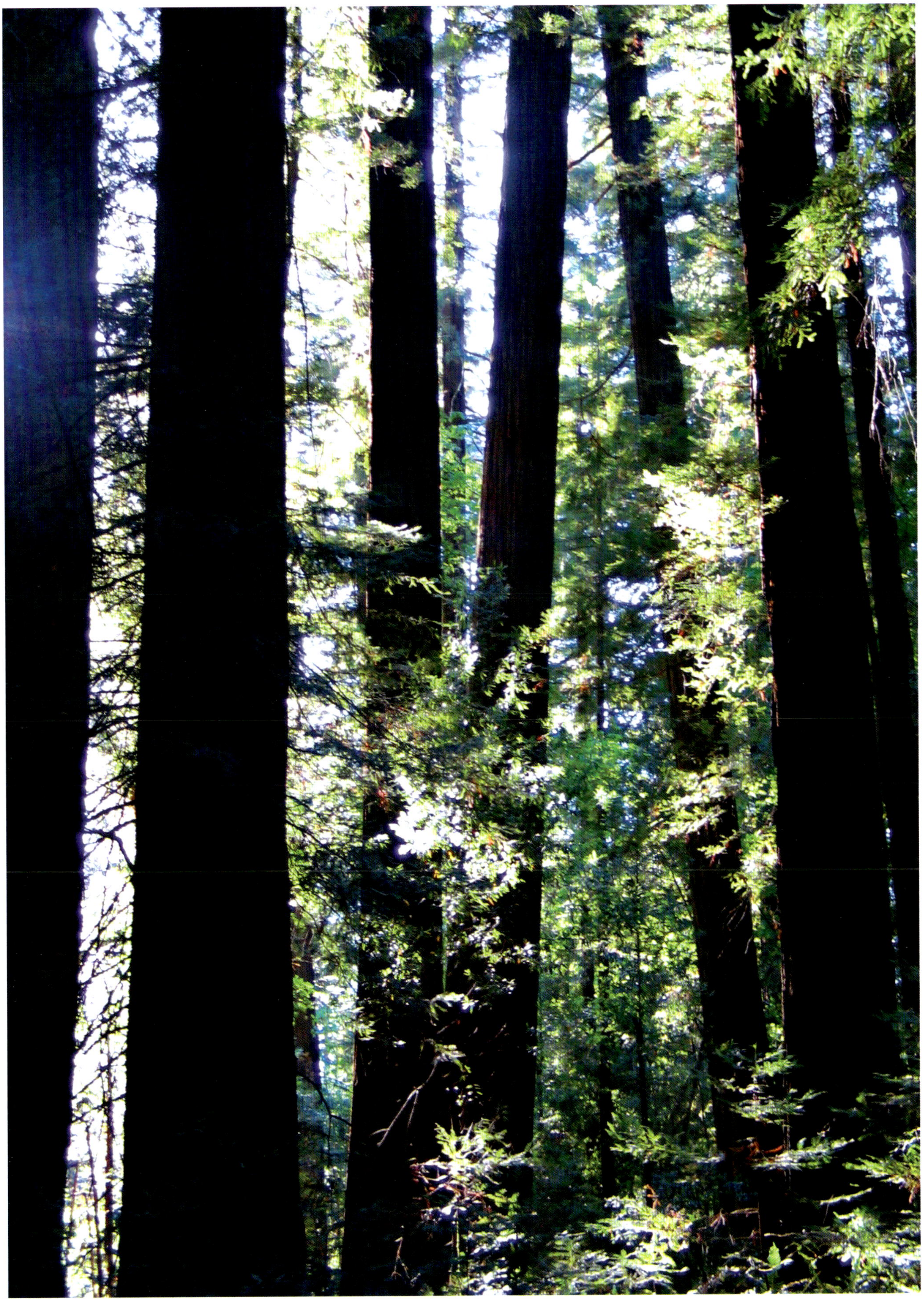

S

SOPHORA japonica
Japanese Pagoda Tree

Introduced in 1753 this heat loving tree won the Award of Garden Merit in 2002 but truthfully is only worth while in the warmer parts of Southern England on south facing sites. Despite its specific and common names, this medium to large, rounded tree is actually a native of China, although widely planted in Japan.

Once mature, panicles of yellow-white, pea like flowers are borne in August, followed by long grey seed pods in autumn. The clone 'Princeton Upright' is so like its parents to be of any consequence. Recently it's changed name to Styphnoiobium japonica, but I struggle to pronounce this so am keeping it listed as before!

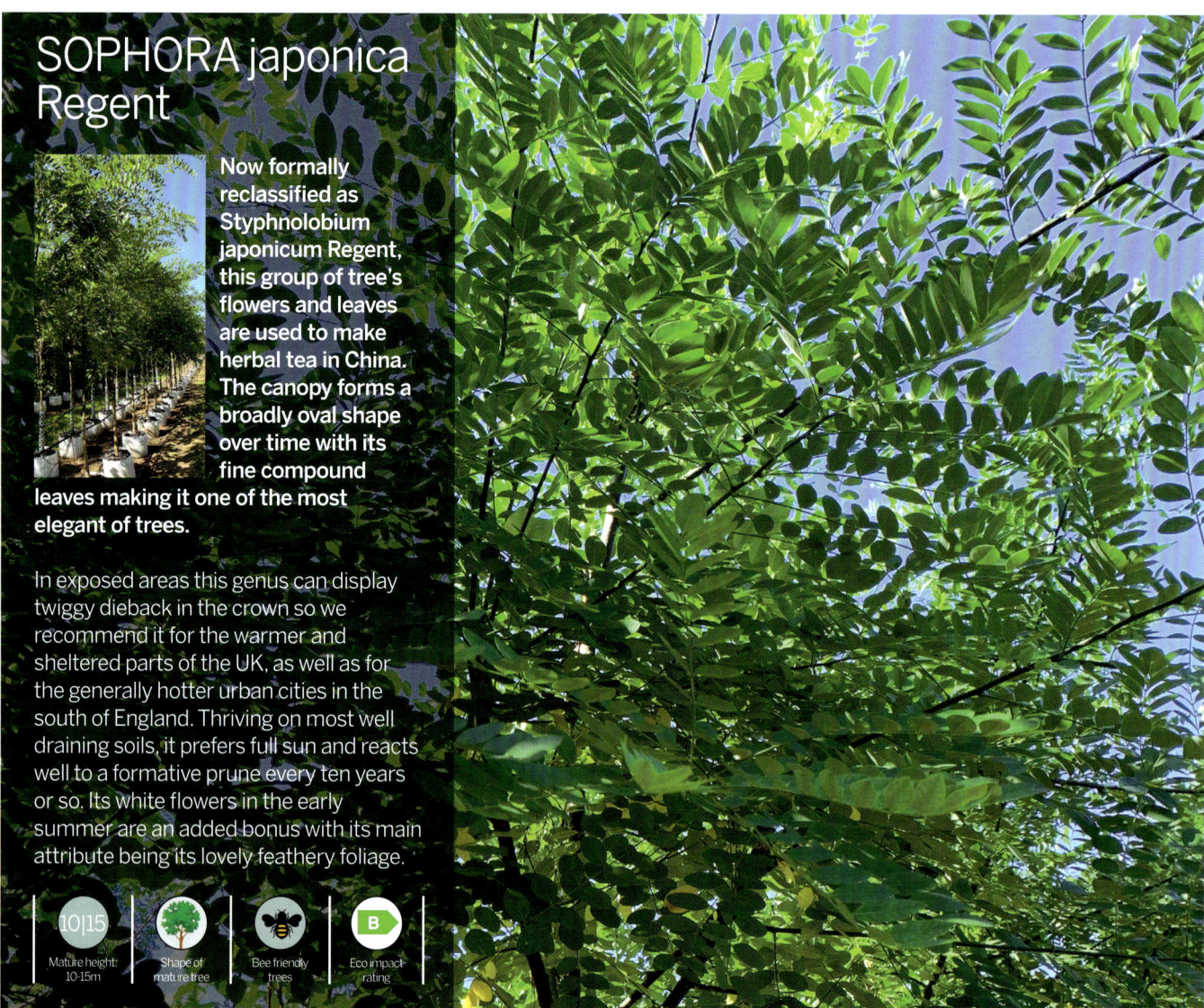

7|12	Shape of mature tree	Garden trees	B
Mature height: 7-12m			Eco impact rating

SOPHORA japonica Regent

Now formally reclassified as Styphnolobium japonicum Regent, this group of tree's flowers and leaves are used to make herbal tea in China. The canopy forms a broadly oval shape over time with its fine compound leaves making it one of the most elegant of trees.

In exposed areas this genus can display twiggy dieback in the crown so we recommend it for the warmer and sheltered parts of the UK, as well as for the generally hotter urban cities in the south of England. Thriving on most well draining soils, it prefers full sun and reacts well to a formative prune every ten years or so. Its white flowers in the early summer are an added bonus with its main attribute being its lovely feathery foliage.

10|15	Shape of mature tree	Bee friendly trees	B
Mature height: 10-15m			Eco impact rating

SORBUS aria Lutescens

This outstanding clone is most attractive in spring and won the Award of Merit in 1952 and the Award of Garden Merit in 2002. A very popular choice for urban gardens, it requires little maintenance and tolerates chalk soils.

The young leaves emerge silvery-white from purple shoots in spring, before hardening to grey-green in summer. This is a small, compact, rounded tree, producing white flowers in April and May and, in good years, orange-red, cherry like fruits in autumn. A very good choice for streets, gardens and parks.

- Mature height: 5-8m
- Shape of mature tree
- Garden trees
- Bee friendly trees
- Eco impact rating: C

SORBUS aria Magnifica

Introduced into general nursery cultivation in the early 1920s, this urban clone has ascending branches and is well equipped to cope with the rigours of reflected heat and light common to developed areas. Although it is not as stunning in the spring as 'Lutescens' it will keep going for longer in the late summer and autumn.

This medium size tree is conical when young, becoming broadly oval at maturity. The large leaves are dark green on top, with silver-white undersides. It has the white flowers and red fruits characteristic of the species, and is a good choice for parks, streets and avenues.

- Mature height: 7-12m
- Shape of mature tree
- Urban trees
- Bee friendly trees
- Eco impact rating: C

SORBUS aria Majestica

This well-known variety is also known as Decaisneana and won the Award of Garden Merit in 2002. In our opinion this clone is synonymous to 'Magnifica' for its overall effect and thrives on most soils including chalky ones.

A tree of medium height with a broad, dense, conical crown, it is of symmetrical form. It has notably large leaves and fruits, and is a splendid choice for parks, streets, gardens and avenues. For further Whitebeam types, refer to Sorbus latifolia and intermedia.

- Mature height: 7-12m
- Shape of mature tree
- Urban trees
- Bee friendly trees
- Eco impact rating: C

Telephone 01353 720 748 | www.barcham.co.uk | www.barchampro.co.uk

SORBUS x arnoldiana Schouten

A reliable, low-maintenance Mountain Ash clone that has proved to be a very popular choice for street planting in London. Unlike many rowan types, it tolerates the reflected heat and light thrown up by hard urban areas.

Budded onto Sorbus aucuparia rootstock, this is a great choice for streets, car parks and urban plantings, because it needs next to no maintenance. It is a small tree with a dense, oval crown, and it has most attractive, green, feathery foliage with golden yellow berries from August onwards.

7|12			C
Mature height: 7-12m	Shape of mature tree	Bee friendly trees	Eco impact rating

This old Barcham favourite has been a rarity over the past few years but we have recently found a good mother plant to take propagational material from so hope to have this tree available again by autumn 2024. We have planted out maidens in our field unit so the next crop for containers is well underway.

SORBUS aucuparia
Rowan / Mountain Ash

We grow this multi-stemmed rather than in standard form as they are not regular in shape and it is better to opt for a clone such as Rossica Major if uniformity is required.

Rowans prefer shorter day lengths and do not thrive in areas with excessive reflective heat and light such as paved and other hard surfaces. Best planted in parkland or verges, it is arguably our prettiest native tree.

| Mature height: 7-12m | Shape of mature tree | Multi-stem | Native trees | Bee friendly trees | Eco impact rating: C |

This wonderful native tree is often associated with Scotland. It certainly suits bird life as the profuse red autumn berries provide a lot of autumnal sustenance.

SORBUS aucuparia Asplenifolia

This Rowan clone is also sometimes referred to as 'Laciniata' and has proved very popular for both urban and rural planting. There are very few cut leaf trees and their addition into the landscape provides lovely foliage contrast.

Highly recommended for streets, verges and garden planting, this medium tree forms a broad pyramid if the leader is retained. It has finely cut, fern like foliage, which turns orange-red in autumn and the red berries are loved by wild birds. Rowans readily thrive on most soils including acid ones.

- Mature height: 7-12m
- Shape of mature tree
- Garden trees
- Bee friendly trees
- Eco impact rating: C

SORBUS aucuparia Cardinal Royal

Introduced by Michigan State University in America, their original plant stands at 12 metres tall by 6 metres wide. This makes it a very good Rowan clone for restricted areas and it is also tolerant of the reflected heat and light associated with urban planting.

The ascending branches of this medium size tree give it a columnar habit at maturity. White flowers in May are followed by red berries in September, which are readily consumed by wild birds. Very good for streets, urban plantings and rural gardens. It will thrive on most soils including acid ones. Out of all the aucuparia types I think this and Sheerwater Seedling are the best performers for the red berried urban clones. It's uniform habit makes it a great choice where minimum maintenance is required.

- Mature height: 7-12m
- Shape of mature tree
- Urban trees
- Bee friendly trees
- Eco impact rating: C

SORBUS aucuparia Cashmiriana

This very pretty garden tree has won a string of horticultural awards over the years including the Award of Garden Merit in 2002. Introduced into the UK in the mid 1930s from its native Kashmir, it remains the daintiest of trees but rarely seen as it is often decimated with Fire Blight, a fungal disorder that kills tree from the top down.

Soft pink flower clusters emerge in May and form good sized white berries by the autumn that often remain hanging on the tree well after the foliage has fallen. Finely serrated leaflets give the tree a charming effect in summer and these can turn from yellow to orange / red in the autumn. Best planted in half / dappled sun positions in lawns of borders.

- Mature height: 5-8m
- Shape of mature tree
- Urban trees
- Bee friendly trees
- Eco impact rating: C

SORBUS aucuparia Edulis

The edible berries of this Mountain Ash can be used to make Rowan jelly. Thought to have been introduced in the very early 1800s, it is sometimes also classified under the varietal names 'Moravica' or 'Dulcis'.

A vigorous and very hardy tree, which is of medium size and broadly oval at maturity. It has larger leaves than the species – and large berries too. A good choice for gardens and urban areas, it thrives on most soils.

| 7\|12 Mature height: 7-12m | Shape of mature tree | Garden trees | Bee friendly trees | C Eco impact rating |

SORBUS aucuparia Golden Wonder

Sometimes classified under the Sorbus arnoldiana group this stocky vigorous rowan makes a fine tree that requires little maintenance. Its lush leaves can turn to a decent orange / red in the autumn before falling.

This pyramidal grower is a good choice for verges, avenues and streets. It makes a medium size, large leaved tree, which produces big bunches of golden yellow fruits from late summer onwards. It thrives on most soils but like all rowans will prefer it slightly acid.

In our opinion this is the best golden berried clone available as it doesn't suffer from the debilitating Fire Blight disease that the variety Joseph Rock can suffer badly from.

| 7\|12 Mature height: 7-12m | Shape of mature tree | Urban trees | Bee friendly trees | C Eco impact rating |

SORBUS aucuparia Joseph Rock

One of the prettiest of rowans it is both a winner of the First-Class Certificate in 1962 and the Award of Merit in 1950. However, it is also the one most susceptible to fire blight which can disfigure the tree to the point of complete demise.

Small narrow green leaflets turn a fantastic red in the autumn and provide a stunning contrast to the creamy yellow berries. A small tree with ascending branches, ideal for gardens. It derives from the Chinese species, has red leaf buds and a dainty overall effect. It is ideal for small gardens and tolerant of most soils.

5|8	Shape of mature tree	Bee friendly trees	C Eco impact rating
Mature height: 5-8m			

SORBUS aucuparia Rossica Major

As trees derived from seed grown Sorbus aucuparia are genetically unique they can be quite variable in habit so if it is uniformity you are after this clone fits the bill. Otherwise it does everything you would expect of our native rowan and requires little or no maintenance.

A strong and fast growing tree, Rossica Major forms a broadly oval crown. Its dark green leaves are attached by red stalks, and it bears its dark red berries from August onwards. A good choice for both urban areas, and rural gardens.

7|12	Shape of mature tree	Urban trees	Bee friendly trees	C Eco impact rating
Mature height: 7-12m				

SORBUS aucuparia Sheerwater Seedling

Along with the clone 'Cardinal Royal' this variety represents the best choice for urban planting where space is restricted. A winner of the Award of garden Merit in 2002, this well known tree has proven to be popular for a number of years.

This medium size, oval tree will also tolerate semi-shade. It thrives on most soils and its ascending branches and dominant leader makes it a tree requiring little maintenance. White flowers are followed by bird friendly red berries by September and the green leaves turn a decent yellow / orange in the autumn.

There is a marked difference on how Rowan types perform in the UK, the further north they are planted the better they are. However, Sheerwater Seedling is a good choice for southern Britain as well as is more tolerant of the occasional hot spell that can come along and its maintenance free habit makes it an ideal prospect for a small urban garden or narrow urban verge.

Mature height: 7-12m | Shape of mature tree | Urban trees | Bee friendly trees | Eco impact rating: C

SORBUS aucuparia Vilmorinii

Discovered by Abbe Delavay and introduced in 1889, this dainty beauty originates from Western China. It makes a lovely little tree requiring little maintenance and giving much enjoyment.

The leaves are dark green and fern-like, turning a red purple in the autumn. Profuse berries hang in drooping clusters, dark red at first then fading to a pink white. Unfortunately, this small tree, like Joseph Rock, is also susceptible to fire blight and is extremely rare to see surviving through to large sizes let alone maturity.

Mature height: 5-8m | Shape of mature tree | Garden trees | Eco impact rating: C

SORBUS commixta Embley
Chinese Scarlet Rowan

Some list this as 'Embley' and some as 'commixta' but we hedge our bets and classify it as one as there is no discernable difference to the vast majority. Originating from Korea and Japan, it was introduced in the early 1880s and won the Award of Merit in 1979.

This small tree of broadly columnar habit is tolerant of most soils and makes a fine choice for garden planting. In autumn its glorious foliage and bright red berries makes it stand out from the rest. Its young trunk is light brown and speckled. Fluffy bunches of small white flowers are produced in the spring.

Mature height: 5-8m | Shape of mature tree | Bee friendly trees | Eco impact rating: C

SORBUS commixta Olympic Flame

Also known as 'dodong' this rowan originates from Japan. Its glossy green foliage is vibrant throughout the growing season and this turns to orange and red in the autumn. Dark orange berries are produced from clusters of white spring flowers by late summer.

Its young trunk is punctuated by lenticels and it thrives on most free draining soils but like all rowan types does not tolerate excessive reflective heat and light from hard areas surrounding it. Selected from seed by a Swedish botanist in 1976, this rowan looks so exotic that it is now firmly established as a favourite Europe wide.

Mature height: 5-8m | Shape of mature tree | Garden trees | Bee friendly trees | Eco impact rating: C

SORBUS discolor

Introduced from its native Northern China in the mid 1880s this clone is often lumped in together with 'Commixta' even though the berry colour is different. One of the earliest rowans to flower in the spring, it makes a lovely garden tree that requires little maintenance.

Creamy-yellow fruits are borne on red stalks by late summer in the manner of 'Joseph Rock' and it forms an open crown made up from ascending branches. It thrives on most soils although like most rowans it will prefer it slightly acid.

- Mature height: 5-8m
- Shape of mature tree
- Garden trees
- Bee friendly trees
- Eco impact rating: C

SORBUS hupehensis

Discovered by Ernest Wilson and introduced from its native western China in 1910, this lovely rowan stands out by its flat blue tinged leaves and light brown trunk. It won the Award of Garden Merit in 2002 and forms a compact broadly oval crown at maturity, but alas can also be susceptible to Fire Blight.

Splendid white berries produced in large clusters and stunning red autumn colour also typifies this small low maintenance tree which thrives on most soils and can tolerate the rigours of the urban environment. Being white, the berries are the last to be taken by birds, so can remain on the tree way past Christmas.

- Mature height: 5-8m
- Shape of mature tree
- Garden trees
- Bee friendly trees
- Eco impact rating: D

SORBUS incana

Thought to have been bred at the Botanical Gardens of Copenhagen, this tough compact tree is incredibly hardy, thriving as an urban tree all over Scandinavia. It rarely flowers and when it does set fruit the berries are orange / red. The foliage puts this tree into the Whitebeam family and its bushy stubby growth needs very little maintenance over its lifespan.

Thriving in most free draining soils it is happy in full sun or semi shade. This is a particularly good prospect for urban planting and gardens in the North of England or Scotland, especially where space is restricted. Its bright green summer leaves turn yellow in autumn. At maturity, its dense crown is broadly oval.

- Mature height: 5-8m
- Shape of mature tree
- Urban trees
- Bee friendly trees
- Eco impact rating: C

SORBUS intermedia
Swedish Whitebeam

The Swedish Whitebeam is widely planted as a street tree in northern Europe. It is a tough tree that can even thrive within view of the coast. Unlike the closely related Sorbus aria clones it is more tolerant of reflected heat and light bouncing of hard areas on urban sites.

A medium size tree with a well formed, rounded crown, its single, dark green leaves have silver-grey undersides. White flowers in May give way to orange-red fruits, produced in small bunches. It is wind resistant and tolerant of calcareous soils and air pollution, making this a really useful candidate for urban planting. We recommend it for streets and avenues.

- Mature height: 7-12m
- Shape of mature tree
- Coastal sites
- Bee friendly trees
- Eco impact rating: C

SORBUS intermedia Brouwers

This Swedish Whitebeam clone has a more pyramidal crown than the species and is more commonly grown by nurseries as the catchall for Sorbus intermedia. Clonal variations can be very similar to their parents but crucially offer a far greater degree of uniformity.

A medium size tree with a conical crown, its single, dark green leaves have silver-grey undersides. White flowers in May produce orange-red fruits. It is wind resistant and tolerant of calcareous soils and air pollution, making this a really tough tree. It will thrive in even the harshest conditions including near the coast.

- Mature height: 7-12m
- Shape of mature tree
- Coastal sites
- Bee friendly trees
- Eco impact rating: C

SORBUS latifolia Henk Vink

A hybrid derived from Sorbus torminalis and Sorbus aria this is a Dutch clone raised for its qualities to thrive within the urban environment. A native of Portugal through to Germany, it is a worthy alternative to the more commonly used Sorbus aria clones.

Round headed and tough, this versatile tree is ideal for streets, verges or parks. White flowers are followed by red berries in the autumn. Its leaves are grey / green and silvery grey beneath to provide a pleasing contrast in windy conditions.

Mature height: 7-12m | Shape of mature tree | Coastal sites | Eco impact rating: C

SORBUS latifolia Atrovirens
Service Tree of Fontainebleau

An improved clone of the hybrid between Sorbus torminalis and aria. Native of Europe, it is seldom used due to it not being known.

Glossy lobed green leaves, grey beneath, are supported by an ascending branch network that broadens out at maturity to become rounded. White flowers in spring form orange fruits that are borne in small bunches. It is a tough tree, withstanding strong winds and coping well with urban conditions. Excellent for verge or street planting.

Mature height: 7-12m | Shape of mature tree | Coastal sites | Bee friendly trees | Eco impact rating: C

S

SORBUS x thuringiaca Fastigiata

Sometimes referred to as Sorbus hybrida, this highly useful urban tree retains the prettiness of Sorbus aucuparia and the toughness of Sorbus aria, its parents. A winner of the Award of Merit in 1924, this tree can get to beyond 10 metres if given the space. The best examples I have seen of this tree are at Calderstones Park in Liverpool, where they have been left long enough, and been given the space to express themselves.

This small tree is columnar when young, but becomes broadly oval as it matures. It is really tough and is well suited to urban plantings, withstanding air pollution very well. It is fine as a street tree and in restricted areas. Clusters of white flowers in spring are followed by bunches of red berries by September. The green/grey foliage can turn a magnificent orange in the autumn. Some recognise this as fastigiate Sorbus intermedia and overlook this clone because of its indigestible name.

- Mature height: 7-12m
- Shape of mature tree
- Urban trees
- Bee friendly trees
- Eco impact rating: D

SORBUS torminalis
Wild Service Tree

The fruits of the Wild Service Tree, which are very sharp but edible when over-ripe, used to be sold as "chequers" in southern England, giving rise to its alternative name of Chequer Tree and the corresponding numbers of pubs taking the same title. The name 'Chequer' is also used to describe the pattern of its bark.

This medium native tree is columnar when young but becomes more rounded as it ages. Its dark brown, fissured bark bears grey scales. Perfect for woodlands, it thrives best under the dappled shade of others and does not react favourably to hot urban areas prone to reflected heat and light. Its attractive green lobed leaves turn a lovely orange / yellow in autumn.

- Mature height: 7-12m
- Shape of mature tree
- Native trees
- Eco impact rating: C

STYRAX japonicus June Snow

This stunning little tree is a real show stopper in June when its mass of single white bell shaped flowers smother the canopy. Their sweet smelling fragrance is very stong on still days. Thriving on most free draining but moisture retentive soils, this is a great tree for a small garden. Its drooping oval fruits are another decorative feature.

We grow this tree as a branched bush with a main supporting trunk. Its green glossy leaves turn to yellow in the autumn. Developed in Holland in the mid 1990's this superb tree has an ascending habit so is ideal where space is at a premium.

5|7	Shape of mature tree	Bee friendly trees	Eco impact rating
Mature height: 5-7m			D

SYRINGA vulgaris cultivars

There are reportedly over 900 varieties of Syringa vulgaris cultivars with many similar to each other but we major on just the four which make fine small multi stem trees. Broad oval deep green leaves are produced by buds on the extremity of the stiffly ascending branch network.

They thrive on most fee draining soils and like full sun to dappled shade. Great for gardens and municipal parks, they are easy to maintain and very reliable. We favour the four classic proven varieties listed below.

- Mature height: 3-5m
- Multi-stem
- Flowering trees
- Bee friendly trees
- Eco impact rating: D

SYRINGA vulgaris Alice Harding
First bought to market way back in 1938, this beautiful white flowering Lilac has fragrant flowers by the end of May and into June.

SYRINGA vulgaris Madame Lemoine
Dating back to 1890, this double white flowering Lilac blooms in mid to late May and prefers a fertile neutral to alkaline soil.

SYRINGA vulgaris Ludwig Spath
Bred by the famous Spath nuersery in Berlin, Germany, in 1883. Marvellous blue / purple scented flowers are borne on large upright spires in May / June.

SYRINGA vulgaris Ruhm von Horstenstein
Introduced from Germany in 1928, this classic variety blooms with scented purple / blue flowers in May. A vigorous grower, perfect for tougher environments.

TAMARIX aestivalis

A native of Europe, Asia and North Africa, this ancient looking tree is incredibly useful in exposed windy areas and will thrive on pretty much any soil apart from shallow chalk. Mostly supplied as bushes, we grow our Tamarix as full standards.

A small genus well suited to coastal locations, tolerating salt laden winds and spray. This variety is virtually identical to Tamarix tetrandra but flowers about a month later, so by a mixed planting of both varieties you can look forward to about six weeks of continuous flower.

- Mature height: 5-8m
- Shape of mature tree
- Coastal sites
- Eco impact rating: C

TAMARIX africana

This lovely foliage tree has whispy grey / bluish green foliage in the summer which brings a unique texture to a garden. Its tiny but numerous soft pink flowers in the spring are a very attractive feature. Tamarix is a very tough tree, even tolerating coastal exposure. Its rounded canopy can be easily shaped by regular pruning.

Thriving on most well drained soils, it is a very wind resistant tree and athough rarely seen inland it makes a fine garden tree.

- Mature height: 5-8m
- Shape of mature tree
- Flowering trees
- Bee friendly trees
- Urban trees
- Coastal sites
- Eco impact rating: C

TAMARIX gallica

This coastal specialist originally from South West Europe has now naturalised along many miles of the English coastline. A great tree to tolerate and diffuse wind.

Better known as a shrub, we grow it as a full standard with a clear stem of 1.8m, best suited for coastal towns or specimen planting inland. Dark brown branches support vivid green foliage and pink fluffy flowers in summer that are borne from new season's wood. Particularly useful on saline soils.

Mature height: 5-8m	Shape of mature tree	Flowering trees	Coastal sites	Eco impact rating: C

TAMARIX tetrandra

The Tamarisk is so evocative of old fashioned, Mediterranean fishing villages. Introduced way back in 1821, this won the Award of Garden Merit in 2002. Although primarily thought of as a coastal plant, it can make a fine garden tree inland, so long as it is not planted on shallow chalk.

We offer this as a small standard tree with a rounded crown. Its light pink flowers are freely produced in May / June. A tough subject, which does well in light, sandy soils. Is very good for coastal locations and is also tolerant of exposed, windy sites.

Mature height: 5-8m	Shape of mature tree	Coastal sites	Eco impact rating: C

TAXODIUM distichum
Swamp Cypress

The Swamp Cypress is the best conifer for wet soils. A native of the Florida Everglades, it is thought of as a pyramidal grower but interestingly the national champion in the USA is 28 metres tall by 29 metres wide suggesting seed variability. Introduced in the early 1640s by John Tradescant it won the updated Award of Garden Merit in 2002.

This large, deciduous, pyramidal conifer has fibrous, brown bark and small, round cones, which are purple when young. It does best in wet soils, and needs plenty of moisture in its first year after planting if it is to succeed. A good choice for parks and often confused with Metasequoia until seen close together.

Foliage is always late to appear in the spring, particularly after planting, but it generally starts growing at full pelt from July onwards.

Taxodium is a wonderful choice to plant near a lake as its autumn display is reflected in the water to double its impact. Its fine leaflets are less prone to silt up ponds in the autumn when compared to larger leaved deciduous trees.

17|22			B
Mature height: 17-22m.	Shape of mature tree	Wet soils	Eco impact rating

TAXUS baccata
English Yew

The native English Yew is a tree of many mystical and religious associations. Incredibly long lived, the oldest reported is in Llangernyw, Wales, and is estimated to be 4000 years old with a circumference of 16 metres. The trees capacity for regeneration is outstanding; especially considering it is a conifer.

A medium tree of conical appearance, its hard wood can support this evergreen to a great age. Often used for hedging, it also makes a fine specimen tree. Very good for parks and gardens. All parts of the tree are poisonous. It can grow on highly calcareous or highly acidic soils, if there is good drainage.

| Mature height: 5-8m | Shape of mature tree | Evergreen trees | Native trees | Eco impact rating: B |

TAXUS baccata Fastigiata
Irish Yew

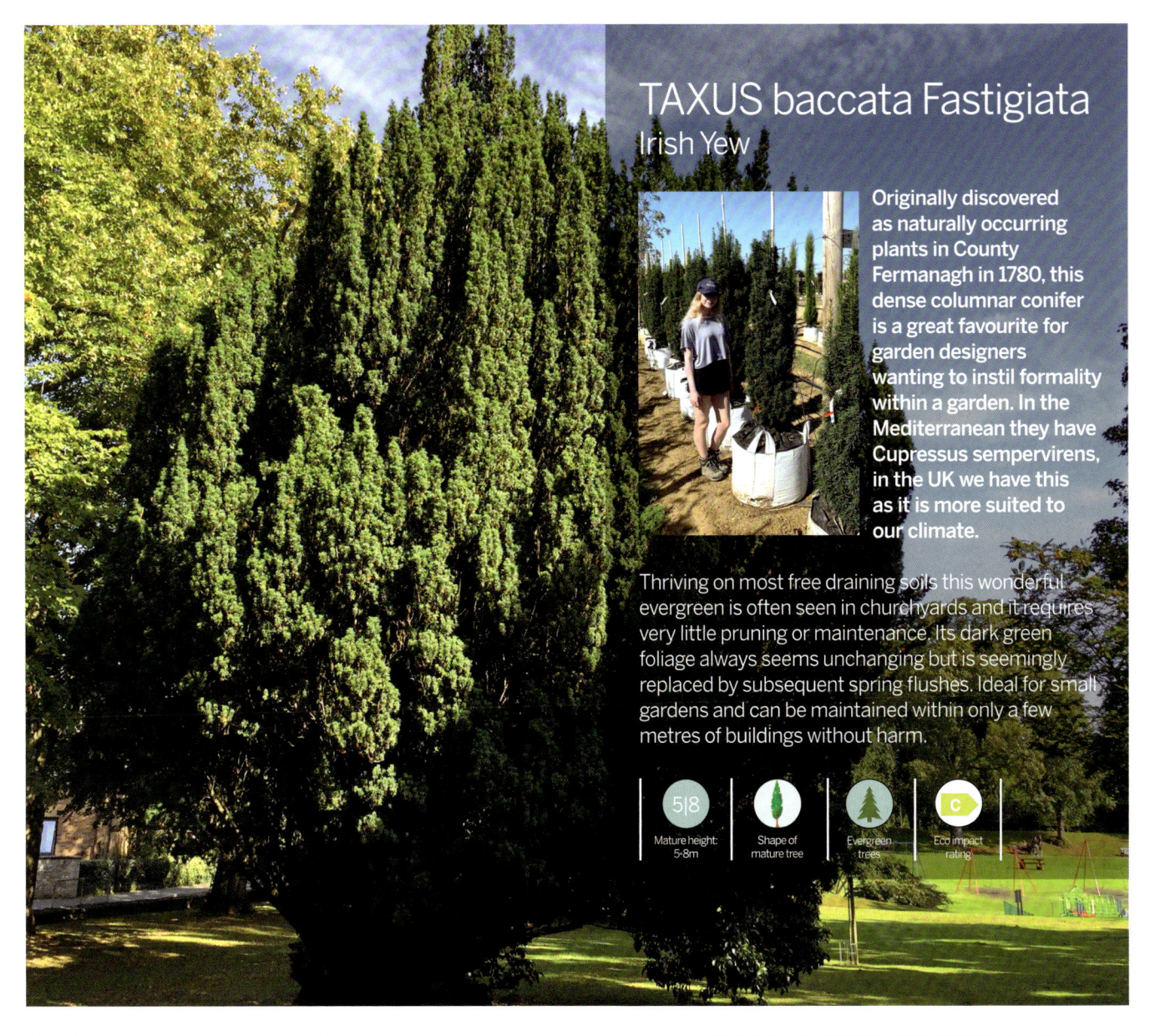

Originally discovered as naturally occurring plants in County Fermanagh in 1780, this dense columnar conifer is a great favourite for garden designers wanting to instil formality within a garden. In the Mediterranean they have Cupressus sempervirens, in the UK we have this as it is more suited to our climate.

Thriving on most free draining soils this wonderful evergreen is often seen in churchyards and it requires very little pruning or maintenance. Its dark green foliage always seems unchanging but is seemingly replaced by subsequent spring flushes. Ideal for small gardens and can be maintained within only a few metres of buildings without harm.

- Mature height: 5-8m
- Shape of mature tree
- Evergreen trees
- Eco impact rating: C

TAXUS baccata Fastigiata Aurea
Golden Irish Yew

A male form discovered later than its female green counterpart back in the 1880s. It forms a dense columnar tree at maturity with gold tipped margined leaves and stiffly ascending branches. Not that it needs much maintenance but Yew is a very adaptable tree to handle as unlike other conifers its shape and size can be reinstated by severe pruning back into old wood in early spring.

It thrives on most free draining soils and is a firm favourite for small gardens up and down the UK where it is planted in multiples when a structured formality is required. The spring flush of foliage is a lighter yellow than its appearance for the rest of the year and it can tolerate full sun or partial shade.

- Mature height: 5-8m
- Shape of mature tree
- Evergreen trees
- Eco impact rating: C

THUJA plicata Atrovirens

A form of the Western Red Cedar. It is an important timber tree in its native North America, although it is more commonly used as a hedging conifer in the UK. The national champion in the States is over 60 metres tall by 18 metres wide. Introduced in the mid 1870s, it won the Award of Garden Merit in 2002.

This large, evergreen conifer does best on wet soils and will tolerate shade. Of pyramidal form if grown as a specimen tree, it is also a fine subject for hedging. In our view superior to Leyland Cypress, but slower growing. Good for parks and gardens, its shiny, green foliage smells of pineapple when crushed.

- Mature height: 17-22m
- Shape of mature tree
- Hedging trees
- Evergreen trees
- Eco impact rating: B

TILIA americana Redmond

This cultivar of the American Lime is of garden origin, and came from Plumfield Nurseries Nebraska, USA, in 1927. It was originally listed under Tilia euchlora but is distinctly different. It is still little known and used in the UK but should not be overlooked.

A pyramidal tree of medium size, this cultivar is barely sensitive to aphids and the associated "dripping", which makes it an ideal lime for street and avenue plantings. The super large leaves, which are a lighter green than those of the species, turn pale yellow in autumn.

Mature height: 12-17m | Shape of mature tree | Avenue trees | Eco impact rating: A

TILIA americana American Sentry

Called 'McKSentry' by American growers to commemorate its breeders, Mackay nurseries in Wisconsin. Its pyramidal habit develops about half as wide as it is high making this a very popular urban tree in the USA. It's tough and has large green leaves that turn to yellow in the autumn. Young stems are a silver grey and sweetly scented flowers are borne in the spring.

This tree has a great symmetry about it so pruning is seldom necessary. It thrives best in full sun for at least six hours of the day and performs well on most free draining soils either side of neutral. Tilia americana was first introduced into the UK in 1752 but this much more recent selection is the one to go for if space is restricted or uniformity is required.

Mature height: 12-17m | Shape of mature tree | Urban trees | Eco impact rating: A

This large tree has a broadly oval crown, with small, heart shaped leaves, which are dark green on top and pale green beneath. Its creamy white flowers are produced in July.

TILIA cordata
Small-Leaved Lime

This well-known native tree won the Award of Garden Merit in 2002 and remains a popular choice within our urban and rural landscapes. It is a good host to mistletoe for the more romantically inclined of you.

It is a relatively sedate grower, is good for avenues and parks, and bears air pollution very well. Like most Lime, it is also a fine candidate for pollarding or pleaching. The trade now widely distributes clonal variations of this tree such as 'Bohlje', 'Erecta', 'Greenspire', and 'Roelvo' which are too close to call apart from the native parent apart at maturity.

- Mature height: 17-22m
- Shape of mature tree
- Native trees
- Eco impact rating: A

This well behaved small leaved lime forms a broadly oval crown. We planted one in a park in Ely about 15 years ago and it has a lovely ascending structure which routinely flowers well in the early summer.

TILIA cordata Erecta

Mature height: 12-17m | Shape of mature tree | Urban trees | Eco impact rating: A

Also referred to as Tilia cordata Select or Tilia cordata Bohlje, this well used and tested clone was first marketed in the 1800s and intially bred in Germany.

It is a good tree for bees and native wildlife in gereral. Thriving on most well draining soils, it is an ideal tough urban tree and has the uniformity to make a fine avenue.

TILIA cordata Greenspire

This American clone derived from the cultivar 'Euclid'. A selection from a Boston Park, it has been in cultivation in the UK since the early 1960s. A winner of the Award of Garden Merit in 2002, it is a very popular choice for urban planting where its uniformity is preferred over the native Tilia cordata.

It maintains a strong leader and well branched crown through to maturity, which distinguishes it over other selections, as the premier clone of Tilia cordata. It thrives well on most soils and copes readily with harsh urban environments given enough soil to exploit. At maturity I would liken it to a great example of Tilia cordata at the same size but with Greenspire you get this every time. Clonal selections give uniformity whereas seed grown trees have a significant degree of genetic variation.

- Mature height: 12-17m
- Shape of mature tree
- Avenue trees
- Bee friendly trees
- Eco impact rating: A

TILIA cordata x mongolica Harvest Gold

This exciting new tree to our range combines the toughness of Tilia cordata with the daintiness of Tilia mongolica. Developed in Manitoba, Canada, it makes an excellent avenue tree with spectacular yellow autumn colour. As it matures the bark exfoliates to give a pleasing patchwork effect. This clone is now used extensively in the States and is already proving its worth as an attractive and durable urban and rural tree.

A tough grower, it forms a lovely oval and ascending crown that broadens with age. From what we have seen it is a very clean tree, producing little flower or fruit, as well as importantly not attracting aphids. We started lining this clone out in our fields in 2008 from young plant material sourced direct from a specialist grower in the States. This new introduction for the UK market is now available from Barcham in our 45 litre Light Pots at 10-12cm & 12-14cm girth.

- Mature height: 12-17m
- Shape of mature tree
- Urban trees
- Eco impact rating: A

TILIA cordata Rancho

This often-overlooked variety is of lesser overall stature than 'Greenspire' but it can be considered neater, with the added bonus of a great and fragrant floral display in early summer. Its branch angles are mechanically strong. It was introduced into the UK in the early 1960s.

Ideal for urban plantings, streets and avenues, this medium tree has a dense, conical habit, and has very shiny, small leaves. Its compact and uniform growing qualities make it ideal for avenue planting, but it is not as well known as Greenspire so rarely gets specified. We rate this clone very highly and it thrives on most soils.

- Mature height: 12-17m
- Shape of mature tree
- Bee friendly trees
- Eco impact rating: A

TILIA cordata Winter Orange

This exiting new variety was found as a seedling in the Netherlands in the 1970s. Whenever we show this tree it is widely appreciated and we never seem to have enough to go around! An ideal prospect for garden pleaching, its orange stems are most unusual.

A medium to large tree with a broadly oval crown, it is distinguished by its red buds and orange shoots in winter. Its white, sweetly scented flowers appear in July. It is a good choice for avenues and tolerates the rigours of the urban environment.

Mature height: 12-17m | Shape of mature tree | Bee friendly trees | Eco impact rating: A

TILIA x euchlora
Caucasian Lime

The result of a cross between Tilia cordata and Tilia dasystyla, this ever popular lime can grow as broad as it is tall, so is often given the wrong sites to grow on. Its flowers can have a narcotic effect on bees, which can sometimes be found on the ground near a tree. Redeemingly, it is free of aphids, so an ideal tree for pleaching or boxing in hard areas.

This Lime reacts well to pollarding, which is a good way of controlling its broadly pendulous habit.

Mature height: 12-17m | Shape of mature tree | Urban trees | Eco impact rating: A

It is a medium to large tree, and as aphids are not attracted to its dark green foliage, the associated "stickiness" is not a problem. Good for wide verges, parks, avenues and urban plantings.

TILIA x europaea
Common Lime

Once the most frequently planted Lime, this is a very long lived tree and commonly planted in central Europe as an urban tree. It is a hybrid between Tilia cordata and Tilia platyphyllos and has been known to reach over 50 metres tall, like the specimen at Duncombe Park in Yorkshire.

A large and impressive, broadly oval shaped tree which is widely used for avenue plantings. It is recognisable by its dense suckering, which forms burrs on the trunk. Its large lush leaves can attract aphids so care should be taken not to plant in hard areas, where the resulting sooty mould will be a problem.

- Mature height: 17-22m
- Shape of mature tree
- Avenue trees
- Eco impact rating: A

TILIA x europaea Pallida
Kaiser Linden

The Kaiser Linden is the Lime of the famous Unter den Linden in Berlin and has been highly rated for many years. It is quick to grow and gives a uniform alternative against seed grown Common Lime that makes it perfect for large avenues.

A large tree of pyramidal form, its pale green leaves have attractive, green-yellow undersides. It thrives pretty much anywhere and is tolerant of most soils. Quick to grow and establish, this is one of our most popular selling limes but as with its parents, care should be taken to avoid hard areas that could be affected by aphid drip.

- Mature height: 17-22m
- Shape of mature tree
- Bee friendly trees
- Eco impact rating: A

TILIA henryana

This rarely seen Lime was discovered in China in 1888 by Augustine Henry. It was introduced into the UK in 1901 by Ernest Wilson and for some reason is still heavily under grown. We are bucking this trend and have been bulking up production numbers but have noticed that in young plants the growth tips can be frost sensitive, so we advise sheltered sites for final placement.

Its ovate leaves are downy to the touch on both sides and edged with bristle-like teeth akin to the outer edges of a Venus Fly Trap. A wonderfully ornamental lime, it flowers in autumn, and is a good choice for south facing parks and gardens within the milder parts of the UK.

- Mature height: 7-12m
- Shape of mature tree
- Garden trees
- Bee friendly trees
- Eco impact rating: C

TILIA mongolica
Mongolian Lime

The Mongolian Lime was introduced from its homeland in the early 1880s. It is both aphid resistant and most unlike the general look of the rest of the Tilia family. Recent plantings in London have been most encouraging and suggest this has great potential for an urban tree in the UK.

This small tree with a rounded habit has all the durability of Lime but is of a size which makes it ideal as a street tree. It has small, serrated, glossy, green leaves, which are similar to those of ivy. A real little beauty requiring little maintenance. It turns to a clear and delicate yellow in autumn and as the leaves are so small for a Lime in the first place, there is not much leaf litter to contend with for an urban environment.

- Mature height: 7-12m
- Shape of mature tree
- Urban trees
- Eco impact rating: C

TILIA platyphyllos
Broad-Leaved Lime

The Broad-leaved Lime is a native of Britain. A winner of the First Class Certificate in 1892, it flowers in June / July and is very tolerant of pruning. It is a compact and stocky tree, the luscious foliage always gives it a healthy demeanour. The clonal selection 'Delft' is a European clone that forms a more pyramidal crown at maturity and could be used where uniformity is required.

A large, fast growing tree with a roughly fissured bark, which remains relatively free of suckers.

This is a good subject for parks and estates, and is also useful for avenue planting. The leaves are almost circular and dark green. It is well suited to urban conditions but thrives best in our countryside.

Mature height: 17-22m | Shape of mature tree | Native trees | Eco impact rating: A

TILIA platyphyllos Delft

This clonal selection of Broad Leaved Lime produces a nicely compact and ascending cown at maturity to form a broadly oval shape. Its floral display of yellow flowers in June and July is particularly favourable for bees. Tilia cordata types are tolerant of tough urban conditions but Tilia platyphyllos cultivars are best planted in green areas away from refected heat and light.

Thiving on most well drained soils, this tidy clone makes a great avenue tree for wide sweeping driveways or as a solitary parkland specimen. As a derivative of our native species, it fits well within the UK landscape.

- Mature height: 17-22m
- Shape of mature tree
- Flowering trees
- Bee friendly trees
- Urban trees
- Eco impact rating: A

TILIA platyphyllos Rubra
Red-twigged Lime

The Red-twigged Lime is a slow grower than its parent and its fresh red twiggy growth is particularly striking when used for pleaching. It has a more ascending habit that the species and it won the Award of Garden Merit in 2002.

This reasonably columnar, medium to large tree is a great choice for avenue planting and areas which suffer from air pollution. Its young shoots are a bright brown-red, and look particularly effective in late winter. It makes a fine choice for a rural landscape and will thrive on most soils given enough room.

- Mature height: 17-22m
- Shape of mature tree
- Bee friendly trees
- Eco impact rating: A

TILIA tomentosa
Silver Lime

The Silver Lime is a handsome tree, but with a rather variable habit. Introduced in 1767 from its native South Eastern Europe, its flowers can be toxic to bees so this should be considered if planting in a rural setting.

A large tree of generally pyramidal habit, the Silver Lime has the advantages of being resistant to both aphids and drought. It grows well in urban areas, although it requires plenty of space. Its dark green leaves have silver-white undersides, creating a beautiful effect when rustled by the breeze. Good for avenues and parks, it will also stand up well to salt-laden coastal winds.

| 17\|22 | Shape of | Urban | Eco impact |
| Mature height: 17-22m | mature tree | trees | rating A |

TILIA tomentosa Brabant

This Dutch clonal selection of Silver Lime was introduced into the UK in the early 1970s and won the Award of Garden Merit in 2002. It is rightly considered to be an excellent urban tree, coping with the rigours of city environments very well. The Belgium variety, 'Doornik' has very similar attributes.

Brabant has a more regularly pyramidal form than the species but is just as large. It is very versatile, being suitable for urban settings, avenues, verges and parks. The striking silver undersides of its foliage makes it a wonderful tree for providing contrast within a landscape and the leaves turn a glorious yellow before falling in the autumn.

| 17\|22 | Shape of | Urban | Eco impact |
| Mature height: 17-22m | mature tree | trees | rating A |

TILIA petiolaris
Weeping Silver Lime

The Weeping Silver Lime is perhaps the most graceful of all large, weeping trees. Often referred to as Tilia tomentosa Petiolaris it has been recently separated to its own species but in my opinion, this is too close to call so doesn't really matter anyway. There is a particularly good specimen to be seen at The RHS garden at Wisley.

Introduced in the early 1840s it won the Award of Garden Merit in 2002. It is fast growing and aphid resistant and is an excellent subject for parks. The flowers are richly scented but narcotic to bees, while its dark green leaves have white, felt-like undersides. Autumn colour is a striking and rich yellow. It thrives on most soils.

- Mature height: 17-22m
- Shape of mature tree
- Parkland trees
- Bee friendly trees
- Eco impact rating: A

TRACHYCARPUS fortunei
Chusan Palm

A remarkable genus of hardy palm introduced by Robert Fortune in 1849. Slow to grow, I have one in my garden that was planted at 60 cm tall, and now stands at a little over 2 metres ten years later. It won the Award of Garden Merit in 2002 and is the best hardy palm for the UK.

While it is hardy in Britain, we recommend planting it in sheltered positions to avoid wind damage to its deep green, fan shaped leaves. Its slender trunk becomes clothed in loose, dark brown fibres and small yellow flowers borne in large panicles are produced in early summer once the plant attains about 2 metres of height.

- Mature height: 7-12m
- Shape of mature tree
- Garden trees
- Evergreen trees
- Eco impact rating

TSUGA canadensis
Eastern Hemlock

Introduced from the Eastern USA in 1736, this broad, often multi stemmed, evergreen conifer grows best on free draining alkaline soils. Ideal for parkland and estates, its architectural network of trunk and mature stems are very pleasing to the eye. Very hardy, its tiny thin leaves look like they are ready for the battle against mountainous climate conditions from where it came.

It thrives in both sun and shade but only where there is adequate drainage. It likes the rarefied air associated with altitude so doesn't do well in urban pollution or times of prolonged drought, so care is needed to keep it watered especially during its establishment period. It does best in the western half of the UK, away from long drying summer winds.

- Mature height: 17-22m
- Shape of mature tree
- Parkland trees
- Eco impact rating: B

ULMUS carpinifolia
Wredei Aurea

This rather slow growing Elm is probably protected against Dutch Elm disease as a result of its size rather than genetic makeup. A sport of 'Dampieri', it won the First Class Certificate in 1893.

A tree of small to medium size and oval habit, it tolerates pollution and salt-laden, coastal winds. Very good for parks, gardens and verges. Its luminescent yellow foliage is particularly striking if planted in a semi shaded area or against a dark backdrop.

- Mature height: 5-8m
- Shape of mature tree
- Garden trees
- Eco impact rating: C

ULMUS glabra Camperdownii
Camperdown Elm

The Camperdown Elm is a form of Wych Elm. The original appeared at Camperdown House, near Dundee, in 1850. It produces clusters of attractive hop like flowers in the spring and its lustrous leaves add well to its effect.

A small weeping tree with a dome shaped head; it looks good growing in a lawn in parks and gardens. It remains neat and compact, and is generally considered to be resistant to Dutch elm disease but only because it doesn't attain the height to attract the infecting beetle.

Mature height: 5-8m | Shape of mature tree | Garden trees | Eco impact rating: A

U

ULMUS Clusius

This Dutch hybrid was raised at Wageningen and released for general cultivation in 1983. It is derived from the same parents as Ulmus Lobel, namely Ulmus glabra Exoniensis and Ulmus wallichiana. This large broadly oval tree is fast growing

This large broadly oval tree is fast growing and well suited to avenue and coastal plantings. It has a resistance to Dutch elm disease but is more susceptible than 'Lutece'.

- Mature height: 17-22m
- Shape of mature tree
- Eco impact rating: A

ULMUS Dodoens

This Elm was seed-raised in the 1950s and eventually released for general cultivation in 1973. It has the same parents as 'Clusius' and has moderate resistance to Dutch elm disease.

This tough large tree, which is good for verges and avenues, forms a broadly pyramidal crown. It is fast growing and a good choice for windy, exposed locations including coastal sites.

- Mature height: 17-22m
- Shape of mature tree
- Eco impact rating: A

ULMUS Lobel

This Elm cultivar was raised at Wageningen in the Netherlands and was selected for its resistance to Dutch elm disease. It has the same parentage as 'Clusius' and was released for general cultivation in 1973.

Large and fast growing, this narrow, columnar tree eventually becomes broader. It will withstand exposed locations, including those on coasts, and is also good for avenues and verges.

Elm is such a versatile and tough tree and it was a tragedy when Dutch Elm Disease swept in to drastically reduce their numbers. Ulmus Lobel has been very successfully planted throughout the UK since then and is one of the better bets when planting this genus.

Mature height: 17-22m | Shape of mature tree | Eco impact rating: A

ULMUS lutece

Also referred to as 'Nanguen' this clone has a complex parentage with Ulmus minor, glabra, Exoniensis and wallichiana all present in its genetic makeup. Originally a Dutch clone, it was discarded for the unfounded fear it was susceptible to Coral Spot fungus but was adopted by the French instead who have planted extensively in Paris and surrounding cities. It rates 5 out of 5 on Dutch field tests regarding Dutch Elm Disease.

Green leaves are late to emerge in May and turn yellow in autumn. It is a tough tree and tolerates urban pollution as well as coastal locations. It is very temperature hardy and has been successfully planted in Scandinavia. It has been subject to 20 years of field trials in France before being released for general planting in 2002.

Mature height: 17-22m | Shape of mature tree | Urban trees | Eco impact rating: A

ULMUS Vada (& Lutece)

I am indebted to Henry Girling for his insights over many years on Ulmus lutece and Ulmus Vada. Indeed it was Henry who convinced us to include these two varieties within our range. With this in mind I would like to include the following article on his observational thoughts on both varieties:

'Since writing the notes to accompany the planting of Ulmus Vada at Keele, I have come into some further information on this important tree and its sister clone, U. Lutèce.

Both trees share a common ancestry, having been bred at the Dutch Willie Commelin Scholten Phytopathologish Laboratorium and the breeder's rights transferred to the French Institute National de la Recherche Agromonique. Both trees are genetically complex, the original cross being between the Exeter Elm, U. glabra var Exoniensis x Himalayan Wych Elm, U. wallichiana. The progeny were crossed and back crossed with other D.E.D. resistant Elms, including Bea Schwartz (early 1930's). The influence of Exeter Elm is apparent in Lutèce, and more so in Vada, with its partially twisted foliage.

Research in French inoculation trials established that Vada outperformed all other clones. Lutèce suffered some minor dieback after inoculation but recovered. In the field. no cases of Lutèce dying from D.E.D. have been reported.

The habit of growth of the two clones is rather different, that of Lutèce ascending steeply with quite a compact crown, growth rate is less than that of earlier disease resistant clones, e.g. U. Lobel, and it is unlikely to make a truly massive tree. Not fussy about soils, which should be well drained and reasonably fertile.

Vada is extremely vigorous, with strong apical dominance. It may, on good sites, increase in height by 1.5m a year; its final form and shape is yet to be established. This clone will withstand an amount of seasonal waterlogging and is extremely wind firm. All the indications are that Vada will grow into a very large tree.

As an Arboriculturalist, it is suggested that Lutèce may be more suited for the urban environment and Vada more suited for rural locations and open spaces. Being fast growing and undemanding as to site requirements, it may be a part replacement for Ash, since they are available in small sizes. Like Ash, they must be planted in a position of good light and require a high level of protection from grazing animals.

As young trees, they tend to have a rather gaunt skeletal appearance, not unlike that of young English Field Elm, they do however rapidly outgrow this adolescent gawkiness.

A word of caution, Elm is a high-water demand species and should not be planted close to buildings founded on high shrinkage clay soils unless the foundations conform to the requirements of Nhbc Standards Chapter 4.2. Incidentally, Elms do not thrive in containers; they will grow rapidly for a year or two and then check.

The long-term value of Lutèce and Vada is yet to be established, nonetheless, the indications are encouraging. At a time when our choice of trees for planting is increasingly constrained by pathological problems, it is time to consider these clones seriously'

Thanks Henry! Time will tell whether these selections are a long-term bet for the UK but early signs are encouraging. In the meantime, I would be cautious about basing your planting plans on Ulmus specifically.

Mature height: 17-22m | Shape of mature tree | Urban trees | Eco impact rating: A

ZELKOVA serrata

This is a medium to large tree with a wide spreading and rounded habit. Its smooth, grey bark flakes attractively, and its foliage displays fine shades of red and bronze in autumn.

A relative of the Elm, this is a native of Japan. Introduced into the UK in 1861, it won the Award of Garden Merit in 2002. It thrives on most soils and is well suited to tolerate the rigours of the urban environment.

Good for avenues and parkland. Zelkovas do best in fertile, sandy, loamy soils.

Mature height: 12-17m | Shape of mature tree | Parkland trees | Eco impact rating: A

ZELKOVA serrata Green Vase

This is a recent American introduction brought into the UK in the 1980s and is widely viewed as the best clonal selection available. It is quick to grow, especially in the first ten years or so, after which it becomes more sedate.

The much tighter, columnar habit of this medium to large cultivar makes it considerably more suitable as a street tree than the species. It also tolerates air pollution and windy sites. The trunk has a soft grey bark and foliage provides very good autumn colour. It thrives on most soils. Similar looking and related to Elm, it is very resistant to Dutch Elm Disease so represents a good and attractive alternative.

Mature height: 12-17m | Shape of mature tree | Autumn colour | Parkland trees | Eco impact rating: A

Telephone 01353 720 748 | www.barcham.co.uk | www.barchampro.co.uk

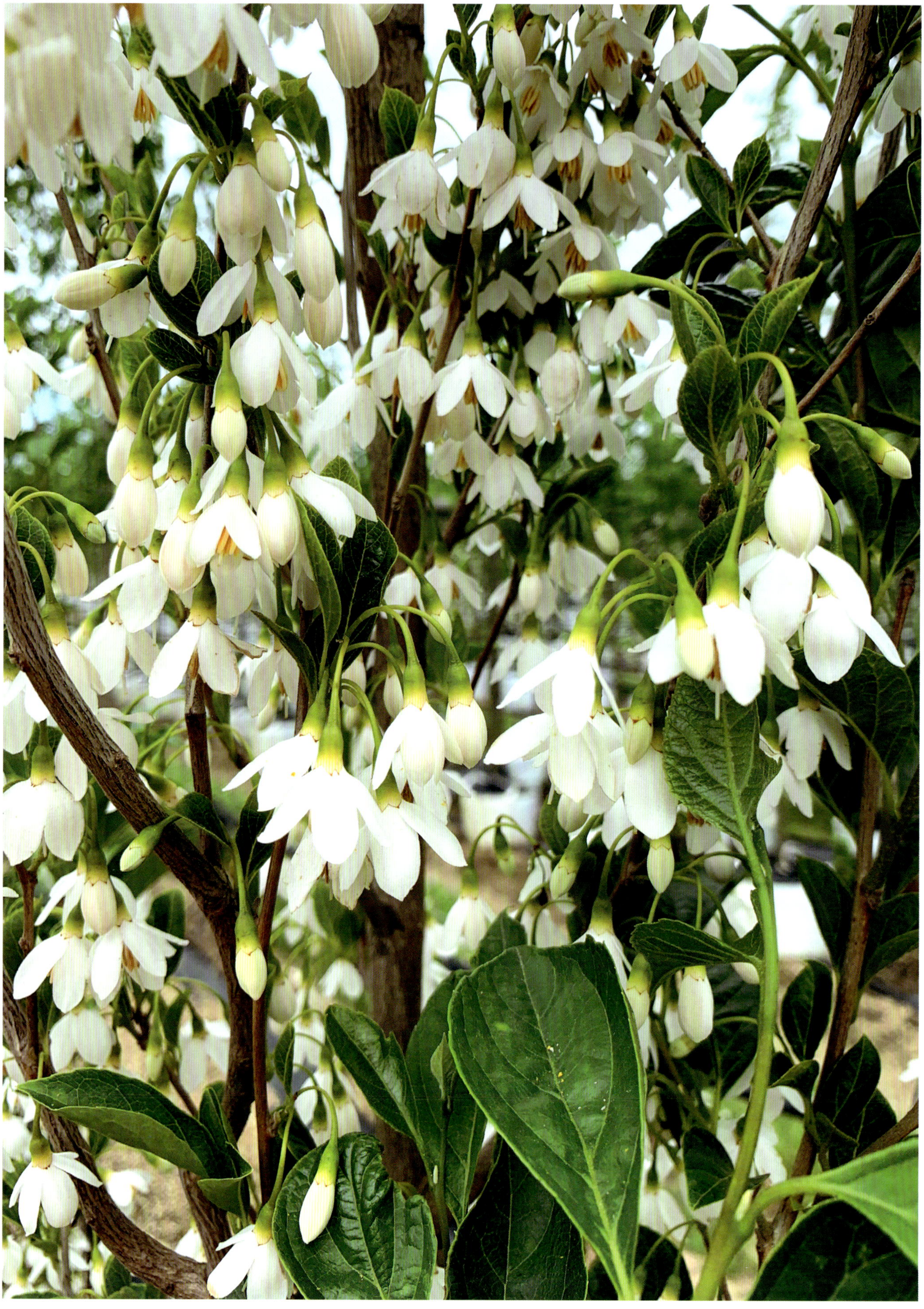

Trees for a Purpose
Choosing the right tree to suit your environment

Autumn Colour

Acer x freemanii Autumn Blaze p.26
Amelanchier lamarckii (Multi-stem) p.65
Liquidambar styraciflua Worplesdon .. p.170
Parrotia persica p.206
Prunus avium Plena p.232

Avenue Trees

Castanea sativa p.89
Platanus x hispanica p.221
Quercus palustris p.267
Tilia cordata Greenspire p.312
Tilia x europaea Pallida p.316

Bark Interest

Acer griseum p.28
Betula albosinensis Fascination p.69
Betula utilis Jacquemontii/Doorenbos p.81
Eucalyptus niphophila p.122
Prunus serrula Tibetica p.249

Clay Soils

Carpinus betulus p.85
Carpinus betulus Fastigiata p.86
Malus Rudolph p.193
Platanus x hispanica p.221
Quercus robur p.272

Coastal Sites

Acer pseudoplatanus Negenia p.44
Populus tremula p.228
Quercus ilex p.266
Sorbus intermedia p.298
Tamarix tetandra p.304

Dry Soils

Gleditsia triacanthos Sunburst p.144
Koelreuteria paniculata p.155
Lagerstroemia indica Rosea p.158
Olea europaea p.203

Edible Fruits

Ficus carica p.134
Malus Cox's Orange Pippin p.182
Mespilus germanica p.197
Olea europaea p.203
Prunus domestica Victoria p.236

Edible Nuts

Castanea sativa p.89
Corylus avellana p.106
Juglans nigra p.153
Juglans regia p.154
Prunus dulcis p.236

Evergreen Trees

Laurus nobilis p.161
Ligustrum japonicum p.162
Magnolia grandiflora p.175
Photinia x fraseri Red Robin p.210
Quercus ilex p.266

Extreme PH, acid or alkaline

Betula pendula p.73
Populus tremula p.228
Quercus cerris p.263
Sorbus intermedia p.298
Sorbus thuringiaca Fastigiata p.300

Flowering

Crataegus laevigata Paul's Scarlet p.110
Davidia involucrata p.119
Magnolia x loebneri Merrill p.179
Paulownia tomentosa p.208
Prunus accolade p.229

Garden

Amelanchier arborea Robin Hill p.63
Betula pendula Youngii p.77
Cornus mas p.105
Corylus avellana Zellernus p.107
Magnolia x loebneri Leonard Messel ... p.178

Hedging

Carpinus betulus p.85
Cupressocyparis leylandii p.117
Fagus sylvatica p.126
Prunus laurocerasus Rotundifolia p.241
Taxus baccata p.306

Narrow Trees

Calocedrus decurrans p.83
Carpinus betulus Frans Fontaine p.87
Malus trilobata p.196
Populus tremula Erecta p.228
Prunus Amanogawa p.230

Parkland trees

Fagus sylvatica p.126
Liquidambar Acalycina p.166
Populus tremula p.228
Prunus padus Watereri p.244
Quercus petraea p.270

Red/Purple Leaves

Acer platanoides Royal Red p.41
Acer pseudoplatanus Spaethii p.44
Fagus sylvatica purpurea p.131
Prunus cerasifera Nigra p.233
Prunus Royal Burgundy p.247

Stilted Screening

Ligustrum japonicum p.162
Magnolia grandiflora p.175
Photinia x fraseri Red Robin p.210
Prunus laurocerasus Novita p.240
Pyrus calleryana Chanticleer p.258

Trees for Bees

Alnus p.56-61
Liriodendron p.172-173
Malus p.181-196
Prunus p.229-256
Tilia p.309-321

Urban Trees

Acer platanoides Emerald Queen p.37
Crataegus prunifolia p.112
Ginkgo biloba p.136
Platanus x hispanica p.221
Tilia tomentosa Brabant p.320

Variegated Trees

Acer negundo Flamingo p.29
Acer negundo Variegata p.29
Acer platanoides Drummondii p.36
Liquidambar styraciflua Manon
  Variegata p.170
Liriodendron tulipifera
  Aureomarginatum p.173

Weeping Trees

Betula Pendula Youngii p.77
Morus alba Pendula p.200
Prunus Shirotae p.250
Salix alba Tristis p.281
Ulmus glabra Camperdownii p.323

Wet Soils

Alnus cordata p.56
Betula nigra p.71
Populus alba p.224
Salix alba Chermesina p.280
Taxodium distichum p.305

Yellow Foliage

Acer platanoides Princeton Gold p.40
Acer pseudoplatanus Worleei p.45
Alnus incana Aurea p.59
Gleditsia triacanthos Sunburst p.144
Robinia pseudoacacia Frisia p.278

Native Trees

Acer campestre p.19
Alnus glutinosa p.57
Betula pendula p.73
Betula pubescens p.79
Carpinus betulus p.85
Corylus avellana p.106
Crataegus monogyna p.111
Euonymus europaeus p.124
Fagus sylvatica p.126
Fraxinus excelsior p.135
Ilex aquifolium p.148
Pinus sylvestris p.218
Populus nigra p.226
Populus tremula p.228
Prunus avium p.231
Prunus padus p.243
Quercus petraea p.270
Quercus robur p.272
Salix alba p.279
Salix caprea p.282
Salix pentandra p.284
Sorbus aria (Lutescens) p.289
Sorbus aucuparia p.291
Sorbus torminalis p.300
Taxus baccata p.306
Tilia cordata p.310
Tilia platyphyllos p.318

Top Trunks Guide

All trees are great environmental contributors so whether they are an 'A' or an 'E' rating they are all doing their bit to lock up carbon by taking carbon dioxide out of the air and converting it into their structures. Barcham Top Trunks gives a guide to the extent carbon is stored per variety. The measurement is estimated dry weight carbon at maturity so the longer a tree lives and the larger it gets the more contribution it delivers.

We are the first nursery to score trees in this way, using data from thousands of trees throughout the UK via the measuring tool 'I Tree'. Many of these trees are either urban trees or trees near buildings in rural locations so we estimate that trees with greater access to space and soil volumes in the wider countryside could store up to three times the volumes shown here.

As yet the measuring systems in place for calculating carbon load are still in their infancy. The carbon locked up below ground in root systems may contribute as much as what we have calculated above ground. What we know for sure is that trees are a great way for our species to help redress the threat of our time, global warming.

The modelling we have used for this study has an abundance of data at genus and species level but we grow a wide range of trees and there was insufficient data to cover all cultivars. With these more obscure varieties we have estimated their eco ratings, taking into account their ultimate size and lifespan compared to their species.

KEY: | VARIETY | LIFE EXPECTANCY (URBAN) | LIFE EXPECTANCY (RURAL) | CARBON CREDIT SCORE (A-E) | CARBON STORED AT MATURITY (KG) |

Variety	Urban	Rural	Score	Carbon (kg)
Abies nordmanniana	150	300	B	4324
Abies fraseri	150	300	B	4324
Abies grandis	150	300	B	4324
Abies koreana	150	300	B	2556
Abies procera	150	300	B	3045
Acacia dealbata	15	35	D	458
Acca sellowiana	15	35	D	90
Acer buergerianum	50	100	C	1174
Acer campestre	150	250	B	2572
Acer campestre Arends	150	250	B	2572
Acer campestre Elegant	150	250	B	2572
Acer campestre Elsrijk	150	250	B	2572
Acer campestre Lienco	150	250	B	2572
Acer campestre Louisa Red Shine	150	250	B	2572
Acer campestre Nanum	50	75	C	1796
Acer campestre Queen Elizabeth	150	250	B	2572
Acer campestre Streetwise	150	250	B	2572
Acer campestre William Caldwell	150	250	B	2572
Acer cappadocicum	75	150	B	2572
Acer cappadocicum Aureum	75	150	B	2572
Acer cappadocicum Rubrum	75	150	B	2572
Acer x freemanii Armstrong	75	150	C	628
Acer x freemanii Autumn Blaze	75	150	C	628
Acer x freemanii Autumn Fantasy	75	150	C	628
Acer ginnala	50	100	C	1040
Acer griseum	75	150	C	628
Acer negundo	50	75	B	2498
Acer negundo Flamingo	25	50	B	2498
Acer negundo Variegatum	50	75	B	2498
Acer palm Dissectum Garnet	50	100	C	514
Acer palmatum	50	100	C	514
Acer palmatum Atropurpureum	50	100	C	514
Acer palmatum Bloodgood	50	100	C	514
Acer palmatum Dissectum Garnet	50	100	C	514
Acer palmatum Fireglow	50	100	C	514
Acer palmatum Osakazuki	50	100	C	514
Acer palmatum Purpurea	50	100	C	514
Acer palmatum Red Emperor	50	100	C	514
Acer platanoides	150	250	A	7250
Acer platanoides Cleveland	150	250	B	4895
Acer platanoides Columnare	150	250	B	4895
Acer platanoides Crimson King	150	250	B	4895
Acer platanoides Crimson Sentry	150	250	C	990
Acer platanoides Deborah	150	250	A	7500
Acer platanoides Drummondii	150	250	B	4895
Acer platanoides Emerald Queen	150	250	A	7250
Acer platanoides Fairview	150	250	B	4895
Acer platanoides Farlakes Green	150	250	A	7250
Acer platanoides Globosum	150	250	C	990
Acer platanoides Olmstead	150	250	B	4895
Acer platanoides Pacific Sunset	150	250	B	4895
Acer platanoides Princeton Gold	150	250	B	4895

KEY:	VARIETY	LIFE EXPECTANCY (URBAN)	LIFE EXPECTANCY (RURAL)	CARBON CREDIT SCORE (A-E)	CARBON STORED AT MATURITY (KG)
	Acer platanoides Royal Red	150	250	B	4895
	Acer platanoides Summershade	150	250	B	4895
	Acer pseudoplatanus	150	250	A	7500
	Acer pseudoplatanus Brilliantissimum	150	250	C	1250
	Acer pseudoplatanus Leopoldii	150	250	B	4895
	Acer pseudoplatanus Negenia	150	250	A	7500
	Acer pseudoplatanus Spaethii	150	250	B	4895
	Acer pseudoplatanus Worleei	150	250	B	4895
	Acer rubrum	75	150	B	3676
	Acer rubrum Bowhall	75	150	B	3676
	Acer rubrum October Glory	75	150	B	3676
	Acer rubrum Red Sunset	75	150	B	3676
	Acer rubrum Scanlon	75	150	B	3676
	Acer saccharinum	100	200	B	4891
	Acer saccharinum Laciniata Wieri	75	150	B	4891
	Acer saccharinum Pyramidale	75	150	B	4891
	Acer x freemanii Celebration	75	150	C	628
	Aesculus californica	150	300	A	5276
	Aesculus x carnea Briotti	150	300	A	5071
	Aesculus x carnea Plantierensis	150	300	A	5071
	Aesculus flava	150	300	A	5276
	Aesculus hippocastanum	200	300	A	7440
	Aesculus hippocastanum Baumannii	150	300	A	5276
	Aesculus indica	150	300	A	7051
	Ailanthus altissima	50	100	A	5138
	Albizia julibrissin Rouge de Tuiliere	15	25	E	44
	Albizia julibrissin Tropical Dream	15	25	E	44
	Alnus cordata	75	100	B	2762
	Alnus glutinosa	75	100	B	2762
	Alnus glutinosa Imperialis	50	75	B	2762
	Alnus glutinosa Laciniata	50	75	B	2762
	Alnus incana	75	100	B	2762
	Alnus incana Aurea	50	75	B	2762
	Alnus incana Laciniata	50	75	B	2762
	Alnus spaethii	75	100	B	2762
	Amelanchier arborea Robin Hill	25	50	C	530
	Amelanchier Ballerina	25	50	C	530
	Amelanchier Lamarckii	25	50	C	530
	Aralia elata	25	50	D	264
	Araucaria araucana	250	750	B	2230
	Arbutus unedo	150	300	D	406
	Betula albosinensis Fascination	50	100	B	3224
	Betula ermanii	50	100	B	3224
	Betula maximowicziana	50	100	C	3224
	Betula nigra	50	100	B	3224
	Betula papyrifera	50	100	B	3224
	Betula pendula	75	100	B	3224
	Betula pendula Crispa	50	100	B	3224
	Betula pendula Dalecarlica	50	100	B	3224
	Betula pendula Fastigiata	50	100	B	3224
	Betula pendula Obelisk	50	100	B	3224
	Betula pendula Purpurea	50	100	B	3224
	Betula pendula Royal Frost	50	100	B	3224
	Betula pendula Tristis	50	100	B	3224
	Betula pendula Westwood	50	100	B	3224
	Betula pendula Youngii	50	100	B	3224
	Betula pendula Zwisters Glory	50	100	B	3224
	Betula pubescens	50	100	B	3224
	Betula ut. Jacquemontii Doorenbos	50	100	B	3224
	Betula utilis Grayswood Ghost	50	100	B	3224
	Betula utilis Jac Snow Queen	50	100	B	3224
	Broussonetia papyrifera	50	100	D	310
	Calocedrus decurrens	350	750	A	5178
	Camelia sasanqua Kanjiro	50	100	C	616
	Camellia japonica Half Std	50	100	C	616
	Camellia sasanqua	50	100	C	616
	Camellia sasanqua cleopatra	50	100	C	616
	Carpinus betulus	150	300	A	6731

KEY:	VARIETY	LIFE EXPECTANCY (URBAN)	LIFE EXPECTANCY (RURAL)	CARBON CREDIT SCORE (A-E)	CARBON STORED AT MATURITY (KG)
	Carpinus betulus Fastigiata	150	250	A	6731
	Carpinus betulus Frans Fontaine	150	250	A	6731
	Carpinus betulus Lucas	150	250	A	6731
	Carpinus japonica	150	250	C	698
	Carya cordiformis	75	150	B	4047
	Carya illinoinensis	150	300	A	7500
	Castanea sativa	150	300	A	6854
	Catalpa bignonioides	50	100	B	2859
	Catalpa bignonioides Aurea	50	100	C	1420
	Catalpa bignonioides Bungei	50	75	C	1420
	Cedrus atlantica	200	300	B	3476
	Cedrus atlantica Glauca	150	300	B	3476
	Cedrus deodara	150	300	B	2107
	Cedrus deodara Aurea	150	300	B	2107
	Cedrus libani	150	300	A	5178
	Celtis australis	150	200	A	5240
	Celtis occidentalis	150	200	A	7115
	Cephalotaxus harr. Fastigiata	50	100	D	61
	Cercidiphyllum japonicum	75	150	B	1287
	Cercis Chinensis Avondale multi-stm	35	75	C	601
	Cercis canadensis Forest Pansy	35	75	D	112
	Cercis siliquastrum	35	75	C	601
	Cercis siliquastrum Alba	35	75	C	601
	Chamaecyparis law.Columnaris Glauca	75	150	C	852
	Chamaecyparis lawsoniana Stardust	75	150	C	852
	Chamaecyparis lawsoniana Yvonne	75	150	C	852
	Chitalpa Summer Bells	25	50	D	294
	Cladrastis kentukea	50	100	D	322
	Clerodendrum tric. Purple Blaze	25	50	D	148
	Clerodendrum trichotomum	25	50	D	148
	Cornus alba Sibirica	35	75	D	292
	Cornus controversa	50	100	D	111
	Cornus controversa Variegata	50	100	D	214
	Cornus Eddie's White Wonder	50	100	D	214
	Cornus kousa	50	100	D	214
	Cornus kousa China Girl	50	100	D	214
	Cornus kousa Chinensis	50	100	D	214
	Cornus kousa Milky Way	50	100	D	214
	Cornus kousa Stella Pink	50	100	D	214
	Cornus mas	50	100	D	111
	Cornus sanguinea Annie's Winter Orange	50	100	D	214
	Corylus avellana Contorta	50	100	C	1454
	Corylus avellana multi-stem	50	75	B	2762
	Corylus avel. Zellernuss multi-stem	50	75	B	2762
	Corylus colurna	50	75	B	2762
	Corylus colurna Teterrra Red	50	100	C	1454
	Cotinus coggygria Royal Purple	35	75	D	108
	Cotoneaster Cornubia	25	50	D	110
	Crataegus laevigata Alba Plena	75	150	C	509
	Crataegus laevigata Paul's Scarlet	75	150	C	509
	Crataegus x lavallei	75	150	C	509
	Crataegus x lavallei Carrierei	75	150	C	509
	Crataegus monogyna	75	150	C	509
	Crataegus monogyna Alboplena	75	150	C	509
	Crataegus monogyna Stricta	75	150	C	509
	Crataegus x prunifolia	75	150	C	509
	Crataegus x prunifolia Splendens	75	150	C	509
	Cryptomeria japonica Elegans	150	300	B	4339
	Cunninghamia lanceolata	250	500	B	3609
	Cupressus arizonica Glauca	50	100	B	2238
	Cupressus macrocarpa Goldcrest	50	100	B	2238
	Cupressus sempervirens	350	750	B	3463
	Cupressus semp. Pyramidalis	350	750	B	3463
	Cupressocyparis leylandii	100	150	B	2245
	Cupressocyparis ley.Castlewellan	50	100	B	2245
	Cydonia oblonga (fruiting varieties)	15	25	D	99
	Davidia involucrata	35	75	D	103
	Diospyros lotus	50	75	C	541
	Diospyros kaki	50	75	C	541
	Eucalyptus debeuzevillei	150	250	A	6433
	Eucalyptus gunnii	150	250	A	7570
	Eucalyptus niphophila	150	250	A	7570
	Eucommia Ulmoides	100	200	C	607

VARIETY	LIFE EXPECTANCY (URBAN)	LIFE EXPECTANCY (RURAL)	CARBON CREDIT SCORE (A-E)	CARBON STORED AT MATURITY (KG)
Euodia hupehensis	25	50	C	571
Euonymus europaeus Red Cascade	50	100	C	527
Exochorda serratifolia Snow White	50	100	D	219
Fagus orientalis Iskander	150	300	A	7008
Fagus sylvatica	200	300	A	7500
Fagus sylvatica Asplenifolia	150	300	A	7500
Fagus sylvatica Black Swan	150	300	B	4216
Fagus sylvatica Dawyck	150	300	B	4216
Fagus sylvatica Dawyck Gold	150	300	B	4216
Fagus sylvatica Dawyck Purpurea	150	300	B	4216
Fagus sylvatica Pendula	150	300	A	7500
Fagus sylvatica Purpurea	150	300	A	7500
Fagus sylvatica Rohan Obelisk	150	300	B	4216
Fagus sylvatica Rohanii	150	300	B	4216
Fagus sylvatica Roseomarginata	150	300	B	4216
Fagus sylvatica Tricolor	150	300	B	4216
Fagus sylvatica Zlatia	150	300	B	4216
Ficus carica	50	100	D	314
Ficus carica Nero	50	100	D	314
Fraxinus americana Autumn Purple	75	150	A	5284
Fraxinus angustifolia Raywood	75	150	A	5284
Fraxinus excelsior	100	200	A	6052
Fraxinus excelsior Altena	75	150	A	5284
Fraxinus excelsior Diversifolia	75	150	A	5284
Fraxinus excelsior Jaspidea	75	150	B	4154
Fraxinus excelsior Pendula	75	150	A	5284
Fraxinus excelsior Westhof's Glorie	75	150	A	5284
Fraxinus ornus	75	150	A	5284
Fraxinus ornus Arie Peters	75	150	A	5284
Fraxinus ornus Louisa Lady	75	150	A	5284
Fraxinus ornus Meczek	75	150	C	871
Fraxinus ornus Obelisk	75	150	B	4154
Fraxinus pennsylvanica Summit	75	150	A	5284
Ginkgo biloba	250	500	B	4954
Ginkgo bilboa Blagon	150	300	C	1434
Ginkgo biloba golden globe	150	300	C	1434
Ginkgo biloba Globosa	150	300	C	1434
Ginkgo biloba Lakeview	150	300	B	2694
Ginkgo biloba Nanum	50	100	C	1134
Ginkgo biloba Princeton Sentry	150	300	C	1434
Ginkgo biloba Tremonia	150	300	C	1434
Ginkgo biloba Tit	150	300	C	1434
Gleditsia triacanthos	100	200	B	3911
Gleditsia tri Draves Street Keeper	75	150	B	2664
Gleditsia triacanthos Inermis	75	150	B	2664
Gleditsia triacanthos Rubylace	75	150	B	2664
Gleditsia triacanthos Skyline	75	150	B	2664
Gleditsia triacanthos Sunburst	75	150	B	2664
Gymnocladus dioica	75	125	C	1176
Halesia carolina	50	100	C	322
Halesia monticola	50	100	C	322
Hamamelis Arnold Promise	25	50	C	225
Hamamelis intermedia Jelena	25	50	C	225
Hamamelis intermedia mollis	25	50	C	225
Hibiscus Resi	25	50	D	113
Ilex x altaclerensis Golden King	150	300	C	1836
Ilex aquifolium	150	300	C	1836
Ilex aquifolium Alaska	150	300	C	1836
Ilex aquifolium Argentea Marginata	150	300	C	1836
Ilex aquifolium J C Van Tol	150	300	C	1836
Ilex aquifolium Pyramidalis	150	300	C	1836
Ilex aqupernyi Dragon Lady	150	300	C	1420
Ilex castaneifolia	150	300	C	1420
Ilex cornuta	150	300	C	1420
Ilex x maserveae Blue Maid	150	300	C	1420
Ilex x Nellie Stevens	150	300	C	1420
Juglans nigra	100	200	A	7094
Juglans regia	100	200	A	5331
Juniperus communis Hibernica	75	150	C	932
Juniperus scopulorum Blue Arrow	25	50	D	328
Koelreuteria paniculata	35	75	D	153

KEY:	VARIETY	LIFE EXPECTANCY (URBAN)	LIFE EXPECTANCY (RURAL)	CARBON CREDIT SCORE (A-E)	CARBON STORED AT MATURITY (KG)
	Liquidambar sty. Stella	150	300	B	2377
	Liquidambar sty. Thea	150	300	B	2377
	Liquidambar sty. Variegata	150	300	B	2377
	Liquidambar styraciflua Worplesdon	150	300	B	2377
	Liriodendron tulipifera	150	300	B	4111
	Liriodendron tulip. Aureomarginatum	100	200	B	4111
	Liriodendron tulipifera Fastigiatum	100	200	B	4111
	Magnolia x brooklynensis Elizabeth	50	100	C	521
	Magnolia x brooklynensis Yellow Bird	50	100	C	521
	Magnolia denudata	50	100	C	532
	Magnolia Galaxy	50	100	C	532
	Magnolia grandiflora	50	100	C	542
	Magnolia grandiflora Gallissoniere	50	100	C	542
	Magnolia grandiflora Praecox	50	100	C	542
	Magnolia Heaven Scent	50	100	C	532
	Magnolia kobus	50	100	C	1270
	Magnolia x loebneri Leonard Messel	50	100	C	521
	Magnolia x loebneri Merrill	50	100	C	521
	Magnolia x soulangeana	50	100	C	521
	Magnolia Spectrum	50	100	C	532
	Magnolia Star Wars Multi Stem	50	100	C	532
	Magnolia Susan	50	100	C	532
	Magnolia Yellow Lantern	50	100	C	532
	Magnolia Yellow River	50	100	C	532
	Malus baccata Street Parade	50	100	C	505
	Malus Bramley Seedling	50	100	C	505
	Malus Butterball	50	100	C	505
	Malus Cox's Orange Pippin	50	100	C	505
	Malus DIrector Moerland	50	100	C	505
	Malus Discovery	50	100	C	505
	Malus Donald Wyman	50	100	C	505
	Malus Egremont Russett	50	100	C	505
	Malus Elstar	50	100	C	505
	Malus Evereste	50	100	C	505
	Malus floribunda	50	100	C	505
	Malus Golden Delicious	50	100	C	505
	Malus Golden Hornet	50	100	C	505
	Malus Howgate Wonder	50	100	C	505
	Malus hupehensis	50	100	C	505
	Malus James Grieve	50	100	C	505
	Malus John Downie	50	100	C	505
	Malus Jonagold	50	100	C	505
	Malus Laxton superb	50	100	C	505

Variety	Urban	Rural	Score	Carbon
Koelreuteria paniculata Fastigiata	35	75	D	113
Laburnocytisus Adamii	35	50	D	60
Laburnum vulgare multi-stem	35	50	C	1034
Laburnum x watereri Vossii	35	50	C	1034
Lagerstroemia indica Alba	35	50	C	503
Lagerostroemia indica Fauriei	35	50	C	503
Lagerstroemia indica Red	35	50	C	503
Lagerstroemia indica Rosea	35	50	C	503
Lagerstroemia ind. Sarah's Favorite	35	50	C	503
Lagerostroemia indica Tuscarora	35	50	C	503
Lagerstroemia indica Violacea	35	50	C	503
Larix decidua	350	750	A	5097
Larix x eurolepis	350	750	A	5097
Larix kaempferi	350	750	A	5097
Laurus nobilis	50	75	D	375
Ligustrum japonicum	75	150	B	4037
Ligustrum lucidum Excelsum Superbum	75	150	B	4037
Ligustrum lucidum variegata	75	150	B	4037
Ligustrum ovalifolium Bush	35	50	D	338
Liquidambar acalycina	150	300	B	2377
Liquidambar styraciflua	150	300	B	2377
Liquidambar sty. Albomarg. Manon	150	300	B	2377
Liquidambar sty.Gumball	25	50	D	377
Liquidambar sty. Lane Roberts	150	300	B	2377
Liquidamber sty. Rotundiloba	150	300	B	2377
Liquidambar sty. Slender Silhouette	150	300	B	2377

KEY:	VARIETY	LIFE EXPECTANCY (URBAN)	LIFE EXPECTANCY (RURAL)	CARBON CREDIT SCORE (A-E)	CARBON STORED AT MATURITY (KG)
	Paulownia tomentosa	150	200	C	1000
	Phellodendron amurense	75	150	B	4047
	Photinia fraseri Red Robin	15	25	D	181
	Phyllostachys aurea	10	25	E	17
	Phyllostachys nigra	10	25	E	17
	Picea abies	100	200	A	5341
	Picea omorika	100	150	C	1746
	Picea pungens Blue Diamond	35	50	D	410
	Picea pungens Glauca	35	50	D	410
	Picea pungens Hoopsii	35	50	D	410
	Pinus cembra	150	300	B	2184
	Pinus nigra	150	300	B	2694
	Pinus nigra austriaca	150	300	B	2694
	Pinus nigra maritima	150	300	B	4960
	Pinus mugo mops	150	300	C	932
	Pinus peuce	150	300	B	3451
	Pinus pinaster	150	300	B	3513
	Pinus pinea	150	300	B	3513
	Pinus radiata	150	300	B	2235
	Pinus strobus	150	300	B	2459
	Pinus sylvestris	150	300	B	3513
	Pinus sylvestris Fastigiata	150	300	B	3513
	Pinus wallichiana	150	300	B	2877
	Platanus x hispanica	250	350	A	7423
	Platanus x hispanica Alphens Globe	150	300	C	1028
	Platanus orientalis Digitata	150	300	B	2877
	Platanus orientalis Minaret	150	300	B	2877
	Populus alba	50	75	B	2476
	Populus alba Raket	50	75	B	2476
	Populus x candicans Aurora	50	75	B	2476
	Populus x canadensis Robusta	50	75	B	2476
	Populus Balsam Spire	50	75	B	2476
	Populus nigra	50	75	B	2476
	Populus nigra Italica	50	75	B	2476
	Populus serotina Aurea	50	75	B	2476
	Populus tremula	50	75	B	2476
	Populus tremula Erecta	50	75	B	2476
	Prunus Accolade	50	75	C	685
	Prunus Amanogawa	50	75	C	685
	Prunus avium	75	100	B	3124
	Prunus avium Kordia	50	75	C	685
	Prunus avium Plena	50	75	B	3124
	Prunus cerasifera Nigra	50	75	C	1644
Malus Mokum	50	100	C	505
Malus Pink Perfection	50	100	C	505
Malus Profusion	50	100	C	505
Malus Red Sentinel	50	100	C	505
Malus Royalty	50	100	C	505
Malus Rudolph	50	100	C	505
Malus sylvestris	50	100	C	505
Malus toringo	50	100	C	505
Malus toringo Brouwers Beauty	50	100	C	505
Malus toringo Scarlet	50	100	C	505
Malus trilobata	50	100	C	505
Mespilus germanica	35	50	C	505
Metasequoia glyptostroboides	350	500	A	5090
Metasequoia glypto Goldrush	250	350	B	4297
Morus alba	75	150	C	524
Morus alba Fruitless	75	150	C	524
Morus alba Pendula	75	150	C	524
Morus alba Platanifolia	75	150	C	524
Morus nigra	150	300	C	524
Nothofagus antarctica	75	150	A	5315
Nyssa sylvatica	350	750	B	4366
Osmanthus armathus std	25	50	D	337
Osmanthus burkwoodii	25	50	D	337
Osmanthus fortunei Aquifolium	25	50	D	337
Ostrya carpinifolia	75	150	B	3454
Parrotia persica	100	150	C	550
Parrotia persica Vanessa	100	150	C	550

Telephone 01353 720 748 | www.barcham.co.uk | www.barchampro.co.uk

KEY:	VARIETY	LIFE EXPECTANCY (URBAN)	LIFE EXPECTANCY (RURAL)	CARBON CREDIT SCORE (A-E)	CARBON STORED AT MATURITY (KG)
	Prunus Cheals Weeping	50	75	C	685
	Prunus domestica Early Rivers	50	75	C	685
	Prunus domestica Hauszwetsche	50	75	C	1644
	Prunus domestica Reine-Claude d'oullins	50	75	C	685
	Prunus domestica Victoria	50	75	C	1644
	Prunus dulcis	50	75	D	340
	Prunus fruticosa Globosa	50	75	D	366
	Prunus x gondouinii Schnee	50	75	C	685
	Prunus x hillieri Spire	50	75	D	375
	Prunus Kanzan	50	75	C	685
	Prunus laurocerasus Caucasica	50	75	D	375
	Prunus laurocerasus Latifolia	50	75	D	375
	Prunus laurocerasus Novita	50	75	D	375
	Prunus laurocerasus Rotundifolia	50	75	D	375
	Prunus lusitanica Angustifolia	50	75	D	349
	Prunus maackii Amber Beauty	50	75	D	340
	Prunus Okame	50	75	C	685
	Prunus padus	50	75	C	685
	Prunus padus Albertii	50	75	C	685
	Prunus padus Watereri	50	75	C	685
	Prunus pissardii Nigra	50	75	C	685
	Prunus Pandora	50	75	C	685
	Prunus Pink Perfection	50	75	C	685
	Prunus Royal Burgundy	50	75	C	685
	Prunus sargentii	50	75	C	612
	Prunus sargentii Rancho	50	75	C	611
	Prunus x schmittii	50	75	C	685
	Prunus serrulata Hokusai	50	75	C	685
	Prunus serrula Tibetica	50	75	C	685
	Prunus Shimidsu Sakura	50	75	C	685
	Prunus Shirotae	50	75	C	685
	Prunus Shirofugen	50	75	C	685
	Prunus subhirtella Autumnalis	50	75	C	685
	Prunus subhirtella Autumnalis Rosea	50	75	C	685
	Prunus subhirtella Pendula	50	75	C	685
	Prunus Sunset Boulevard	50	75	C	685
	Prunus Tai Haku	50	75	C	685
	Prunus Ukon	50	75	C	685
	Prunus Umineko	50	75	C	685
	Prunus Yedoensis	50	75	C	685
	Pseudotsuga menziesii	350	750	B	3796
	Pterocarya fraxinifolia	150	250	A	5255
	Pyracantha Navaho	25	50	E	11
	Pyrus Beurre Hardy	35	75	D	286
	Pyrus calleryana Chanticleer	75	150	C	996
	Pyrus calleryana Redspire	75	150	C	996
	Pyrus communis Beech Hill	35	75	D	286
	Pyrus communis Conference	35	75	D	286
	Pyrus communis Gieser Wildeman	35	75	D	286
	Pyrus Doyenne du Comice	35	75	D	286
	Pyrus salicifolia Pendula	35	75	D	286
	Quercus castaneifolia	150	300	A	7500
	Quercus cerris	150	300	A	7500
	Quercus coccinea	150	300	B	4568
	Quercus frainetto	150	300	A	7500
	Quercus hispanica Waginengen	150	300	A	7500
	Quercus Ilex	150	300	A	7500
	Quercus imbricaria	150	300	A	7250
	Quercus nigra	150	300	A	7104
	Quercus palustris	150	300	A	6589
	Quercus palustris Green Dwarf	150	300	C	1028
	Quercus palustris Green Pillar	150	300	A	6589
	Quercus palustris Helmond	150	300	A	6589
	Quercus petraea	150	300	A	7500
	Quercus phellos	150	300	B	4936
	Quercus Regal Prince	150	300	A	7500
	Quercus robur	150	300	A	7500
	Quercus robur Fastigiata	150	300	A	7500
	Quercus robur Fastigiata Koster	150	300	A	7500
	Quercus rubra	150	300	A	7500
	Quercus suber	150	300	A	7500
	Quercus x turneri Pseudoturneri	150	300	A	7282
	Rhus typhina	25	50	E	20
	Robinia pseudoacacia	100	150	A	5247
	Robinia pseudoacacia Bessoniana	50	100	B	2697
	Robinia pseudoacacia Casque Rouge	50	100	B	2697
	Robinia pseudoacacia Frisia	50	100	B	2697
	Robinia pseudo Umbraculifera	25	50	C	1050
	Salix alba	50	75	B	2680
	Salix alba Belders	50	75	B	2680
	Salix alba Chermesina	50	75	B	2680
	Salix alba Liempde	50	75	B	2680
	Salix alba Tristis	50	75	B	2680
	Salix caprea	50	75	B	2680
	Salix caprea Pendula	50	75	D	295
	Salix daphnoides	50	75	C	591
	Salix matsudana Tortuosa	50	75	C	591
	Salix pentandra	50	75	D	295
	Sambucus nigra Black Lace	25	50	C	957

KEY:	VARIETY	LIFE EXPECTANCY (URBAN)	LIFE EXPECTANCY (RURAL)	CARBON CREDIT SCORE (A-E)	CARBON STORED AT MATURITY (KG)
	Sequoiadendron giganteum	750	2500	A	5132
	Sequoiadendron giganteum Glauca	350	750	B	3609
	Sequoia sempervirens	350	750	A	5132
	Sophora japonica	100	150	B	2728
	Sophora japonica Princeton	50	75	B	2728
	Sophora japonica Regent	50	75	B	2728
	Sorbus aria	50	100	C	1016
	Sorbus aria Lutescens	50	100	C	1016
	Sorbus aria Magnifica	50	100	C	1016
	Sorbus aria Majestica	50	100	C	1016
	Sorbus x arnoldiana Schouten	50	100	D	295
	Sorbus aucuparia	50	100	C	530
	Sorbus aucuparia Asplenifolia	50	100	C	530
	Sorbus aucuparia Cardinal Royal	50	100	C	530
	Sorbus aucuparia Cashmiriana	50	100	C	530
	Sorbus aucuparia Edulis	50	100	C	530
	Sorbus aucuparia Golden Wonder	50	100	C	530
	Sorbus aucuparia Joseph Rock	50	100	C	530
	Sorbus aucuparia Rossica Major	50	100	C	530
	Sorbus aucuparia SheerwaterSeedling	50	100	C	530
	Sorbus aucuparia Vilmorinii	50	100	C	530
	Sorbus commixta	50	100	C	593
	Sorbus commixta Embley	50	100	C	593
	Sorbus commixta Olympic Flame	50	100	C	593
	Sorbus discolor	50	100	C	593
	Sorbus hupehensis	50	100	D	295
	Sorbus incana	50	100	C	1409
	Sorbus intermedia	50	100	C	1409
	Sorbus intermedia Brouwers	50	100	C	1409
	Sorbus latifolia Atrovirens	50	100	C	1409
	Sorbus latifolia Henk Vink	50	100	C	1409
	Sorbus x thuringiaca Fastigiata	50	100	D	216
	Sorbus torminalis	50	100	C	1409
	Styrax japonicus June Snow	50	100	D	219
	Syringa pekin.Beijing Gold	50	100	D	219
	Syringa vul. D'Alice Harding	50	100	D	219
	Syringa vul. Ruhm Von Horstenstein	50	100	D	219
	Syringa vulgaris Ludwig Spath	50	100	D	219
	Syringa vulgaris Madame Lemoine	50	100	D	219
	Tamarix aestivalis	50	100	C	1449
	Tamarix africana	50	100	C	1449
	Tamarix gallica	50	100	C	1449
	Tamarix tetrandra	50	100	C	1449
	Taxodium distichum	250	750	B	2907
	Taxus baccata	250	500	B	2230
	Taxus bac.Fastigiata Aureomarginata	150	300	C	1731
	Taxus baccata Fastigiata Aurea	150	300	C	1731
	Thuja plicata Atrovirens	350	750	B	4413
	Tilia americana American Sentry	150	300	A	5019
	Tilia americana Redmond	150	300	A	5019
	Tilia cordata	150	300	A	5019
	Tilia cordata Erecta	150	300	A	5019
	Tilia cordata Greenspire	150	300	A	5019
	Tilia cordata x mongolica Harvest Gold	150	300	A	5019
	Tilia cordata Rancho	150	300	A	5019
	Tilia cordata Winter Orange	150	300	A	5019
	Tilia x euchlora	150	300	A	5019
	Tilia x europaea	150	300	A	5019
	Tilia x europaea Pallida	150	300	A	5019
	Tilia henryana	150	300	C	1633
	Tilia mongolica	150	300	C	877
	Tilia platyphyllos	150	300	A	5019
	Tilia platyphyllos Delft	150	300	A	5019
	Tilia platyphyllos Rubra	150	300	A	5019
	Tilia tomentosa	150	300	A	5019
	Tilia tomentosa Brabant	150	300	A	5019
	Tilia tomentosa Petiolaris	150	300	A	5019
	Trachycarpus fortunei	50	75	E	12
	Tsuga heterophylla	250	500	B	4006
	Ulmus carpinifolia Wredei Aurea	100	200	C	1250
	Ulmus glabra Camperdownii	100	200	A	6903
	Ulmus Clusius	100	200	A	6903
	Ulmus Dodoens	100	200	A	6903
	Ulmus Lobel	100	200	A	6903
	Ulmus lutece	100	200	A	6903
	Ulmus Vada	100	200	A	6903
	Zelkova serrata	150	250	A	5341
	Zelkova serrata Green Vase	150	250	A	5341

Honey Bees Need Trees...

It's easy to take trees for granted, as they stand majestically throughout the seasons. However, they do not just provide us with ornament bearing flowers and fruit for our pleasure but provide a much needed food source for Honey bees.

Planting a collection of trees that flower for each month of the bees foraging year, provides continuous forage for the bees throughout the year. Start off with Alder, which has masses of pollen that is much needed early in the year when the bees are feeding their brood.

Amelanchier, which is pretty, provides lots of nectar which is collected to make honey stores for winter, and then Whitebeam, Lime, Sweet Chestnut and Pride of India for the summer months. It is believed that 5 or 6 trees provide more forage for bees than an acre of wildflower meadow. It's so much easier to plant a tree than to try and grow an abundance of flowers.

Honey bees also use the sticky resin from buds and trees to produce propolis, which varies in composition and colour from colony to colony, season to season depending on the sources available.

This sticky resin is metabolised and then used to seal and protect the hive. Propolis has sterile qualities and therefore helps to keep disease and draughts at bay.

Detailed below are trees which are beneficial to bees by season.

Early Spring: Alnus, Cornus mas, Corylus.
Late Spring/Early Summer: Amelanchier, Crataegus, Cydonia, Malus, Mespilus, Prunus, Pyrus, Sorbus.
Mid-Summer: Castanea, Koelreuteria, Liriodendron, Tilia cordata, Tilia platyphyllos.
Autumn: Prunus subhirtella Autumnalis

Planting Guide

Our trees are generally measured by girth size in centimetres. This measurement is taken one metre from ground level and is the circumference around the trunk at this point.

1. Water regularly and slowly during the first two growing seasons after planting. If the water doesn't drain away within ten minutes you are in danger of over watering.

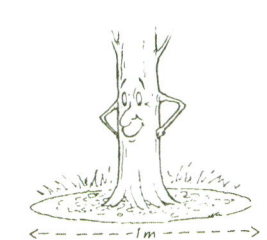

2. All grass and weed competition around the base of the tree should be eliminated (an area of at least one metre around the base of each tree is recommended). Tree trunks will take up herbicides so take care not to spray stems.

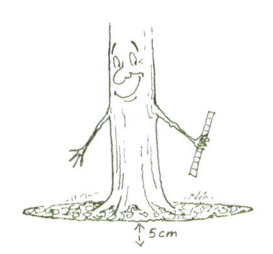

3. The area kept free from weed and grass competition can be mulched annually to a depth of five centimetres to prevent subsequent weed growth.

4. The tree can be staked either side of the container root system to avoid excess movement during establishment, and to prevent the stakes damaging the root system when they are driven into the ground.

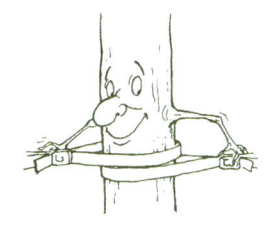

5. All ties should be adjusted as necessary to allow the tree to grow freely, without constriction.

6. All damage from strimmers and other mowing equipment is to be avoided.

7. Trees hate to be planted deep. Once the pot has been removed for planting, the top of the compost should be at finished ground level after installation.

Girth Size	Approx Height	Pot	Height	Width	Approx Weight
8-10cm girth	= 7-9ft	20L	30cm	30cm	25kg
10-12cm girth	= 9-11ft	35L	25cm	30cm	35kg
12-14cm girth	= 11-13ft	45L	35cm	40cm	50kg
14-16cm girth	= 13-15ft	55L	35cm	45cm	55kg
16-18cm girth	= 15-17ft	65L	40cm	45cm	75kg
18-20cm girth	= 17-19ft	100L	40cm	60cm	100kg
20-25cm girth	= 19-21ft	150L	55cm	60cm	155kg
25-30cm girth	= 20ft+	250L	65cm	70cm	255kg
30-35cm girth	= 25ft+	350L	70cm	80cm	355kg
35-40cm girth	= 25-30ft+	500L	75cm	95cm	505kg
40-60cm girth	= 25-35ft+	750L	80cm	110cm	755kg
		1000L	100cm	120cm	1,005kg
		1750L	100cm	150cm	1,755kg
		3000L	125cm	175cm	3,015kg

How to find us

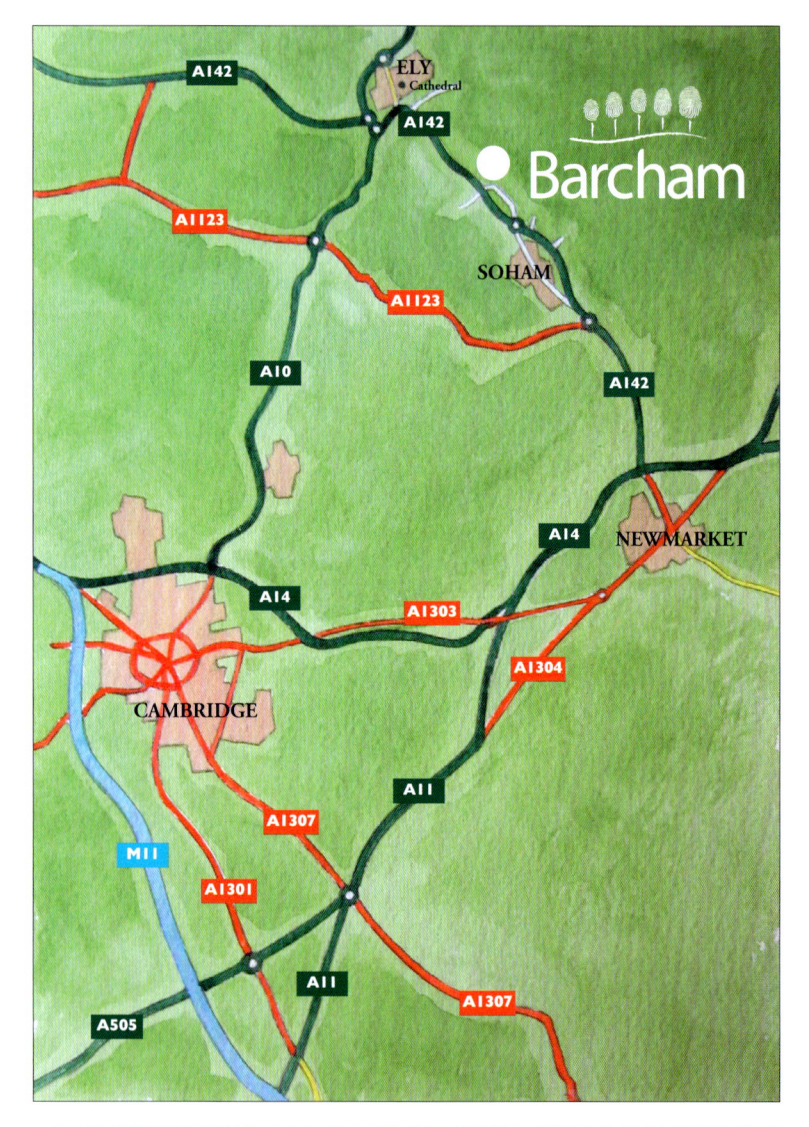

We are located between Ely and Soham on the A142. Disregard signposts to Barcham until you get to one saying Barcham & Eye Hill. Follow this road for a few hundred yards and our entrance is on the left. Our drive takes you to our reception where we have a cup of tea or coffee waiting for you!

If you are travelling by train, we are only 3 miles from Ely mainline train station. There are always taxis there but if you phone ahead we would be pleased to collect you. It takes about one hour to get from Kings Cross to Ely on some services so this may be a better option for those of you travelling from London.

Barcham
The Tree Specialists

Barcham Trees PLC,
Eye Hill Drove,
Ely, Cambridgeshire,
CB7 5XF

Tel: 01353 720 748
Fax: 01353 723 060
Email: sales@barchamtrees.co.uk

www.barcham.co.uk
www.barchampro.co.uk

Terms & conditions

Availability
All plant material listed is offered subject to availability on receipt of order.

Prices
Barcham Trees is a wholesale business therefore all prices are ex-nursery and do not include VAT at the prevailing rate.

Ordering
Orders placed on the telephone must be confirmed in writing via email or in the post.

Credit Accounts & Invoice Terms
Barcham has its invoices credit insured by Coface UK. Accounts are vetted by our insurer and credit limits issued. If a credit limit is not issued, payment is required on a pro-forma basis. Terms are stated on the invoice and should be strictly complied with to avoid insurer collection. Until payment has been received in full, our trees are still the property of Barcham Trees Plc and can be recovered as such.

Warranty
Whilst every effort is made to keep nursery stock healthy and true to name and type, our liability for plants supplied is limited to the replacement of those plants. No warranty expressed or implied is given as to the growth or suitability of those plants to their ultimate location. If you are not completely satisfied, contact must be made to this office within 7 days of delivery or collection, and confirmed in writing. Failure to do so will deem those goods as being accepted by the customer.
No responsibility is accepted for replacements, as so much depends on the planting, soil and weather conditions. Barcham Trees Plc takes no responsibility for the cost of replanting failed trees.

Guarantee
All our container trees are guaranteed for twelve months after delivery if supplied and planted between the months of October through to March. No liability is taken for stock supplied in bud and leaf between April and September unless the concern is registered within three days of delivery. Our guarantee is subject to drought, flood, vandalism and poor practice.

These terms and conditions shall take precedence over any other that customers may attach to their orders, any variation to these terms and conditions shall not be valid unless agreed in writing. In placing an order a customer is deemed to have accepted these terms and conditions.

Barcham Technical Guides

Barcham has produced a series of handy A5 guides, written by Keith Sacre, which are full of technical information for the tree specifier. To request a copy please email us, info@barchamtrees.co.uk

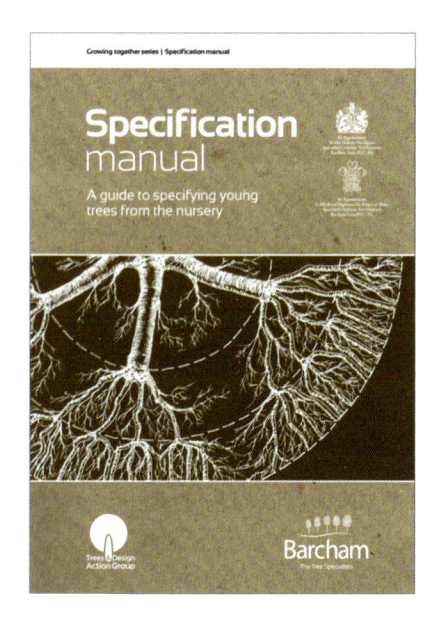

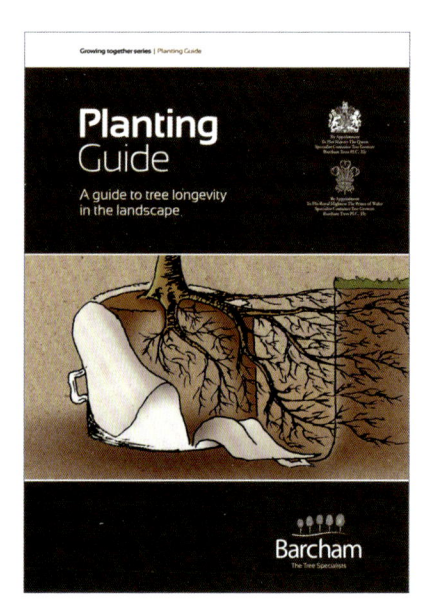

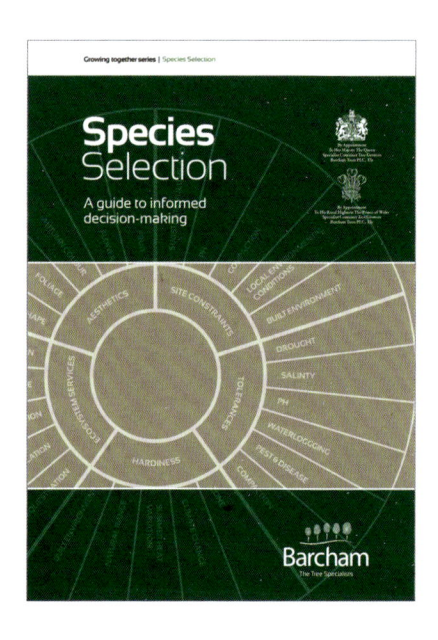

English to Latin translator

Alder ....Alnus & varieties
Almond ....Prunus dulcis
Amur Cork Tree..................................Phellodendron amurense
Amur Maple ....Acer ginnala
Angelica Tree ....Aralia elata
Antarctic Beech ....Nothofagus antarctica
Apple ....Malus
Ash..Fraxinus & varieties
Aspen ....Populus tremula & varieties
Atlas Cedar ....Cedrus atlantica & varieties
Austrian Pine ....Pinus nigra Austriaca

Bamboo..Phyllostachys & varieties
Bastard Service Tree ....Sorbus thuringiaca Fastigiata
Bay Laurel...Laurus nobilis
Bay Willow ....Salix pentandra
Beech ....Fagus & varieties
Birch..Betula & varieties
Bird Cherry..Prunus padus & varieties
Blue Spruce ....Picea pungens & varieties
Bournemouth Pine ....Pinus pinaster
Box ....Buxus
Bottle Brush..Callistemon laevis
Box Elder ....Acer negundo & varieties
Broad-Leaved Lime ....Tilia platyphyllos
Bhutan Pine ....Pinus wallichiana

Cabbage Tree ....Cordyline australis
Camperdown Elm........................Ulmus glabra Camperdownii
Canadian Maple ....Acer rubrum & varieties
Candyfloss Tree.............................Cercidiphyllum japonicum
Cappadocian Maple...............Acer cappadocicum & varieties
Cedar ....Cedrus & varieties
Cedar of Lebanon..Cedrus libani
Celtic Maple ....Acer pseudoplatanus & varieties
Cherry..Prunus & varieties
Chestnut-Leaved Oak............................Quercus castaneifolia
Chinese Date..Ziziphus guiggiolo
Chinese Privet............................Ligustrum lucidum & varieties
Chusan Palm..Trachycarpus fortunei
Coastal Redwood ....Sequoia sempervirens
Contorted Willow............................Salix matsudana Tortuosa
Common Lime ....Tilia europaea & varieties
Cork Oak...Quercus suber
Copper Beech....................................Fagus sylvatica Purpurea
Cornelian Cherry ....Cornus mas
Crab Apple ....Malus & varieties
Crape Myrtle ....Lagerstroemia indica & varieties
Cypress.....................................Cupressus arizonica Glauca &
                                                     Cupressus macrocarpa Goldcrest
Cypress Oak....................Quercus robur Fastigiata & varieties

Date Plum..Diospyos lotus

Dawn Redwood ....Metasequoia glyptostroboides & varieties
Deodar Cedar..Cedrus deodara
Desert Willow...............Chitalpa tashkentensis Summer Bells

Dogwood..Cornus & varieties
Dove Tree ....Davidia involucrata

Elm ....Ulmus & varieties
English Oak..Quercus robur
Eucalyptus ....Eucalyptus & varieties

False Acacia..Robinia & varieties
Flowering Ash..................................Fraxinus ornus & varieties
Field Maple ....Acer campestre & varieties
Fig..Ficus
Fir..Abies
Foxglove Tree ....Paulownia tomentosa
Fraser Fir..Abies fraseri

Giant Redwood...........................Sequoiadendron giganteum
Golden Rain..Laburnum & varieties
Golden Ash ....Fraxinus excelsior Jaspidea
Great Western Cedar.........................Thuja plicata Atrovirens
Gum Tree ....Eucalyptus & varieties

Hackberry ....Celtis occidentalis
Handkerchief Tree..Davidia & varieties
Hawthorn...Crataegus & varieties
Hazel ....Corylus & varieties

Holly..Ilex & varieties
Holm Oak ....Quercus ilex
Honey Locust..Gleditsia & varieties
Hop Hornbeam...Ostrya carpinifolia
Hornbeam ....Carpinus & varieties
Horse Chestnut..Aesculus & varieties
Himalayan Birch ....Betula utilis & varieties
Hungarian Oak..Quercus frainetto

Incense Cedar ....Calocedrus decurrans
Indian Bean Tree..Catalpa & varieties
Irish Juniper ....Juniperus communis Hibernica
Irish Yew................................Taxus baccata Fastigiata & Aurea
Italian Alder..Alnus cordata
Italian Cypress................................Cupressus sempervirens

Japanese Angelica Tree ....Aralia elata
Japanese Cedar ....Cryptomeria
Japanese Maple ....Acer palmatum & varieties
Japanese Pagoda Tree ....Sophora japonica & varieties
Jelly Palm..Butia capitata
Judas Tree................................Cercis siliquastrum & varieties
June Berry..Amelanchier & varieties

Common Name	Botanical Name
Katsura	Cercidiphyllum japonicum
Keaki	Zelkova serrata & varieties
Kentucky Coffee Tree	Gymnocladus dioica
Killarney Strawberry Tree	Arbutus unedo
Kilmarnock Willow	Salix caprea Pendula
Korean Fir	Abies koreana
Kusamaki	Podocarpus
Larch	Larix & varieties
Laurel	Prunus rotundifolia/laurocerasus
Leyland Cypress	Cupressocyparis leylandii & varieties
Lilac	Syringa v& varieties
Lime	Tilia & varieties
Lobels Maple	Acer lobelii
Lombardy Poplar	Populus nigra Italica
London Plane	Platanus hispanica
Magnolia	Magnolia & varieties
Maidenhair Tree	Ginkgo & varieties
Manna Ash	Fraxinus ornus & varieties
May Tree	Crataegus & varieties
Medlar	Mespilus germanica
Mongolian Lime	Tilia mongolica
Mountain Ash	Sorbus aucuparia & varieties
Monkey Puzzle	Araucaria araucana
Monterey Pine	Pinus radiata
Mulberry	Morus & varieties
Nettle Tree	Celtis australis
Nordmann Fir	Abies nordmanniana
Norway Maple	Acer platanoides & varieties
Norway Spruce	Picea abies
Oak	Quercus & varieties
Olive	Olea europaeus
One-Leaved Ash	Fraxinus excelsior Diversifolia
Oriental Plane	Platanus orientalis & varieties
Paper Birch	Betula papyrifera
Paper Mulberry	Broussonetia papyrifera
Paperbark Maple	Acer griseum
Pear	Pyrus & varieties
Pecan	Carya Illinoinensis
Pencil Cedar	Cupressus sempervirens
Persian Iron Wood	Parrotia persica & varieties
Pin Oak	Quercus palustris
Pine	Pinus & varieties
Pineapple Guava	Feijoa sellowiana
Plum	Prunus domestica
Poplar	Populus & varieties
Portugal Laurel	Prunus lusitanica
Pride of India	Koelreuteria paniculata & varieties
Privet	Ligustrum & varieties
Purple Leaf Plum	Prunus cerasifera Nigra
Pussy Willow	Salix caprea
Redbud	Cercis & varieties
Red Maple	Acer rubrum & varieties & Acer freemanii Autumn Blaze
Red Twigged Lime	Tilia platyphyllos Rubra
Red Oak	Quercus rubra
Redwood	Sequoia
River Birch	Betula nigra
Rose of Sharon	Hibiscus
Rowan	Sorbus aucuparia & varieties
Rubber Tree	Eucommia ulmoides
Scarlet Oak	Quercus coccinea
Scarlet Willow	Salix alba Chermesina
Scots Pine	Pinus sylvestris
Sentinel Pine	Pinus sylvestris Fastigiata
Serbian Spruce	Picea omorika
Serviceberry	Amelanchier & varieties
Sessile Oak	Quercus petraea
Shingle Oak	Quercus imbricaria
Silver Birch	Betula pendula & varieties
Silver Maple	Acer saccharinum & varieties
Silver Lime	Tilia tomentosa & varieties
Silver Wattle	Acacia dealbata
Small-Leaved Lime	Tilia cordata & varieties
Smoke Tree	Cotinus coggygria Royal Purple
Swedish Birch	Betula Dalecarlica
Swedish Upright Aspen	Populus tremula Erecta
Sweet Gum	Liquidambar & varieties
Snakebark Maple	Acer
Snow Gum	Eucalyptus & varieties
Snowy Mespilus	Amelanchier & varieties
Stone Pine	Pinus pinea
Sumach	Rhus typhina
Sugar Maple	Acer saccharum & varieties
Swamp Cypress	Taxodium distichum
Swedish Whitebeam	Sorbus intermedia & varieties
Sweet Chestnut	Castanea sativa & varieties
Sweet Gum	Liquidambar & varieties
Swiss Mountain Pine	Pinus mugo
Sycamore	Acer pseudoplatanus & varieties
Thorn	Crataegus & varieties
Tree of Heaven	Ailanthus altissima
Trident Maple	Acer buergerianum
Tulip Tree	Liriodendron tulipifera
Tupelo	Nyssa sylvatica
Turkish Hazel	Corylus colurna
Turkey Oak	Quercus cerris
Violet Willow	Salix daphnoides
Victoria Plum	Prunus domestica Victoria
Walnut	Juglans & varieties
Wedding Cake Tree	Cornus controversa
Weeping Birch	Betula pendula Tristis & Youngii
Weeping Willow	Salix alba Tristis (Chrysocoma)
Whitebeam	Sorbus aria & varieties
Witch Hazel	Hamamelis & varieties
White Willow	Salix alba
Wild Cherry	Prunus avium & varieties
Wild Service Tree	Sorbus torminalis
Willow	Salix & varieties
Wing Nut	Pterocarya fraxinifolia
Western Red Cedar	Thuja plicata & varieties
Yellow Wood	Cladrastis kentukia
Yew	Taxus baccata

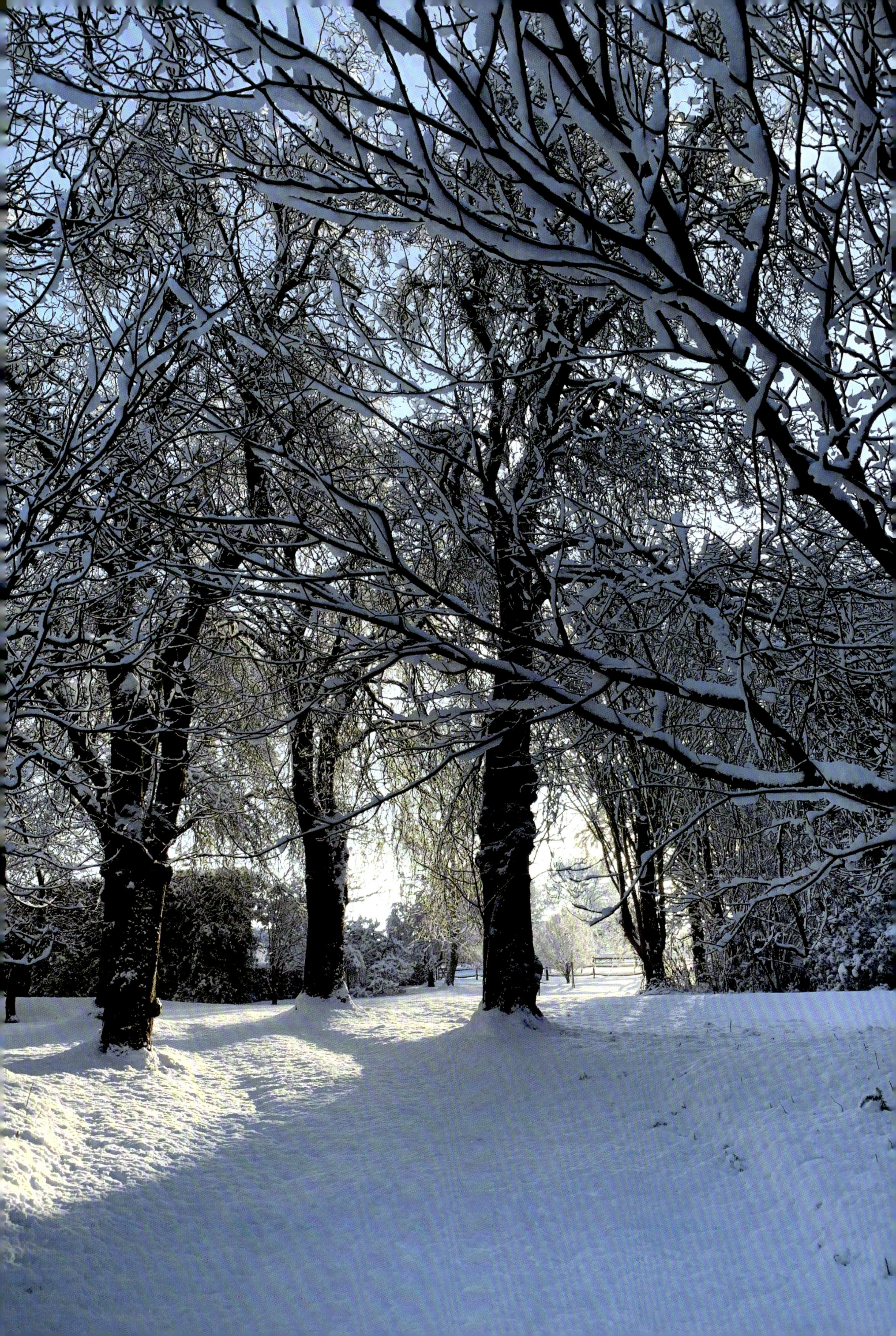

Tree Index

Abies fraserii	17
Abies nordmanniana	17
Acer buergerianum	18
Acer campestre	19
Acer campestre Arends	19
Acer campestre Elegant	20
Acer campestre Elsrijk	20
Acer campestre Lienco	21
Acer campestre Louisa Red Shine	22
Acer campestre Nanum	23
Acer campestre Queen Elizabeth	23
Acer campestre William Caldwell	23
Acer cappadocicum	24
Acer cappadocicum Aureum	24
Acer cappadocicum Rubrum	25
Acer x freemanii Armstrong	25
Acer x freemanii Autumn Blaze	26
Acer x freemanii Autumn Fantasy	27
Acer ginnala	27
Acer griseum	28
Acer negundo	29
Acer negundo Flamingo	29
Acer negundo Variegata	29
Acer palmatum	30
Acer palmatum Bloodgood	30
Acer palmatum Dissectum Garnet	30
Acer palmatum Fireglow	31
Acer palmatum Osakazuki	31
Acer palmatum Purpurea	32
Acer palmatum Red Emperor	32
Acer platanoides	33
Acer platanoides Cleveland	33
Acer platanoides Columnare	33
Acer platanoides Crimson King	34
Acer platanoides Crimson Sentry	35
Acer platanoides Deborah	35
Acer platanoides Drummondii	36
Acer platanoides Emerald Queen	37
Acer platanoides Fairview	37
Acer platanoides Farlakes Green	38
Acer platanoides Globosum	38
Acer platanoides Olmstead	38
Acer platanoides Pacific Sunset	39
Acer platanoides Princeton Gold	40
Acer platanoides Princeton Gold Upright	40
Acer platanoides Royal Red	41
Acer pseudoplatanus	42
Acer pseudoplatanus Brilliantissimum	43
Acer pseudoplatanus Leopoldii	43
Acer pseudoplatanus Negenia	44
Acer pseudoplatanus Spaethii	44
Acer pseudoplatanus Worleei	45
Acer rubrum	45
Acer rubrum Bowhall	46
Acer rubrum October Glory	46
Acer rubrum Red Sunset	47
Acer rubrum Scanlon	47
Acer saccharinum	48
Acer saccharinum Laciniata Wieri	48
Acer saccharinum Pyramidale	49
Aesculus californica	49
Aesculus x carnea Briotii	50
Aesculus x carnea Plantierensis	50
Aesculus flava	51
Aesculus hippocastanum	51
Aesculus hippocastanum Baumannii	52
Aesculus indica	53
Ailanthus altissima	54
Albizia julibrissin Rouge de Tuiliere	55
Albizia julibrissin Tropical Dream	55
Alnus cordata	56
Alnus glutinosa	57
Alnus glutinosa Imperialis	58
Alnus glutinosa Laciniata	58
Alnus incana	58
Alnus incana Aurea	59
Alnus incana Laciniata	60
Alnus X spaethii	61
Amelanchier arborea Robin Hill	62,63
Amelanchier Ballerina	64
Amelanchier lamarckii	65
Aralia elata	66
Araucaria araucana	66
Arbutus unedo	67
Betula albosinensis Fascination	68,69
Betula ermanii	70
Betula maximowicziana	71
Betula nigra	71
Betula papyrifera	72
Betula pendula	73
Betula pendula Dalecarlica	74
Betula pendula Fastigiata	74
Betula pendula Obelisk	75
Betula pendula Purpurea	75
Betula pendula Tristis	76
Betula pendula Westwood	77
Betula pendula Youngii	77
Betula pendula Zwisters Glory	78
Betula pubescens	79
Betula utilis Jacquemontii/Doorenbos	80,81
Betula utilis Snow Queen	82
Broussonetia papyrifera	82
Calocedrus decurrens	83
Camellia sasanqua Cleopatra	84
Camellia sasanqua Kanjiro	84
Camellia sasanqua Rosea	84

Carpinus betulus 85	Cryptomeria japonica Elegans 114
Carpinus betulus Fastigiata 86	Cupressus arizonica Glauca 115
Carpinus betulus Fastigiata Frans Fontaine 87	Cupressus macrocarpa Goldcrest 115
Carpinus betulus Lucas 87	Cupressus sempervirens 116
Carpinus japonica 88	Cupressocyparis leylandii 117
Carya cordiformis 88	Cupressocyparis leylandii Castelwellan 117
Carya Illinoinensis 89	Cydonia oblonga 118
Castanea sativa 89	
Catalpa bignonioides 90	Davidia involucrata 119
Catalpa bignonioides Aurea 91	Diospyros lotus 120
Catalpa bignonioides Bungeii 92	Diospyros kaki... 120
Cedrus atlantica 92	
Cedrus atlantic Glauca 93	Eucalyptus debeuzevillei 121
Cedrus deodara 94	Eucalyptus gunnii 122
Cedrus deodara Aurea 95	Eucalyptus niphophila 122
Cedrus libani 95	Eucommia ulmoides 123
Celtis australis 96	Euodia hupehensis 123
Celtis occidentalis 96	Euonymus europaeus Red Cascade 124
Cercidiphyllum japonicum 97	Exochorda serratifolia Snow White 125
Cercis canadensis Forest Pansy 97	
Cercis Chinensis Avondale 98	Fagus orientalis Iskander 125
Cercis siliquastrum 98	Fagus sylvatica 126
Cercis siliquastrum Alba 99	Fagus sylvatica Asplenifolia 127
Chamaecyparis lawsoniana Columnaris Glauca 99	Faus sylvatica sylvatica Black Swan 128
Chamaecyparis lawsoniana Stardust 99	Faus sylvatica Dawyck 128
Chamaecyparis lawsoniana Yvonne 100	Fagus sylvatica Dawyck Gold 129
Chitalpa tashkentensis Summer Bells 100	Fagus sylvatica Dawyck Purple 130
Cladrastis kentukia 100	Fagus sylvatica Pendula 130
Clerodendrum trichotomum 101	Fagus sylvatica Purpurea 131
Cornus alba Sibirica 101	Fagus sylvatica Rohanii 132
Cornus controversa 102	Fagus sylvatica Roseomarginata 133
Cornus controversa Variegata 103	Fagus sylvatica Zlatia 133
Cornus Eddie's White Wonder 103	Ficus carica 134
Cornus kousa China Girl 103	Fraxinus americana Autumn Purple 135
Cornus kousa Chinensis 104	Fraxinus angustifolia Raywood 135
Cornus kousa Milky Way 104	Fraxinus excelsior 135
Cornus kousa Stella Pink 105	Fraxinus excelsior Altena 135
Cornus mas 105	Fraxinus excelsior Diversifolia 135
Cornus sanguinea Annie's Winter Orange 106	Fraxinus excelsior Jaspidea 135
Corylus avellana 106	Fraxinus excelsior Pendula 135
Corylus avellana Contorta 107	Fraxinus excelsior Westhofs Glorie 135
Corylus avellana Zellernus 107	Fraxinus ornus 135
Corylus colurna 108	Fraxinus ornus Arie Peters 135
Corylus colurna Te-Terra Red 109	Fraxinus ornus Louisa Lady 135
Cotinus coggygria Royal Purple 109	Fraxinus ornus Meczek 135
Cotoneaster Cornubia 109	Fraxinus ornus Obelisk 135
Crataegus laevigata Paul's Scarlet 110	Fraxinus pennsylvanica Summit 135
Crataegus x lavallei 110	
Crataegus x lavallei Carrièrei 111	Ginkgo biloba 136
Crataegus monogyna 111	Ginkgo biloba Blagon 136
Crataegus monogyna Stricta 112	Ginkgo biloba Golden Globe 137
Crataegus x prunifolia 112	Ginkgo biloba Lakeview 138
Crataegus x prunifloia Splendens 113	Ginkgo biloba Nanum 138

Ginkgo biloba Tremonia	139
Ginkgo biloba Princeton Sentry	139
Gleditsia triacanthos	140
Gleditsia triacanthos Draves Street Keeper	141
Gleditsia triacanthos Inermis	141
Gleditsia triacanthos Ruby Lace	142
Gleditsia triacanthos Skyline	143
Gleditsia triacanthos Sunburst	144
Gymnocladus dioica	144
Halesia monticola & carolina	145
Hamamelis x intermedia Arnold Promise	146
Hamamelis x intermedia Jelena	146
Hibiscus x Resi	147
Ilex x altaclerensis Golden King	148
Ilex aquifolium	148
Ilex aquifolium Alaska	149
Ilex aquifolium Argentea Marginata	150
Ilex aquifolium J C Van Tol	150
Ilex aquifolium Pyramidalis	151
Ilex castaneifolia	151
Ilex x Nellie Stevens	152
Juglans nigra	153
Juglans regia	154
Juniperus communis Hibernica	154
Koelreuteria paniculata	155
Koelreuteria paniculata Fastigiata	156
Laburnocytisus Adamii	156
Laburnum x watereri Vossii	157
Lagerstroemia indica Fauriei Natchez	158
Lagerstroemia indica Rosea	158
Lagerstroemia indica Sarah's Favorite	159
Lagerstroemia indica Tuscarora	159
Lagerstroemia indica Violacea	160
Larix decidua	160
Larix x eurolepis	160
Larix kaempferi	161
Laurus nobilis	161
Ligustrum japonicum	162,163
Ligustrum lucidum Variegata	164
Ligustrum ovalifolium	165
Liquidambar acalycina	166
Liquidambar styraciflua	167
Liquidambar styraciflua Gumball	167
Liquidambar styraciflua Lane Roberts	168
Liquidambar styraciflua Rotundifolia	168
Liquidambar styraciflua Slender Silhouette	169
Liquidambar styraciflua Stella	169
Liquidambar styraciflua Thea	169
Liquidambar styraciflua Manon Variegata	170
Liquidambar styraciflua Worplesdon	170,171
Liriodendron tulipifera	172
Liriodendron tulipifera Aureomarginatum	173
Liriodendron tulipifera Fastigiatum	173
Magnolia x brooklynensis Elizabeth	174
Magnolia x brooklynensis Yellow Bird	174
Magnolia denudata Yellow River	174
Magnolia Galaxy	175
Magnolia grandiflora	175
Magnolia grandiflora Gallisoniensis	176
Magnolia grandiflora Praecox	176
Magnolia Heaven Scent	177
Magnolia kobus	177
Magnolia x loebneri Leonard Messel	178
Magnolia x loebneri Merrill	179
Magnolia x soulangeana	179
Magnolia Spectrum	180
Magnolia Susan	180
Malus baccata Street Parade	181
Malus Bramley Seedling	181
Malus Butterball	182
Malus Cox's Orange Pippin	182
Malus Director Moerland	183
Malus Donald Discovery	183
Malus Donald Wyman	184
Malus Egremont Russett	185
Malus Elstar	185
Malus Evereste	186
Malus floribunda	187
Malus Golden Delicious	187
Malus Golden Hornet	188
Malus Howgate Wonder	188
Malus hupehensis	189
Malus James Grieve	189
Malus John Downie	189
Malus Jonagold	190
Malus Laxton's Superb	190
Malus Mokum	191
Malus Profusion	191
Malus Red Sentinel	192
Malus Royalty	193
Malus Rudolph	193
Malus sylvestris	194
Malus toringo	194
Malus toringo Brouwers Beauty	195
Malus toringo Scarlet Brouwers Beauty	195
Malus trilobata	196
Mespilus germanica	197
Metasequoia glyptostroboides	198
Metasequoia glyptostroboides Goldrush	199
Morus alba	200
Morus alba Fruitless	200
Morus alba Pendula	200

Morus nigra 201	Prunus domestica Reine-Claude d'oullins 235
	Prunus domestica Victoria 236
Nothofagus antarctica 202	Prunus dulcis 236
Nyssa sylvatica 202	Prunus fruticosa Globosa 237
	Prunus x gondouinii Schnee 237
Olea europaea 203	Prunus x hillieri Spire 238
Osmanthus armatus 203	Prunus Kanzan 239
Osmanthus burkwoodii 204	Prunus laurocerasus Caucasica 240
Osmanthus fortunei aquifolium 204	Prunus laurocerasus Novita 240
Ostrya carpinifolia 205	Prunus laurocerasus Rotundifolia 241
	Prunus lusitanica angustifolia 241
Parrotia persica 206	Prunus maackii Amber Beauty 242
Parrotia persica Vanessa 207	Prunus Okame 243
Paulownia tomentosa 208,209	Prunus padus 243
Phellodendron amurense 210	Prunus padus Albertii 244
Photinia x fraseri Red Robin 210	Prunus padus Watereri 244
Phyllostachys aurea 211	Prunus Pandora 245
Phyllostachys nigra 211	Prunus Pink Perfection 246
Picea abies 212	Prunus Royal Burgundy 247
Picea omorika 212	Prunus sargentii 248
Picea pungens Hoopsii 213	Prunus sargentii Rancho 248
Pinus nigra austriaca 214	Prunus x schmittii 248
Pinus maritima 215	Prunus serrula Tibetica 249
Pinus mugo Mops 215	Prunus Shimidsu Sakura 250
Pinus peuce 215	Prunus Shirotae 250
Pinus pinaster 216	Prunus Shirofugen 251
Pinus pinea 216	Prunus x subhirtella Autumnalis 252
Pinus radiata 217	Prunus x subhirtella Autumnalis Rosea 252
Pinus strobus 217	Prunus Sunset Boulevard 253
Pinus sylvestris 218	Prunus Tai haku 254
Pinus sylvestris Fastigiata 219	Prunus Ukon 255
Pinus wallichiana 220	Prunus Umineko 255
Platanus x hispanica (acerifolia) 221	Prunus x yedoensis 256
Platanus orientalis Digitata 222	Pterocarya fraxinifolia 257
Platanus orientalis Minaret 223	Pyrus Beurre Hardy 257
Populus alba 224	Pyrus calleryana Chanticleer 258
Populus alba Raket 224	Pyrus calleryana Redspire 259
Populus balsamifera 225	Pyrus communis Beech Hill 259
Populus x candicans Aurora 225	Pyrus communis Conference 260
Populus nigra 226	Pyrus communis Gieser Wildeman 260
Populus nigra Italica 227	Pyrus Doyenne du Comice 261
Populus serotina Aurea 227	Pyrus salicifolia Pendula 261
Populus tremula 228	
Populus tremula Erecta 228	Quercus casteneifolia 263
Prunus Accolade 229	Quercus cerris 263
Prunus Amanogawa 230	Quercus coccinea 264
Prunus avium 231	Quercus frainetto 265
Prunus avium Kordia 232	Quercus x hispanica Wageningen 265
Prunus avium Plena 232	Quercus ilex 266
Prunus cerasifera Nigra 233	Quercus imbricaria 267
Prunus Cheals Weeping 234	Quercus palustris 267
Prunus domestica Early Rivers 234	Quercus palustris Green Dwarf 268
Prunus domestica Hauszwetsche 235	Quercus palustris Green Pillar 269

Quercus palustris Helmond 269	Sorbus latifolia Henk Vink 299
Quercus petraea 270	Sorbus latifolia Atrovirens 299
Quercus phellos 271	Sorbus x thuringiaca Fastigiata 300
Quercus Regal Prince 271	Sorbus torminalis 300
Quercus robur 272,273	Styrax japonicus June Snow 301
Quercus robur Fastigiata (Koster) 274	Syringa vulgaris Alice Harding 302
Quercus rubra 274	Syringa vulgaris Madame Lemoine 302
Quercus suber 275	Syringa vulgaris Ludwig Spath 302
Quercus X turneri Pseudoturneri 275	Syringa vulgaris Ruhm von Horstenstein 302
Rhus typhina 276	Tamarix aestivalis 303
Robinia pseudoacacia 276	Tamarix africanus 303
Robinia pseudoacacia Bessoniana 277	Tamarix gallica 304
Robinia pseudoacacia Casque Rouge 277	Tamarix tetrandra 304
Robinia pseudoacacia Frisia 278	Taxodium distichum 305
Robinia pseudoacacia Umbraculifera 278	Taxus baccata 306
	Taxus baccata Fastigiata 307
Salix alba 279	Taxus baccata Fastigiata Aurea 307
Salix alba Chermesina 280	Thuja plicata Atrovirens 308
Salix alba Liempde 280	Tilia americana Redmond 309
Salix alba Tristis (x sepulcralis Chrysocoma) 281	Tilia americana American Sentry 309
Salix caprea 282	Tilia cordata 310
Salix caprea Pendula 282	Tilia cordata Erecta 311
Salix daphnoides 282	Tilia cordata Greenspire 312
Salix matsudana Tortuosa 283	Tilia cordata x mongolica Harvest Gold 313
Salix pentandra 284	Tilia cordata Rancho 313
Sambucus nigra Black Lace 284	Tilia cordata Winter Orange 314
Sequoiadendron giganteum 285	Tilia x euchlora 315
Sequoiadendron giganteum Glauca 286	Tilia x europaea 316
Sequoia sempervirens 286,287	Tilia x europaea Pallida 316
Sophora japonica 288	Tilia henryana 317
Sophora japonica Regent 288	Tilia mongolica 317
Sorbus aria Lutescens 289	Tilia platyphyllos 318
Sorbus aria Magnifica 289	Tilia platyphyllos Delft 319
Sorbus aria Majestica 289	Tilia platyphyllos Rubra 319
Sorbus x arnoldiana Schouten 290	Tilia tomentosa 320
Sorbus aucuparia 291	Tilia tomentosa Brabant 320
Sorbus aucuparia Asplenifolia 292	Tilia tomentosa Petiolaris 321
Sorbus aucuparia Cardinal Royal 292	Trachycarpus fortunei 321
Sorbus aucuparia Cashmiriana 292	Tsuga canadensis 322
Sorbus aucuparia Edulis 293	
Sorbus aucuparia Golden Wonder 293	Ulmus carpinifolia Wredei Aurea 322
Sorbus aucuparia Joseph Rock 294	Ulmus glabra Camperdownii 323
Sorbus aucuparia Rossica Major 294	Ulmus Clusius 324
Sorbus aucuparia Sheerwater Seedling 295	Ulmus Dodoens 324
Sorbus aucuparia Vilmorinii 295	Ulmus Lobel 325
Sorbus commixta Embley 296	Ulmus lutece & Ulmus Vada 325, 326
Sorbus commixta Olympic Flame 296	
Sorbus discolor 297	Zelkova serrata 327
Sorbus hupehensis 297	Zelkova serrata Green Vase 327
Sorbus incana 298	
Sorbus intermedia 298	
Sorbus intermedia Brouwers 298